This book must be returned immediately if is asked for by the librarian,
and in any case by the last date
stamped below.

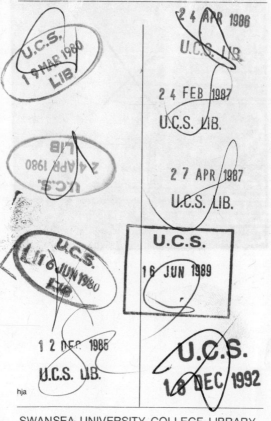

D0271412

Making the news

Making the news

Peter Golding
Philip Elliott

Longman
London and New York

Longman Group Limited London
Associated companies, branches and representatives
throughout the world

Published in the United States of America
by Longman Inc., New York

First published 1979

British Library Cataloguing in Publication Data

Golding, Peter
  Making the news.
  1. Radio broadcasting – Social aspects.
  2. Television broadcasting of news – Social aspects. 3. Broadcast journalism – Social
  aspects.
  I. Title   II. Elliott, Philip
  301.16′1   PN1990.83   78–41006

  ISBN 0–582–50460–0

Printed in Great Britain by Richard Clay (The Chaucer Press) Ltd, Bungay, Suffolk

Contents

Foreword

Professor James D. Halloran
Director
Centre for Mass Communication Research
University of Leicester

The General Conference of UNESCO at its fifteenth session in November 1968 authorised the Director General, in co-operation with the appropriate international and national organisations, to undertake research about, and promote the study of, the part played by 'the media of mass communication in modern society'.

The outcome of this decision was 'a meeting of experts' held in June 1969 in Montreal. The experts who came from over 20 different countries were given the task of examining the development, current state and potential of mass communication research, and were asked to make recommendations and provide guidelines for research developments in the future.

I was asked by UNESCO to prepare the working paper for this meeting, and an extended version of this plus a summary of the discussions and an outline of the recommendations for future action were published by UNESCO with the title – Mass Media in Society: The Need of Research.[1]

This was by no means the first time that UNESCO had published reports, made recommendations and suggested action in the general field of mass communication research. But the Montreal meeting, as reflected in the aforementioned publication, is widely held to be of particular importance because it is seen as marking a new direction in UNESCO's approach to mass communication research.

As far as the research reported in this book by Peter Golding and Philip Elliott is concerned, the implications of this change and of the meeting generally were quite crucial. Attending the meeting, as an observer, was Mr Arthur D. Morse, Executive Director of the recently formed International Broadcast Institute (now International Institute of Communications), and he was particularly impressed by the emphasis which was given to the desirability of establishing close co-operative working relationships between researchers and broadcasters at both national and international levels. He was also quick to accept one of the underlying principles, namely that ideally mass communication should be studied as a social process and that this, inter alia, called for intensive studies of media institutions and production processes. This was quite unusual for a broadcaster in the late sixties, and it showed Arthur Morse to have been well ahead of his time in the acceptance of the need for critical research in this area. This progressive view was further confirmed when he followed up his acceptance of the principles with a willingness to explore the possibility of IBI sponsoring and funding research by the Centre for Mass Communication Research at the University of Leicester, which had been established in 1966, and where such research was already being pioneered.

As a result of these explorations, and following further discussions the Executive Committee of IBI approved and agreed to fund a research proposal 'to study the television news process in three or four countries' which I submitted to them at a meeting in Rome in late 1969.

Before the research actually started in mid-1970 the three countries were chosen, and the design was slightly amended to incorporate some suggestions from members of the IBI Executive and Board of Trustees which had been put forward at further meetings in Rome and in Racine, Wisconsin. However, it needs to be made clear that, although IBI was always available for consultation, it was accepted from the outset that the research was undertaken on a completely independent basis, and that IBI would not in any way seek to influence the study or the composition of the final report. This again was quite unusual, and the credit for this open, liberal and generous approach must go to members of the IBI Executive, particularly to Olof Rydbeck, the chairman at the time, Sig. Mickleson who succeeded him, Christopher Kolade, Arthur Morse, and Edward Ploman, who succeeded Arthur Morse as Executive Director following the tragic death of Arthur Morse in 1971.

The planning, development, organisation and execution of this research project represent a significant step forward in broadcaster-researcher co-operation in a hitherto neglected area. There can be little doubt that the project marks an important point – perhaps even a breakthrough – in the history of mass communication research, and the part played in this by the broadcasters mentioned earlier, and by those who co-operated so willingly in Ireland, Nigeria and Sweden needs to be put on record.

I would also like to put on record my own personal appreciation and admiration of the scholarly, imaginative and thorough way in which Golding and Elliott responded to the challenge presented by this unusual project and successfully overcame the several obstacles, expected and unexpected, which were encountered in the course of the research.

Their joint efforts provide valuable insights, not only into the development of news broadcasting and the context and production of broadcast news, but also into the profession of broadcast journalism. The book is a valuable contribution to the sociology of broadcasting.

Note

1. Reports and Papers on Mass Communication, No. 59, UNESCO, Paris, 1970.

Acknowledgements

Most of the data on which this study is based were collected inside the newsrooms of broadcasting organisations in Sweden, Ireland and Nigeria. Our greatest debt is to the broadcasters and journalists in these countries whose unfailing courtesy and tolerance enabled the study to take place. To the broadcasting executives whose generosity in opening their institutions to our inquiries guaranteed the survival of the research we owe a particular debt, in the hope that their example will persuade others that more good than harm must come from the informed study of the most powerful cultural machines of our time. Tom Hardiman in Ireland, Olof Rydbeck, Otto Nordenskiöld, Håken Unsgaard and Örjan Wallquist in Sweden, Victor Badejo, Christopher Kolade, Teju Oyeleye, V. I. Maduka, and Alhaji A. Zorru in Nigeria, all authorised a degree of access and penetration into the organisations they commanded with unusual candour and sympathy for the needs of research. All gave their own time and assistance unhesitatingly.

It would be impossible to name the many individual journalists who made our task easier. We hope our efforts to understand and explain their work are some repayment for their assistance and co-operation throughout the research periods. We are especially indebted to Jim McGuinness, Desmond Fisher, Rory O'Connor and Mike Burns in Ireland, Gert Engström, Oloph Hansson and Sam Nilsson in Sweden, and Biola Olasope and Horatio Agedah at the Nigerian Broadcasting Corporation (NBC), T. Shenjobi and Kunle Adeleke at the West Nigeria Broadcasting Corporation (WNBC) in Ibadan, and Mohammed Ibrahim at Radio-Television Kaduna. As Heads of News in their respective organisations all helped ease our entry into and disruption of their departmental good order.

We would also like to thank the many others, too numerous to mention by name, in the broadcasting organisations, the press, the agencies and academia who gave freely of their time to answer our enquiries, discuss issues with us, help us to a better acquaintance with their countries and generally to facilitate the research.

Many of the broadcasters made useful comments on the first draft of this book. We are especially grateful to Desmond Fisher of Radio Telefis Eireann (RTE), Horatio Agedah of NBC and Ivar Ivre of Sveriges Radio (SR). Many academic colleagues gave us useful reactions to early drafts, and we would like particularly to thank Philip

Schlesinger and Jeremy Tunstall for their detailed and insightful commentaries. Jen Golding applied much helpful remedial skill to the final manuscript. Many helpful suggestions were also received from Nick Garnham, Richard Collins, Howard Davis and Pertti Hémanus, as well as from friends and colleagues at the Leicester Centre for Mass Communication Research.

The fieldwork in Ireland was carried out by Jim Halloran and Adrian Wells. Their crucial contribution to this research requires more than passing acknowledgement, and we are totally indebted to them for their work both in Ireland and in later analysis and discussion.

The finance which largely supported the research reported in this book was provided by the International Broadcast Institute (now International Institute of Communication) and arranged by Professor J. D. Halloran and the late Arthur Morse, then executive director of the Institute. We are grateful to them and to the present executive director, Edward Ploman, who made many interesting comments on the research report on which the book is based.

No researcher interested in the mediation of ideas through production can be unaware of the critical role of a good typist. To Jean Goddard, Enid Nightingale, Sue Pyne, Brigid Travers and Dorothy Brydges our heartfelt thanks.

Peter Golding
June 1978 *Philip Elliott*

To Jen and Wen

Chapter 1

Introduction

Among the many attempts to characterise the times in which we live is the recurrent observation that we are the victims of an information explosion. Like many such instant diagnoses, the idea of an information-rich environment hides more than it reveals. Most important it mistakes a technological for a social revolution. Nevertheless it remains true that, over the last 100 years or so, vast industries have evolved for the production and distribution of information. Among them are the news media. In the manufacture of knowledge these organisations rank supreme as providers of what a famous American journalist, Walter Lippmann, long ago referred to as a pseudo-environment. By this he meant that our knowledge of the world beyond our everyday experience is structured by the symbols, values and selective criteria of others (Lippmann, 1922, Ch. 1).

News, whether provided by the newspaper press or broadcasting, is a central part of the pseudo-environment. Whatever functions it performs for individuals, and many studies have tried to tease out this complex relationship between product and consumer, it is clear that the news is badly missed when not available. A study by American researchers during a newspaper strike in New York in 1945 concluded that 'the reading of the newspaper has become a ceremonial ritualistic or near-compulsive act for many people' (Berelson, 1949). The news has become a crucial source of beliefs and values with which people try to make sense of their own lives and the world around them. This book is an attempt to examine this much taken-for-granted product, and to question its nature and sources.

We have done this by investigating the production and content of broadcast news in three countries. The research attempts to answer two questions:
1. What picture of the world is provided by broadcast news?
2. How is this picture related to the routine demands of news production in broadcasting organisations?

Of course these basic questions throw up wider issues about the social role of journalism, the ideological nature of news and, not least, the possibility of change. It is our hope that if the research cannot resolve these wider issues it can at least clarify them. We do not pretend, however, that the book has no opinion. We view the evidence presented here as strong support for an interpretation of broadcast news as a systematically partial account of society, an interpretation with disturbing implications for broadcasters' claims of neutrality, and not least for our understanding of how political and social opinions are formed.

The three countries in which the study was carried out were Nigeria, Sweden and Ireland. In Nigeria the research was conducted at the three main broadcasting organisations, the Nigerian Broadcasting Corporation in Lagos, Western Nigeria Broadcasting Corporation in Ibadan and Radio-Television Kaduna in Kaduna. In Sweden and Ireland the research was conducted at the national broadcasting corporations, Sveriges Radio and Radio Telefis Eireann, respectively. The researchers spent three main periods at each station observing news production, and finally conducting more formal interviews with the journalists in each department. Additional interviews and archive research were conducted for historical and organisational material. The output of the news departments was examined by means of an analysis of the content of 28 bulletins from each news programme during two 14-day periods in November 1971 and April/May 1972.

Most informed commentaries on news broadcasting deal with the specific situation in their own countries. Very often the explanations of practice and content are specific to the situation they describe, and indeed there is every reason they should be. This research, however, is aimed at those fundamental aspects of news which transcend the particular problems of a single country or organisation. This does not mean a search for the 'essential character' of news, but it does focus attention on those aspects of news production that cannot be explained away as eccentricities of a particular place or time. But comparative study usefully allows us to examine not only the universals of news production, but also the differences, the alternative solutions which arise in different situations to the varying problems of broadcast journalism. There are two further reasons for the multinational character of this study.

First, news is an international commodity. A large though variable proportion of the news broadcast in any country is produced elsewhere. This makes journalists increasingly aware of news gathering and production elsewhere and introduces an element of comparison in their own evaluation of the work they do. It is hoped this awareness will be aided and substantiated by the comparative elements in this study. The second point is that journalism as a set of occupational practices has never developed in national isolation. Whether through formal training, chance contacts or foreign residence the ideas and methods of journalism have diffused throughout the world to produce a number of interesting variations on a theme.

The three countries chosen for the research appear, at first sight, an oddly assorted trio. There are three primary reasons for their selection. First, we wanted to have a fairly wide range of socio-economic conditions so as to widen the range of contexts within which news broadcasting departments could be examined (see Table 1.1). Sweden is a technically advanced European nation with a high per capita income and a predominantly industrial work force. Nigeria, by contrast, despite its much heralded oil boom of the last decade, remains a poor country with a vast population (roughly one in four black Africans is Nigerian), the majority of whom are small farmers living below, at or occasionally just above subsistence level. Ireland, though a member of the European Economic Community, is nonetheless one of the less wealthy nations of Europe and has a comparatively large agricultural sector. In cultural terms too these three provide an enormous range of traditions and history, much of which impinges in interesting and complex ways on the evolution and practice of journalism.

Table 1.1 Contrasted features of the countries studied

	Sweden	Ireland	Nigeria
Population (millions)*	8.22	3.16	64.75
National income per cap. (US $)†	7557	2040	201
Econ. active pop'n in agriculture (%)‡	8.1	25.9	84.7
TV sets/100§	34.8	17.8	0.18
Radios/100§	37.8	28.7	6.9
Daily newspapers/100	53.6	23.6	0.9

Notes: *Estimates based on most recent censuses.
  †Sweden 1975, Ireland 1974, Nigeria 1973.
  ‡Figure for Nigeria is that of population in rural areas.
  §Nigerian figures based on licences and therefore probably a considerable underestimate.

Second, these three countries offered an intriguing variety of traditions and philosophies. Clearly the British influence in Nigeria and Ireland is important, but less so in Sweden; the background of a nationalist press in the first two also produced contrasts of some significance. The European notion of objective reporting and the fourth estate has been challenged by some African writers who see a totally different role for journalism in a developing nation, and this dimension added to the range of contrasts available.

Finally, there is the less theoretically pure but highly relevant problem of access. Their willingness to co-operate with the research may make the broadcasting organisations of these three countries drastically unrepresentative. However, accounts of news departments in other countries suggest that this is not the case. The research was conducted on the understanding that we had guaranteed access to all relevant people, places and documentation. Naturally this created doubts and anxieties. News departments are invariably politically sensitive, and are understandably suspicious of research. We were received in all departments with unfailing good will, and developed relationships of, at best, close *rapport*, at the least sceptical tolerance, which were sustained over many weeks of observation in newsrooms and on newsbeats. We have no reason to suppose such patience or candour are so unique to these countries as to make our findings unrepresentative.

Chapter 2 sets out the basic questions underlying our research, and situates them in the growing body of research into broadcast journalism. Chapter 3 shows how news broadcasting has evolved, and how occupational beliefs and traditions have developed historically. In Chapter 4 the wider context of news broadcasting is discussed, particularly its relationship with broadcasting generally, and with the state. Chapter 5 reports our findings about the production of news and attempts to display the structures and routine behind the apparent chaos of television newsrooms. The result of this hidden order is examined in Chapter 6, which looks at the findings of our analysis of the content of television news. Chapter 7 is concerned with the journalists themselves, their beliefs, values, careers, commitments and characteristics. Finally Chapter 8 returns to our preliminary argument in the light of the research, and looks closely at possibilities for change in broadcast news.

Chapter 2

The study of news

It sometimes puzzles people that sociologists have appeared to worry so much about the media, and in particular the news media, in recent years. Is it a frustrated desire to associate with more glamorous institutions than those of academia, a mischievous attempt to elevate leisure pursuits to objects of serious research, or simply a relentless ambition to subject more and more areas of daily life to the dreary embrace of academic study? In this chapter we look at the way sociologists have examined news, and contrast it with the puzzled or hostile reaction their work has provoked among journalists. We then briefly outline the ideas that our own research was intended to explore.

Sociologists and journalists

Cecily: What field of endeavour are you engaged in?
Felix: I write the news for CBS
Cecily: Oh! Fascinating!
Gwendolyn: Where do you get your ideas from?
Felix: (*He looks at her as though she's a Martian*) From the news.
Gwendolyn: Oh, yes, of course. Silly me ...

(Simon, 1966, p. 82)

For Felix, as for many journalists, the idea that news is manufactured is entirely alien. Indeed, this idea is foreign to most popular conceptions of news. News just is what it is, everybody recognises it when they see it, though the professional journalist is endowed with a more refined sense that he refers to, with great pride, as a 'nose for news'. It is only in comparatively recent years that questions have been raised about the news and its production. This contrasts sharply with other knowledge-producing institutions, for example education, whose structures and purposes have come under close scrutiny and enquiry over the last twenty years. It is worth considering what has retarded equivalent examination of news production.

There is a school of thought which denies that the news is at all structured or socially patterned. This argument suggests that the news derives from a series of chance reactions to random events. John Whale, who has written frequently and thoughtfully on his work as a journalist, puts it as follows (1970, p. 510):

Our product is put together by large and shifting groups of people, often
in a hurry, out of an assemblage of circumstances that is never the same
twice. Newspapers and news programmes could almost be called random
reactions to random events.

Almost, but not quite. For in taking understandable umbrage at what
he sees as an attempt by sociologists to reduce the complexities of the
journalists' trade to academic formulae, John Whale misreads the
argument. That no charter is proclaimed, no rule book or credo issued
to guide the production of news, is no proof that it lacks consistent
pattern. News production is no more an indeterminate anarchy than
other social processes, and where there is social process there is order.
The sociologist attempts to discern the regularities in this order.
Journalists do not, of course, work by heaven-sent criteria against which
events are measured for newsworthiness. But simply because 'large
shifting groups of people' are working 'often in a hurry' there have to be
routines of practice which lessen the burdens of unpredictability, and
make manageable the colossal task of transmuting the events of the
world into news.

John Whale concedes this. He points to some aspects of this order in
the same piece, when he writes of the 'banal technicalities' that militate
against the coverage of certain places and events, the commercial
considerations which have to be brought to bear in evaluating the
worthy but dull, the competitive strategies of competing media or
journalists. These are indeed the stuff of sociological accounts of news,
suggesting that the content of news is related to the inevitable routines
which are to a great extent required for its production.

Not all antipathy to a sociology of journalism derives from the thesis
that the news is inherently inexplicable. Another long tradition accounts
for news in the romantic deeds of the great men of the trade. The
Hollywood caricature of the world-weary pro, in rolled-up sleeves and
eye-shade, barking pithy orders at a zealous corps of awed reporters,
remains for many both inside and outside journalism a stylised but
plausible image of how news is made. His is the word made flesh. Most
standard histories of journalism are replete with the 'great man theory of
history', the view that a few dominant personalities with iron will and
clarity of vision have caught history by the tail and twisted it in the
direction they desire. In Britain we still speak of 'the Northcliffe
Revolution' in labelling that colossal and gradual change in the
commercial nature of the press that came in the wake of the 'retail
revolution' in the mid-nineteenth century. The history of journalism in
the United States often reads like a serial biography of men like James
Gordon Bennett, Horace Greely and William Randolph Hearst. Of
course these 'impressarios of journalism' as Francis Williams, probably
the best writer of this kind of popular history of the press, has termed
them, did carry enormous personal influence (Williams, 1957, 1969).
Indeed, their like will feature prominently in the historical perspectives
of Chapter 3.

The trouble with the great man theory of history is that there is an awful lot of history and not many great men. The great editorial figures immortalised in films like *Citzen Kane* crystallised rather than created; they gave imaginative and energetic momentum to existing movements of style, organisation or strategy, none of which can ever be reduced to personal invention. It just never explains enough to isolate the genius or originality of a few dominant figures, often really remembered because of their flamboyance and eccentricity in tales of dubious authenticity.

Gay Talese, in writing the story of the *New York Times*, subtitles his book 'the story of the men who influence the institution that influences the world', and his book is a tribute to the thesis that the chain of influence runs in that direction (Talese, 1971). This is much like the notion that the length of Cleopatra's nose determined the course of Roman history. It is in fact the John Whale thesis writ large. It suggests that just as newsrooms react randomly to random events, so the accidental arrival of great men on the scene of history provokes unpredictable changes, and history is indeed 'just one damn thing after another'. Our research proceeds with the contrary assumption that individual personalities can indeed make a considerable impact on their environment, but within an historical and organisational context which they inherit and unavoidably confront.

A further objection to a sociological account of journalism is raised by those who feel that in a closed and complex world like the press or broadcasting no outsider can ever hope to comment intelligently without his comments exposing his unfamiliarity. This is aimed partly at ignorance of technology and practice. The outsider cannot analyse practices whose purpose and importance he scarcely comprehends. For example, a study of the making of a television series (Elliott, 1972a), while welcomed by many in broadcasting, was accused by one senior practitioner of misunderstanding what it had described, a misunderstanding which could be avoided by placing emphasis 'on the need for the training of any research worker who hopes to study mass communication to include a period of practical work within a broadcasting organisation' (Wyndham Goldie, 1972, p. 519). Despite the odd equation of studying mass communication with broadcasting alone, this is not an unreasonable suggestion. It is important, however, not to confuse becoming proficient in the analysis and observation *of* something with becoming proficient *at* it. Not many ornithologists can achieve flight, yet we generally trust their analysis of its accomplishment by birds.

Of course, there is no excuse for ignorance of terminology and practice, and all the researchers involved in this study had conducted previous studies inside broadcasting organisations. This does not make them trained professionals. But it did provide a working knowledge of professional practice which eased relationships with the journalists being studied, and prevented observation periods being dissipated in an an endless barrage of naive questioning of the obvious.

There is a deeper level to this argument however, and again it was raised in Mrs Wyndham Goldie's review. She suggests a non-professional will actually misinterpret what he sees because the professionals do not articulate their motives and objectives, 'the overall purpose of the team, which is so well understood by them that it doesn't have to be stated' (Wyndham Goldie, 1972, p. 517). In a reply to this review two colleagues of the study's author raised some important objections to Mrs Wyndham Goldie's position. They note that 'She seems to assume that research is about what people say, not what they do', and go on to challenge her dismissal of case studies.

> Yet if she is right, her belief that generalisation from case studies of production is impossible is surely absurd, since only if there are recurrent problems met and resolved in similar ways can these common understandings she believes so mysterious be workable or even exist. And generalisation is precisely about these recurrences. If she is wrong, and the activities in the media are no more or less obscure than those in other industries, then the search for regularities and routines is a perfectly valid procedure (Croll and Golding, 1972, p. 541).

Jeremy Tunstall makes a similar point in his important study of British specialist journalists, when drawing attention to the segmented nature of journalism (Tunstall, 1971, p. 3). His point is that so complex is the occupation that it is *only* the outsider who is able to provide a coherent and balanced view of how journalism works.

Part of the dispute arises from the similarity some commentators perceive in the purposes of sociology and journalism. Many journalists see sociology as an academic word-game, characterised by inelegant jargon, woolly-minded naivety and intellectual arrogance based on ignorance of 'real life'. Many sociologists still use the term 'jounalistic' for those essays by colleagues they judge to be superficial, ill-judged, over-hasty and over-written. To many in both camps the two pursuits are indeed alternative methods of investigating and explaining the social life of the world (Jacobs, 1970; Hill, 1972). Suffice to say that a sociological account of journalism is indeed that of an outsider. This research was conducted in the belief that this was an advantage providing a breadth of vision unavailable to the practitioner. It was also rooted in the view that a sociological account would at the very least provide an alternative to that of the 'insider', offering insights of as much value to him as to the non-professional.

We can look at these alternative perspectives in a little more detail. Journalists are very often concerned about the comprehensibility of news, wondering if the assumptions that are made about audience knowledge and intelligence are valid. Thus improvements are often seen in terms of simpler vocabulary, more graphic assistance, and of course that question-begging panacea, more background. Journalists, in other words, are concerned with the short-term and deliberate manipulation of news, and with its immediate and direct effect on viewers. The sociologist has a different perspective, being concerned rather more with the long-term, routine and non-deliberate manufacture of news, and by corollary, with the long-term and cumulative influence on viewers, This distinction can be graphically summarised:

	Short-term	Long-term
Deliberate	A. *Bias* Campaigns Comprehension tests	B. *Policy* Propaganda
Non-deliberate	C. *Unwitting bias* Inferential structures Unintended effects	D. *Ideology* Audience consciousness

Essentially the journalist's perspective is in box A, or sometimes B, the sociologist's has been in C, and more recently, in D. This difference explains some of the tensions arising from sociological commentaries on news. What the sociologist describes as a necessary consequence of the organisation of production, the journalist sees as an accusation of bias or incompetence. The sociologist is only applying to journalism, however, a perspective applied equally to other culture-producing institutions, notably education. If journalists think they have been unfairly ravaged by sociology they should attend a conference on the sociology of education![1]

Many journalists have themselves written quizzical appraisals of their craft in books, lectures or articles. Of course this is not a recent innovation. Even if one disregards the earlier critiques in Britain by working journalists like William Cobbett, or before him Milton, Defoe, Steele, Addison and their like, leading figures of journalism have regularly reflected in print on the role and character of their work. In this century the writings of Walter Lippmann stand out among such works, born of his conviction that 'In an exact sense the present crisis of western democracy is a crisis in journalism' (Lippmann, 1920, p. 5). Lippmann's eloquently expressed view that democracy depends on the quality of the information available to its citizens is presented with considerably more sophistication than the frequent rhetorical displays in favour of a 'free press' which have succeeded him. It is with the growth in broadcast journalism that the literature on journalism by journalists has lengthened most dramatically. There are several reasons for this.

First, and most simply, the expansion in the numbers of journalists has, among other things, expanded the number of potential book writers employed in press and broadcasting. Like many academics, the journalist is often found to have the bones of the great novel in his desk drawer, or if not the great novel the definitive solution to the crisis of contemporary democracy. Not unnaturally, this creative urge often finds outlet in informed criticism of that area of the world he knows best, his own occupation. Second, broadcast news has placed journalism in the shop window of an entertainment medium of absorbing interest to an enormous public. The domestic habits and personal idiosyncrasies of 'newscasters' have acquired a not dissimilar fascination to those of other media personalities. Sunday newspapers provide exciting behind-the-scenes accounts of television newsrooms, and even television itself pores over its own machinations with narcissistic fondness. Not surprisingly this prompts the men in the spotlight to offer their own portrayals to an eager audience.

More serious professional reviews assess the relationship between the press and news broadcasting, and men who have worked in both have been anxious to examine their impact on one another and their comparative effectiveness. John Whale's conclusion that newspapers are better equipped to explain political affairs was a stimulus both to his own return to print journalism from television, and to his book on political journalism (Whale, 1967). Several professionals have written, sometimes defensively, at other times anxiously, of the involvement of journalism in the issues reported, for example the supposed exacerbation of violence by its televised portrayal, or the huge impact of television on election campaigning. Several events have brought these issues to a head, among them the televised coverage of the Vietnam war, and the argument as to whether it stimulated popular opposition to the war or inured the American population to atrocity and thus hypnotised it into sublime indifference. This issue was followed by the battle of attrition between Vice-President Agnew and the American news media, concern about the role of the media in Northern Ireland, and parallel skirmishes throughout the world. Universally professional journalists have found themselves under attack, and have been forced to articulate the previously implicit conventions and purposes of their activities. In the United States this gave rise to an internal debate about 'the new journalism', a creed developed as a self-consciously iconoclastic rationale for the subjective reportage of writers like Tom Wolfe and Truman Capote. The quarry they were after was the journalistic faith in objectivity, though the extent to which they pursued or destroyed it will be examined in Chapter 8.

In many ways it is the expansion of television news that has stimulated the debate about news in general. The novelty, and vividness of television news, and the sheer scale of television news audiences have made this debate more urgent, more public, and more political.

Televison is quite simply the largest mass medium and for most people the most important. Most people in industrialsied countries spend more of their leisure time watching television than doing anything else. In less technically advanced countries radio broadcasting, at least since the 'transistor revolution' of the early 1960s, is the primary medium, and television is still embryonic. For this reason the Nigerian sections of this study are concerned with both radio and television (indeed, as in many small broadcasting organisations, the functional division between the two media is incomplete and sometimes non-existent in Nigeria and other African countries).

To illustrate this expansion briefly, in 1950 Africa, South America and 'Oceania' contained not a single television set, while there were only 11 million in the whole world. By 1963 this total had soared to 130 million, and UNESCO estimated the total by 1971–2 to be 288 million. The advance of radio in Africa is equally dramatic. In 1950 there were 0.7 sets per 100 people; in 1962 there were 2.3 sets; by 1971 five countries had more than 15 per 100 and 14 countries had between 5 and 10 sets per 100, while the average figure had risen to 5.5 per 100. This is still vastly below the level in Europe and North America, but it is a rapid increase in audience use by any standards, particularly allowing for the common practice of multiple use of a single receiver.

Of course these figures make no sense without a comparative look at the press. In many advanced societies it appears that newspaper circulations reach a saturation point beyond which rising costs, the competition of broadcasting and pressures on advertising revenue combine to weed out the market. In particular the recent rapid rise in newsprint costs and concern for the conservation of remaining sources have hit the world's press severely. In aggregate, world press circulations have remained more or less stable in the last decade, while the number of titles has declined, particularly in Europe.

The displacement of the press by broadcasting has led some observers to forecast a split in function between the two media, with broadcasting providing immediate coverage and up-to-date transmission of facts, while the press provides more leisurely discussion and analysis. This may or may not prove to be the case. But simply in terms of the statistics of consumption more people than ever before receive the majority of their news from broadcasting.

These bald statistics of the expansion of broadcasting, of course, offer no direct evidence of the increased consumption of *news* broadcasting. However, most research indicates two important developments. First, news broadcasting is in fact a popular item of broadcast provision. In many countries the major evening news bulletins regularly secure places among the top rated programmes. Major dramatic news events can secure the rapt attention of more or less whole populations in front of their sets, as at the time of Kennedy's assassination or a moon landing.

The second relevant research finding is the very high credibility of television news. Invariably, when asked which account they would be more likely to accept if the same event were reported in the press and on television, the majority of people put their faith in television.[2] Partly this is rationalised in terms of the visual component of television news – 'well you can actually see it happening'. Yet the same trust is placed in radio. It may have something to do with the aura of established impartiality which attaches to broadcasting institutions by virtue of their usual constitutional position. Newspapers are perceived as avowedly partisan, by contrast with the seemingly apolitical status of broadcasting.

We shall touch on some of these issues in examining what it is that sociologists have had to say about news.

Sociologists and the news

> As part of our new glamour, we are invited especially often these days to sit with society's measurers in exotic places so they can tell us about the impact of what we do. (Frank, 1970)

Mass communications research, especially in the United States, developed very largely independently of social scientific thinking. As a result the bulk of the research was, if not indistinguishable from market research, at least concerned with similar problems, those of the extent and nature of exposure to the media and the effects of such consumption. Not surprisingly social scientists largely accepted the research priorities this implied, and in any case gave little attention to the mass media since they were presumably being studied in schools of journalism, mass communications and the like. They were not, and an optimistic version of the history of mass media research would see it as an emancipation from the wilderness of 'mass communications' studies into the havens of social science. This emergence has an important secondary aspect, the shift from the study of effects to the study of production. Logically if not chronologically this development has had three turning points.

It began by conceiving the production of mass communications as a chain along which messages passed, were selected and rejected and finally processed for distribution to the public. This sequence was akin to the opening and shutting of a series of gates and the problem was to identify the gatekeeper and discover the criteria upon which his selections were based (White, 1950 Donohue, *et al.* 1972). The 'gatekeeper' tradition has been heavily criticised in recent years. It is an easy target. Its essential naivety is not difficult to identify or pillory. Undoubtedly its limitations were not invisible to many of the hundreds of graduate students who sat by the elbow of their local 'Mr Gates' and dutifully calibrated the pile of rejected carbons in his waste bin. But the research was easy to conduct, conceptually simple, readily quantifiable, and not without a useful conclusion, that news production was often mechanical, routine, passive and systematic. That most of the studies concentrated on small-town papers in the United States does not detract from the significance of this much maligned research tradition.

Nonetheless its simplistic nature is obvious, and researchers turned to more sophisticated analysis of newsmaking. Their concern was to get away from the notion of 'bias', the deliberate manipulation of news for political or personal ends, which so regularly confines the thoughts of media critics to the short term and the deliberate. The notion of bias implies a position of balance from which news can be dragged by the weights of prejudice, intrigue or the malign influence of political and commercial outsiders. It has two crucial limitations. One is the impossibility of establishing quite where that position of balance lies. The subtle problems that derive from this dilemma lay behind much of the recent discussion of objectivity which will be examined in later chapters. The other is the temptation to assume that if these various weights can be removed, and the journalist liberated from the conspiratorial chains that bind him, professional autonomy will guarantee the untainted impartiality and completeness of the news (Merrill, 1974). Much later research (including our own) has been aimed at showing how professionalism, and its attendant values and practices, itself adds an important constraint on the news produced.

Researchers attempted to go beyond the discovery of deliberate distortion and document what they called 'unwitting bias'. This was achieved by the detailed analysis of the way in which a particular event was handled by the news media. Kurt and Gladys Lang conducted the seminal study of this kind in 1951 when Chicago laid on a triumphal rally to welcome General Douglas MacArthur to the city. The event took place against the backdrop of MacArthur's dispute with President Truman, who had sacked him from his post of command in Korea when the General had threatened to exceed the Truman–Acheson strategy. MacArthur came home to declare sentimentally before Congress that he intended quietly, as old soldiers do, to 'fade away'. Instead Chicago offered him whistles, fire-crackers, church bells and a hero's welcome (Lang and Lang, 1953, 1970).

Thirty-one observers were scattered round the city and instructed to note in detail all that happened. They found that people on the streets were disappointed by the tranquillity of the event; in contrast to television viewers who witnessed the crowded hullaballoo the press had led them to expect. The drama and excitement of the televised version of the parade derived from television's anxiety to keep the occasion alive and adequate to its pre-publicity. In doing so, *unwittingly and incidentally*, an impression of widespread support for MacArthur, and by extension his politics, was diffused into public consciousness and popular history.

Such research rests on a comparison of media coverage with what 'really happened', which of course begs a whole range of questions. One partial solution is to demonstrate the systematic way prior expectations about an event shape its coverage by the media, and to suggest the way this might structure the portrayal of the event, regardless of the validity of such a portrayal. The researchers' reality may be as distorted as the journalists', and the epistemological issues that raises are beyond the present discussion. But as a way of locating 'unwitting bias' this method is at least suggestive. A study much influenced by the work of the Langs was conducted by researchers at an anti-Vietnam war rally in London in 1968 (Halloran *et al.*, 1970). For weeks prior to the rally press coverage had concentrated on the possibility of a violent confrontation between police and demonstrators. These expectations were heightened by comparing the rally to political demonstrations earlier in the year in the Paris (May) 'événements' and the battles at the Democratic Party Convention in Chicago. The political content and context of these different occasions were largely displaced by concentrating on their presumed similarity as examples of violent dissidence confronting the forces of law and order. The London demonstration was very largely a peaceful and orderly affair marred by violence between a small breakaway group and the police. Yet press and television coverage was almost entirely focussed on these incidents. The authors of the study concluded that coverage of the event both reflected the expectations raised by the media in the 'build-up' period, and in turn reinforced the retrospective perception of the demonstration as a violent, irrational and indeed non-political confrontation, a view which has passed into history (Murdock, 1973).

Both these studies studiously avoid imputations of conscious distortion, but speak of 'unwitting bias' or 'inferential structures' which act as templates guiding the selection of events and their presentation. The third point along the road of production studies is to turn away from the production of news about single events and to extend the analysis to the long-term, routine processes which underlie the daily task of news production. Studies of this kind are few and far between for some fairly obvious reasons.

First, by definition they require time, the longer the better, to observe the difference between the accidental surface events of a particular period and the more fundamental practices which persist beyond them. This is a luxury rarely available to researchers. Second, it requires long-term access to journalists and their working environment. Intruding on someone's work, observing what they do, asking difficult, awkward, occasionally ignorant questions, with every likelihood that the end product will be a questioning or critical account of what has been observed, is to place a very great strain on tolerance and hospitality. It is well for sociologists studying media professionals, and indeed occupations in general, to imagine how they would react to a request from a student of the sociology of social research who wanted to perch obtrusively by their desk for a couple of months. Add to these practical and personal restraints the invariable sensitivity of broadcast news departments and it is not difficult to understand the scarcity of studies of production.

Nonetheless some important studies have been carried out which have thrown up suggestive leads. In a study of the major American network news organisations, particularly NBC, Epstein drew attention to the way in which the needs of the organisation were paramount in constructing news programmes (Epstein, 1973). In the heavily commercial environment of American broadcasting, what Epstein terms the economic logic, the problems of scheduling, audience maintenance and cost control, swamp journalistic demands. At the same time concern for audience interest compels a packaging of news in story models, presented by personalities, in a production environment entirely geared to the pre-planned, digestible and limited product organisational imperatives require. Altheide has drawn much the same picture in a study of a local television station in Arizona (Altheide, 1976). He argues that the demands of programming and entertainment produce a preconceived, prepackaged journalism or 'news perspective', which severely curtails what is sought for and accepted in broadcast news. In a similar context, outside broadcasting, Sigelman has suggested how these organisational demands are impressed on to working journalists through the mechanisms of socialisation and selective recruitment. The ideals and objectives of the organisation are operationalised, he suggests, in the occupational mythology which journalists acquire in the course of their induction into the job and progression upward through a career. Such is the concentration on the routine manipulation of limited skills, a narrow and technical definition of journalism, that autonomy is not felt to be threatened. In Sigelman's words the job is 'more a feat of engineering than of architecture' (Sigelman, 1973; see also Roshco, 1975).

Studies of the permanent structure of news production in broadcasting elsewhere are rare indeed. Two recent studies in Britain should be mentioned; Philip Schlesinger's account of news production in the BBC, and Michael Tracey's study of current affairs and political television (Schlesinger, 1978; Tracey, 1977). Both emphasise the organisational contexts which become translated into routines in the production of television news, and both thus adopt the sociological perspective of Box D in our earlier diagram. There are, of course, other scattered studies, but it would be a litany of the bibliographically obscure to list them all here.[3] Few studies of broadcast news production have been conducted, and not that many more of the press (see, however, Tunstall, 1971; Chibnall, 1977).

A slightly different tack has been taken by researchers indeed concerned with the long-term and non-deliberate basis of news production, but at the level of the journalists themselves, their values, attitudes and assumptions. The largest such study was a telephone survey of well over a thousand American journalists carried out by a team of researchers at Illinois University (Johnstone *et al.,* 1976). They produced a great deal of basic data on training, education, careers and specialisation. But most interesting was their attempt to relate these characteristics to two basic attitudes among their respondents, which, borrowing their terms from Cohen (1963), the authors term neutral and participant. For the 'neutral' journalists, 'the news media constitute an impartial transmission link dispensing information to the public: news is seen to emerge naturally from the events and occurrences of the real world, and it is sufficient for the journalist to be a spectator to the ongoing social process and to transmit faithfully accurate communications about it' (Johnstone, *et al.,* 1976, p. 114). The 'participant' journalist, by contrast, takes a more active and creative role in the discovery of news, giving primacy to relevance, context and investigation. This distinction is discussed and summarised in many reviews of journalism (Merrill, 1974; Janowitz, 1975). The Illinois researchers found that 'participants' were more highly educated, younger, more mobile and more ambitious than the 'neutrals'. We return to this issue in Chapter 7. Of course this gap between the active–critical, and passive–consensual approaches has appeared in various spheres with the growth of a radical critique within the professions in the last two decades. In journalism, as distinct from say education or social work, it has a pre-history in the political origins of the craft. But we shall be exploring its implications for broadcast journalism throughout this study.

Other researchers have concentrated less on this division than on what they see as a more fundamental view of the world shared by all journalists. Obviously this theme appears in any study of journalism. In the work of some sociologists influenced by phenomenological or ethnomethodological schools of thought, however, it has become dominant. Bensman and Lilienfeld, for example, describe what they call the 'journalistic attitude' as a particular occupational way of seeing the world, akin to others in the world of the arts and culture (Bensman and Lilienfeld, 1973). Molotch and Lester, more solidly rooted in the new phenomenological sociology, conclude their review of the way journalists produce accounts of reality with the rather mundane discovery that 'all events are socially constructed and their "newsworthiness" is not contained in their objective features' (Molotch and Lester, 1974, p. 110). Not all the work in this vein is quite so jejune however. One of the most interesting of these researchers is Tuchman, who has attempted to capture the categories employed by journalists in coping with the reality they have to report (Tuchman, 1973b). Judgements about news, she suggests, become absorbed into the 'common-sense' knowledge of everyday journalism. They further become organised into 'typifications' which in turn determine the organisation of work. These basic insights are well explored by Tuchman in describing the strategies employed by journalists to deflect criticism (Tuchman, 1972). One is left with the problem in this work, however, of the relative weight of work routines in determining 'typifications', or, as sometimes seems to be claimed, the categories determining the organisation of work. As with all studies emphasising values, attitudes and mental categories, one is left yearning for a little history or analysis of production.

We are left with the conclusion that research to fill out our Box D is scarce, scattered and inconclusive. There are rather more studies which look at the product itself, and we shall mention some of these in Chapter 6.

The twin dilemmas of news broadcasting

The journalist gives content and direction to the opinions of a mute multitude. But he is nevertheless forced to listen, combine, and guess what the tendencies of this multitude are, and what it desires to hear and have confirmed, and whither it wants to be led. (Georg Simmel, 1964)

Criticism of broadcast news often comes from groups or individuals who detect bias in the way they are presented by the news, or who feel their activities are deliberately ignored. The charges impute intentional distortion, suppression or aspersion by journalists as individuals or by media organisations. That these sins are committed is beyond dispute. That they are normally endemic to journalism and systematically part of its daily practice is not. Indeed, it is the theme of this research that deliberate manipulation of material with intent to disseminate partial views of the world is so peripheral a part of the manufacture of news as to be largely irrelevant to its explanation. Journalists are as venal as other men in their daily pursuits, and as partisan in their judgements about the world. But commitments to objectivity, accuracy and honesty in broadcast journalism are usually sincere and serious. It will be our contention that despite these tenets broadcast news provides only a partial account of the world, an account whose deficiencies are consistent and rooted in the working routines and beliefs which sustain the daily practice of news production. In other words, we suggest it is the structure of news-making rather than bias which needs examination and explanation.

What we shall be examining in this study is the way this structure conflicts with the occupational values and intentions of broadcast journalists. This conflict derives from two basic dilemmas. First, the news attempts to be a *comprehensive* account of significant events in the world. Yet also, being finite, it has to be *selective*. Part of journalism's task is the intelligent selection of events in the world as newsworthy and the application to them of criteria of importance and priority. Much therefore is omitted, and selection necessitates partiality and the intrusion of personal judgement and organisational need. The second dilemma derives from the commitment of news to convey *objective*, factual accounts of events, and at the same time to make them *meaningful* and comprehensible to audiences. But even the simplest of contexts or explanatory additions will compromise complete objectivity. If news is restricted to the brief narration of unadorned reports it is reduced to a meaningless collage of separate facts; unrelated, pointless and random. If it expands to include explanation and background it introduces meaning with the inevitable intrusion of opinion and tendentiousness.

These two intractable dilemmas are not new, nor unique to broadcast news. They are rooted in the clash of demands made on news media since the emergence of a commercial press, and thus of audience-seeking strategies on the one hand, and the legitimating creeds of objectivity and impartiality on the other. Broadcasting has added to the dilemmas because of its technological demands, its problematic relationship with the state and its massive audiences. Broadcasting organisations try resolutely to confirm their authority by claims to comprehensive, credible, and objective news coverage, yet they suffer acutely from the limitations of time, thus exacerbating the first dilemma. At the same time broadcasting serves a heterogeneous and widespread audience which it seeks to entertain, and serve with comprehensible, popular, meaningful news. Yet constitutional and legislative restraints prohibit the broadcasting of opinion, extreme dissent, or excessive controversy, thus heightening the second dilemma.

In this study we will be examining the way these dilemmas are resolved in the daily production of broadcast news in three very different societies. We will be examining two ideas in particular. First, we suggest that the attempt to translate legislative demands into operational practice has been doomed to failure. In aiming at objectivity or impartiality broadcasting practice merely falls back on the historically bred routines and values of commercial journalism. For several reasons broadcasting is a relatively passive form of journalism, highly dependent on the news-producing groups in society, whose values and cultural definitions it inevitably reproduces and relays. Second, we will argue that the resulting content of broadcast news portrays a very particular view of the world that we can label ideological. Lacking two crucial dimensions of descriptive structure, process and power, it is inherently incapable of providing a critical account of events in the world. This is not the result of a conspiracy within newsrooms or of the inadequacies, professional or political, of broadcast journalists. It is a necessary result of the structure of news gathering and production, and of the routines and conventions built into professional broadcasting practice. News is the end product of patterned routines whose management is the process of news production.

Academics are often assumed to be obsessed with definitions; neat, tidy pigeon-holes in which to sort reality. When it comes to news, journalists have often succumbed to the same temptation. 'History in a hurry', 'blood, broads and money', and Charles Dana's 'what makes the reader say "gee-whizz"' are among the more snappy attempts by journalists to encapsulate their craft (see, inter alia, Brucker, 1973). Half a century ago Lippmann suggested that 'the news is not a mirror of social conditions but the report of an aspect that has obtruded itself' (Lippmann, 1922, 216). These views at least begin to accept that news is structured.

In attempting to unearth this structure and examine the ideas outlined in this chapter we shall begin by describing the evolution of news broadcasting in the three countries in our study.

Notes

1. This misunderstanding is at the heart of many debates between journalists and their academic observers. See for example some of the contributions in Halloran and Gurevitch (1970). In Britain two recent examples have been the response to a study of industrial relations news on television (Glasgow University Media Group, 1976), and in the discussion of news by the Annan Committee report on the future of broadcasting (Home Office, 1977, Ch.17). The latter is a classic case of mistaking analyses of the

necessary structures of news production for criticisms of professional ability, thus concluding that improvement is to arise from better professional training.

2. This finding is, not surprisingly, confirmed recurrently in audience research produced by broadcasting organisations. Research at the Leicester Centre for Mass Communication Research has also suggested the high credibility of television news. See also, *inter alia*, Bogart (1968–9).

3. Several interesting studies have been conducted by researchers interested in organisations rather than the media, who happen to have alighted on broadcasting or newspapers. Two examples by British industrial sociologists are Warner (1971), and Burns (1977). An American example is Argyris (1974). A pioneering production study in current affairs television in Britain is Blumler (1969). As befits their origins in doctoral theses, both Tracey (1977) and Schlesinger (1978) provide fairly thorough bibliographies of production studies.

Chapter 3

The evolution of
news broadcasting

Most of the ideas and activities that constitute contemporary journalism have evolved through a long historical cycle. This chapter reviews that cycle in each of the three countries. Obviously it would be misleading to reduce the scattered events in vastly different settings to an ordered scheme, but it is possible to detect an underlying similarity, a pattern around which variations are created by the individual circumstances of national history.

The development of journalism is frequently portrayed as the heroic and passionate struggle of journalists for a free press, the creation of which ennobles both their own profession and the democracy it helps sustain. Without seeking to debunk this view, never without an element of truth whatever its romantic excesses, it may be more useful to subject journalism to the prosaic considerations of *cui bono*; news for whom. News, like any product, is subject to pressures of supply and demand. On the one hand changes in the technology, both of production and distribution, in the organisation of news gathering and production, and in the purposes, political or economic, which prompt production in the first place, all shape the form and context of journalistic activities. On the other hand, there is no news without an audience to be informed by it. Changes in the size and distribution of populations, in literacy levels, and in the different needs various audience groups bring to journalism, all play a significant part in the evolution of some types of news media rather than others. The cycle through which these various factors operate seems roughly similar in most European countries. In outline, it is as follows.

Printers develop news-sheets to the point where they secure the attention of absolute monarchs who subject them to licence. An official news gazette of some kind is the first regular publication. Licensing is challenged and eventually diminished, and where a 'bourgeois revolution' occurs the rising commercial classes provide a rapidly expanding audience for the new press, while the political parties engendered in the challenge to the old order are ready patrons and sponsors of the art of political journalism. Advances in production techniques, better transportation and increasing populations all facilitate higher circulations, newspapers prosper and the publisher-printer gives way to the publisher-editor in the rapidly differentiating industry. The growing power of legislative bodies is often used to repress over-zealous journalism but either by persistent opposition or the steady rapprochement of press and political elites the press secures constitutional recognition. Political journalism emerges as a full-time occupation. Urbanisation, road and rail communications, cheaper paper and faster presses all foster lower prices and higher circulations. The political press gives way to a more obviously commercial press concerned to burst the limits of explicit partisanship and appeal to wider readerships with new techniques and styles of 'reporting'. The reporter replaces the journalist; his skills are accuracy, conciseness, speed, verbal simplicity and objectivity. The further growth of advertising supplies a new economic base for journalism, and the search for mass readerships creates the mass popular press of the twentieth century. The subsequent decline and restructuring of the newspaper press are of less relevance to us here than the three crucial legacies which are bequeathed by this cycle to the subsequent development of broadcast journalism.

First, the almost universal constitutional recognition of the press, guaranteeing its freedom from censorship and granting it licence to comment, is the first stage in that special relationship with the state which becomes so much more central in the organisation of broadcasting. Second, this process produced a large autonomous body of men called journalists whose job, quite separately from any involvement in politics, was the manufacture of news. A profession had been created (Elliott, 1978). Third, the journalists created a set of beliefs about how their job should be done and what characterised its most laudable practices. Most important of these beliefs was the discovery of objectivity in reporting. Before turning to these three legacies, it is necessary to flesh out the historical scheme a little.

The emergence of journalism in Europe

There is no need here to dig back as far as the *Acta Diurna* which kept the citizenry of Julius Caesar's Rome informed 2,000 years ago. European journalism begins in the handwritten newsletters of the early sixteenth century or earlier. Circulating particularly between trading companies, these furnished their wealthy patrons with news of military, political and economic events throughout the continent.

Printers had moved from the German centres of their craft along the trade routes, setting up shop, not in centres of learning in university towns, but in the newly thriving trade towns like Basel, Venice and, in 1483, Stockholm. They quickly saw the opportunity to supplement the limited income available from books and soon developed the 'corantos' or news-sheets (most notably in Holland) to provide the information so essential to the merchant groups for whom they were written. The news-sheets were quite different from the newsletters in two ways. They were serially produced, albeit not always at exactly regular intervals, and they were compilations rather than accounts of a single event like the 'trewe encountre of the battle of Flodden Field' that some enterprising publicist had produced in 1513 in England. These digests for businessmen were well established in most northern European countries by the mid-seventeenth century. As Steinberg notes: 'in northern Europe the net of international trade which the Hanse towns had spun from Russia to England and from Norway to Flanders now provided easy openings for the printers' craft' (Steinberg, 1974, p. 46). A technical invention plus a commercial need had established the new form of communication.

The first newspapers date from the very early seventeenth century, run by publisher-printers who collated a variety of 'intelligences' from around the Continent. These were rigorously licensed in most countries and the only regular publication was some form of official Gazette. Many of these date from the early seventeenth century and several have survived in various mutations to the present day. Among these were *Ordinari Post Tijdender* founded in Sweden in 1645. At first its main function was to give the official version of events in the Thirty Years War. Its publication followed the successful introduction of a newspaper in German for the German territories then occupied by the Swedes under King Gustavus Adolphus (Pers, 1966).

The establishment of a daily press awaited the expansion of trade and the liberalisation or abolition of licensing (1695 in England, 1766 in Sweden, the first continental country to remove censorship). Daily newspapers soon followed, dating for example from 1702 in England, 1772 in France. In Sweden the first news-sheet had appeared in 1598, the first weekly in 1624. The abolition of censorship in 1766 led directly to the first daily newspaper, *Dagligt Allehanda* (Olson). Swedish mercantile power in the Baltic and north Germany stimulated a rapid growth in the provincial and Stockholm newspapers. Freedom of publication was restricted between 1772 and 1809 with the restoration of Royalist power but after the dethronement of Gustav IV in 1809 when the ripples of the French Revolution hit Stockholm, the liberal freedoms were restored. The Swedish law of press freedom adopted in 1812 was one of the four fundamental laws making up the Swedish constitution. Like many such laws, however, it was initially a two-edged weapon and distaste for journalistic excess was reflected in the punishment prescribed for violation of some of its statutes – death, exile or lashing and imprisonment. The law was modified in 1865, and again in 1922. New constitutional legislation on the freedom of publication was passed in 1949. This followed an enquiry into authoritarian tendencies in the Second World War. To prevent anything similar in future times of crisis 'the text of the legislation sought by all conceivable means to guarantee against encroachments upon the press by the powers of State' (Gustafsson and Hadenius, 1976). In 1975 a parliamentary commission put forward a proposal for a new fundamental law to include all the mass media. Legislation to extend and strengthen the freedom of expression, information and publication is expected.

Although the chronology is not the same everywhere, the general pattern is similar. Growing commercial prosperity secures the economic independence of the press, and eventually some form of constitutional guarantees of its autonomy. This second 'struggle for freedom' normally occurs in the wake of the French Revolution. In France over 400 new papers appeared after the publication of the *Declaration of the Rights of Man* in 1780. The reality of the political autonomy of the press proclaimed by its apparent emergence as a 'Fourth Estate' is subject to some suspicion. But true or not, it was a myth of some power and significance. As Boyce has argued in describing this myth in its British context, '. . . the idea of the Fourth Estate had served its purpose: it had enabled the British press to stake a claim for a recognised and respectable place in the British political system, even in the British constitutional system, and to justify breaking away from government repression and subsidies. The credibility of the press lay in its apparent independence from the party political machine . . .' (Boyce, 1978, p. 26–7). Often the press splits into a radical faction labouring under the repressive legislation of newly evolved parliamentary assemblies, and a bourgeois press serving the commercial middle class increasingly predominant in the legislatures. In Germany, the party press developed in the nineteenth century only to be turned by Bismark into his 'reptile press', as he put it, crawling on its belly under severe control. More exemplary is Belgium where the 1830 constitution proclaimed that 'the press is free; censorship may never be re-established and no surety may be extracted from writers, editors, or printers' (Olson, 1966). This last phrase is interesting, indicating the further differentiation of the industry.

Leonore O'Boyle has contrasted the emergence of full-time journalism in England, France and Germany in the nineteenth century. In France the shortage of political posts after the 1815 restoration left a large surplus of job-seeking, unskilled, but educated men who saw journalism as a stepping stone to a political career. The growing power of political journalism is captured in a *Quarterly Review* description of the upheavals of 1848 as 'the accidental audacity of . . . the spawn of two printing houses'. Journalism proper was not to expand substantially until the popular cheap entertainment press, 'La presse a un sou', after 1860. In Germany too, some of the educated but unemployable professionals who sought refuge in the vast civil service also found their way into journalism. While political parties were as yet embryonic, nonetheless nationalists and liberals frequently sought a voice through journalism (O'Boyle, 1968). England, by contrast, produced an economically viable press before 1850. *The Times*, in particular, representing the voice of acceptable reform, expanded its circulation from about 6,000 in 1822 to over 50,000 in the 1850s. Papers like this could afford higher salaries for full-time journalists. The occupation thus became selfconsciously distinct from the political–literary hybrid it had been hitherto.

Before the emergence of the popular mass-entertainment press, crucial developments in supply and demand were required. On the production side the introduction of steampowered printing, and of cheap, mechanised paper production facilitated faster production at lower prices of higher print-runs. On the demand side populations were increasing in numbers and becoming more literate.

In Sweden, Lars Johan Hierta started *Aftonbladet* in 1830, and the success of his paper, together with the growth of Sweden's industrial population and railway system, heralded a period of rapid advances in the newspaper industry. By 1850 there were 58 provincial newspapers (Olson). Sweden had possibly the highest literacy level in Europe by the mid-nineteenth century, the combined effect of Lutheran teaching and a 1686 law proclaiming that children had to learn to read. Most literacy figures derive from tests on captive populations and it may be indicative either of high literacy or the elevated social composition of the Swedish criminal classes that only 7 per cent of an 1857 sample of Swedish prisoners were illiterate (Cipolla, 1969, p. 76).

Irish literacy was also high, almost certainly higher than in England. The National School system, forty years ahead of England, was established in 1831, and the number of children on roll went up nearly five-fold between 1833 and 1849 (Akenson, 1970). The Irish population doubled between 1800 and 1840 before the twin crises of famine and emigration in mid-century. Illustrating the point that developments in different countries take place at politically equivalent historical junctures rather than simultaneously is the rise of the Irish provincial press. By analysing the dates of establishment of surviving papers two peaks emerge. The Dublin Gazette (*Iris Oifiguil*) was established in 1711. There was only one daily at the end of the eighteenth century, *Saunder's News Letter*, published daily since 1777, but mainly an advertising sheet (Madden, 1867, Vol. II, Ch. V). Stewart estimates a total of about 65 papers in Ireland at the time of the French Revolution, a third of them in Dublin (Stewart, 1962). These were largely one-man enterprises, and, interestingly, they were all in English, though Irish was the majority language of all but the elite groups in the population. Most secure were the pro-British, Royalist, Ascendancy 'Castle press' papers, though they probably had very small circulations. The opposition papers, and the term covers a wide spectrum from mild liberal convictions to rampant radicalism, were financially vulnerable, particularly the smaller local papers, and Inglis concludes that 'by the summer of 1789 not a newspaper of any importance remained in the provinces that had not been either frightened or seduced into support of the administration' (Inglis, 1954, p. 72). The small provincial papers carried little local news and served a thinly scattered, impoverished population. It was the politicisation of the peasantry between 1830 and 1860 that lit the fuse for a major explosion of publications. This fizzled out in the stagnant years of the 1860s and 1870s until the resurgence of the Home Rule issue and economic recovery prompted the birth of many newspapers in the 1880s and 1890s. These two peaks of course are not at all chronologically coincident with the pattern in the English provincial press though the relationship with industrial and demographic changes is very similar (see Madden, 1867, II, pp. 164–5 and also Munter, 1967).

The transformation of a 'political' press, particularly a party-based press, to a mass circulation popular press, is a complex process which is only roughly the same in different countries. But there are essentially similar features that can be abstracted. The major change is in the economic base of the press. The 'retail revolution' results in competitive selling of branded products and an advertising industry to promote them. Newspapers are the ideal medium to convey such advertising to their consumer-readers, which gradually replaces sales to a greater or lesser extent as a source of revenue. Consequently, newspaper prices can be reduced and the seeds of the popular mass circulation press are sown.[1] The political party-based press often persists through this 'revolution' though normally forced to concede to the economic logic of the process. Where advertising is limited, political parties may be the only source of subsidy, thus sustaining a party-based press (see Hoyer, *et al.* 1975). Alternatively, where the provincial press has a much higher aggregate circulation than the nationals (as in Ireland), nationals may represent the persistance of the party press while local papers look more like the results of the 'pure' process. Late industrialisation in many countries delays the development of a Labour press.

The journalistic consequences of this process are important. The search for new and larger readerships draws the press away from a strident factionalism and toward a more central band of opinion, in which a mix of apparent neutrality and entertainment make a paper attractive as much as influential. Two journalistic strategies emerge to achieve this change of emphasis. The first is ideological, stressing the objective and authoritative nature of the news being supplied. The second is a matter of style and presentation, the 'new journalism'. There is obviously some tension between these two strategies, and as we shall see this tension becomes the basis for many of the anxieties of broadcast news, a hybrid form of information in an entertainment medium. These two outcomes of rapid commercialisation can be described in slightly more detail. Fact and opinion are distinguished. Their new relative value is captured in the famous 1921 dictum of C. P. Scott, editor of the English *Manchester Guardian*, that 'Comment is free, facts are sacred'. Opinions are caged in editorial columns, facts command the news pages. The distinction is institutionalised in the contrast between the reporter and the journalist, correspondent or columnist.

Mott's history of the American press brings this out very well. The division of labour within news organisations detracted from the omnipotence of the editor-in-chief, himself less and less likely to be proprietor, and drew attention to the diffuse news items gathered by a corps of reporters (Mott, 1962, p. 312). As *Putnams Monthly* put it in 1855, 'the great journals are now rather corporate institutions than individual organs'. As local papers were forced to take cognisance of local events, so too they were forced to have reporters to cover them. What Mott calls 'the triumph of the news principle' was complete by the mid-century (Mott, 1962, p. 384). He quotes a contemporary observation that 'the American reader will abandon a paper of his own political creed for one that has superior enterprise in publishing the latest and fullest items of events'. Another writer quite simply concluded that 'for the majority of readers, it is the reporter, and not the editor, who is the ruling genius of the newspaper' (Mott, 1962). The widespread use of the byeline was testimony to this judgement. With the 'triumph of the news principle' came the complementary strategy of capturing a wider credibility in the creed of objectivity. Arising from a style part-American, part-telegraphic, terse, brief 'reporting' came to replace lengthy discursive commentaries as the mark of efficient newspaper work.

The new style of journalism was seen at its earliest development in the American 'penny press', beginning in the 1830s (Tunstall, 1977). This press made two claims. First, in the words of James Gordon Bennett's *New York Herald*, vintage 1835, 'We shall support no party, be the organ of no faction or coterie, and care nothing for any election of any candidate from President down to constable.' Such independence was bought by successful selling. The second claim of the new papers was their popular appeal, based on a demotic and entertaining prose retailing the human interest and crime stories already familiar to readers of, for example, the English Sunday papers. Of course, the latter, in adopting the interests of their real antecedents, the broadsheets and street literature of the eighteenth century, were merely making a virtue of necessity. If they carried political information they were subjected to taxes as newspapers and faced financial subjugation. The entertainment style of the American penny press was an important influence, but it can be overstated. Bleyer has argued that the reliance on police court news and the more sensational trials as audience-grabbers were practices adopted by some American papers from English examples, particularly the Bow Street stories appearing in papers like the London *Morning Herald* (Bleyer, 1927).

A second element in the new style was the unadorned prose and pithy syntax of the 'New Journalism'. It has been argued that the cost of cables put a premium on verbiage and directly encouraged this terser use of language, and a more 'objective style' (Shaw, 1967). A third aspect was the use of the interview, or explicit presentation of the verbal evidence on which a news story was based (Turnbull, 1936). Nilsson traces this directly to the penny press extension of court question-and-answer procedure to its own methods (Nilsson, 1971). It became a primary and increasingly refined tool of the reporter, and its successful employment a mark of his skill.

Fourth, reporting was marked by speed; the early delivery of intelligence. The spur to haste was competition, its reward the 'scoop'. Horace Greely, publisher of the *New York Herald Tribune*, giving evidence before a House of Commons Committee in 1851, told a slightly astonished member of the committee of the urgency with which news should be delivered to the reader. 'Does the interest of the intelligence evaporate so soon?' he was asked. 'Not that, but a subscriber must have the paper that gives him his news in the morning before he goes to work' (House of Commons, 1851, para. 2649). As early as 1759 the *Northampton Mercury* in England responded to the stimulus of competition by getting its news in 'so expeditious a manner ... as to cause equal amazement and envy'. The feat is proudly explained as the result of 'very extraordinary Expences (one of which is ... having no less than 4 Horses stationed on the road every Saturday) for the quick Reception of News; for the extraordinary Dispatch in Printing it; and for the speedy Conveyance of it through so many different Counties' (Cranfield, 1962, pp. 259–60).

Thus new technology and economic organisation provided the basis for a new journalism. The day of the political journalist was far from over of course. The newspaper as an adjunct of party politics remained a powerful weapon in the hands of such men as Hjalmar Branting in Sweden. He was editor-in-chief 1887–1917 of the major organ of the Labour movement, *Social-Demokraten*, and subsequently became prime minister in 1920. Similarly, in Ireland the *Irish Press* was founded as late as 1931 by Eamon de Valera as the voice of his Fianna Fail party and remains the second highest circulation daily in the Republic. The *Irish Independent*, the country's most successful daily, was for many years controlled by the Murphy family, heirs to the William Martin Murphy who devotedly led Irish employers to climactic battle with the unions before the First World War.

But the party paper was an increasingly heavy burden on party funds, and for the 'new journalist' it was a straitjacket on his newly defined autonomy and integrity. In the battle for readers, newspapers have been drawn to the centre of the political spectrum.[2] Lars Furhoff has examined the process in Sweden by which 'newspapers are forced to compete for the same marginal readers and ... they therefore tend to similarity in large things and small' (Furhoff, 1968). This despite the ostensible persistence of a party press in Sweden. He cites the intertwined history of *Dagens Nyheter*, established in 1864 as a 'penny newspaper' and *Stockholms-Tidningen*, founded in 1889. The latter took a circulation lead over *Dagens Nyheter* for many years, but by 1941 it had lost ground again after the circulation spiral of the 1920s. Prior to 1920, newspapers had been politically polarised around the issues of extension of the franchise, temperance and trade tariffs. Overt factionalism declined in the circulation battles, even though *Stockholms-Tidningen* was taken over in 1956 by L.O. (Landsorganisationeni Sverige), the Swedish Trade Union Federation. In 1966 it was closed down, and indeed by that date over a third of Swedish newspapers had closed since the war. Between 1945 and 1968, 69 Swedish newspapers closed, representing a loss of 39 per cent of published titles. Most were small second papers competing with a larger paper in the same area but seven had circulations of more than 20,000 (Høyer *et al.*, 1975). Inevitably, newspapers which become local monopolies are both forced to mute explicit factionality and can afford to do so.

This is a common pattern, and its later consequences in the newspaper industry are beyond the brief of this book. Before examining the history of broadcast journalism, it is necessary to consider the evolution of Nigerian journalism to the start of broadcasting.

Early journalism in Nigeria

While in general the history of African journalism is a contracted version of the European pattern, it is neither so recent in origin nor so passive an offspring of colonial forebears as is sometimes supposed. Nonetheless, many living Nigerian journalists have witnessed the greater part of this history in their own lifetimes, and the traditions and origins of the occupation are crucially important to complete our comparative picture.

Nigeria generally lagged behind other areas of 'British West Africa', and printing presses first appear in Sierra Leone at the end of the eighteenth century (Rowand, 1972; Jones-Quartey, 1959). They were required by missionaries in their task of introducing literacy in English. The missionaries arrived in West Africa as printing in Europe was undergoing a technical revolution, and materials and skills diffused quickly, especially in Sierra Leone and Liberia. The first printing press in Nigeria appears to have been set up by the Presbyterian Mission in Calabar in 1846. The transition from a missionary press to political journalism is characterised by three factors. First, the inhospitable climate of the West African coast discouraged large European settlements – unlike East Africa – so that large publics could only be created among the indigenous population. Second, the area is densely populated and in Yorubaland urbanisation was relatively advanced in the nineteenth century. Third, the production by missionary zeal of a formally educated indigenous stratum, and by British traders of an indigenous commercial stratum willing to conduct transactions in the interior so disliked by the British, threw up two ambitious groups bound to be frustrated by the yoke of colonial control. As Omu (1978, p. 11) points out, 'the early press was inevitably a political press'. The missionary papers, like the bilingual *Iwe Irohin*, started in 1859, were an example for these groups when seeking a way of expressing their frustrations a generation later. At this early stage, as in Europe, newspapers were limited to information sheets for the colonial administrators. As Mazrui (1972b, p. 162) puts it, 'The Adam and Eve of newspapers in Africa were government gazettes.' In fact, it has been claimed that in northern Nigeria a government press was operating prior to British penetration in the form of a monthly *Kano Chronicle*, published in Arabic and Hausa by the Kano Emirate Administration

(Jose, quoted in Wilcox, 1974, p. 60).

The mid-century was the era of publisher-printers, for whom printing was one of the few commercial enterprises open. They were mostly West Indians driven from Liberia and Sierra Leone by the monopoly practices of British trading companies to the as yet freer prospects in Lagos and the Gold Coast. These papers, like Robert Campbell's *The Anglo-African* (1863), were comparatively inoffensive, though Governor Freeman was all for introducing a paper tax in 1862 to curb what he described as 'a dangerous instrument in the hands of semi-civilised Negroes' (Omu, 1968, p. 288).

The departure of the West Indians in the early 1870s left the way clear for the first Nigerian indigenous papers. The consolidation of monopoly power by the Royal Niger Company in 1886 intensified the blockage of entrepreneurial advance by Nigerians, while the growth of trade in Lagos increased demand for the shipping intelligence and news of market conditions that have always been the backbone of infant newspaper industries. Richard Beale Blaize, a Sierra Leone Yoruba, started the fortnightly *Lagos Times and Gold Coast Advertiser* in 1880 and set the tone for many similar ventures to follow it.

The steady advance of nationalist ideas found ready expression in the pages of the embryo press. Journalism was a narrow avenue of advance for educated Nigerians with political ambitions, and politician-proprietors running one-man papers dominated the press until after the First World War. They wrote in the 'long winded and baroque' (July, 1968, Ch. 17) style beloved of the Victorian colonial intelligentsia, and fed on the upsurge of cultural nationalism in the 1890s, especially after the unpopular Education Ordinance of 1882 making English compulsory. The flowering nationalism of these papers was consistently watered by self-interest. The proprietors were frequently traders who supported the British 'pacification' of the interior while at the same time hurling verbal abuse at the Royal Niger Company. The growing severity of British control after 1900, however, focussed their opposition, and their strengthening vigilance prompted the Newspaper Ordinance of 1903.

In fighting the battle for the liberal freedoms the Nigerian press placed the local administration in a considerable dilemma. Aware that press liberty was, in Junius' ringing phrase 'the great palladium of the British freedoms', Nigerian journalists courted support from liberal British opinion, and the Colonial Office was forced to restrain the more repressive of its officers (Omu, 1968). In looking at the offences which led to the 1909 Seditious Offences Ordinance one Colonial Office official was struck that 'much worse things are said and done in Ireland and no action is taken'. In fact, the Ordinance was little used, there were only three prosecutions in 25 years despite the contempt Governor Lord Lugard held for what he called the 'scurrilous local yellow press'. The battle for 'freedom of the press' was not strictly equivalent to the European movement. As Wilcox (1974, p. 76) notes, 'in Africa, . . . press development did not stem from the concepts of *individual* freedom but from the historical background of *national* freedom from colonial rule'.

The inter-war years saw a rapid advance both in the number of newspapers and in circulations. The 1922 Clifford Constitution opened the way to political parties, and despite economic depression the politician-editors of this period revived what had been a crumbling industry, giving it new purpose, the inter-party struggle, and a degree of financial security. The comparative freedom granted these papers is explained by Omu (1965, p. 273–4): 'as African nationalism acquired momentum and inspired constitutional changes which produced African participation in government, and as the nationalist parties increasingly turned against one another, British administrators apparently became less disposed to limit the freedom of the press'. (Omu, 1965, p. 273–4). The proprietors who fostered this party press were still professionals first, politicians second and journalists last. 'Ownership and control were in the hands not of trained journalists but of lawyers, doctors, chemists, businessmen and even surveyors and architects.' (Coker, 1960). Their style is captured in Coker's portrayal of them as 'black Victorians'. Even the legendary Herbert Macauley, who bought and revivified the *Lagos Daily News* in 1927, was a civil engineer by training. Ikoli's *Nigerian Daily Times* (1926) was the first successful daily, and introduced new styles of journalism and new aggressive selling techniques. The dailies dropped their price to a penny and therefore sought large circulations from the widening literate public. Headlines, news on the front page, better typography, all helped attract this still very limited audience, while prize competitions and other promotional schemes secured their loyalty. It was this that provided financial security for the successful papers. There was little local advertising revenue, except from the purveyors of quack medicines, and expatriate firms were loathe to support the more virulent anti-government press despite its circulation.

Financial support also came from the parties, and the major editors in the 1920s were still leading political figures. In effect, as Omu puts it, 'newspapers shifted their focus from that of political group supporters to organs of political parties', (Omu, 1968, p. 321). With economic security came the gradual emergence of limited companies in the 1930s. The culmination of this process was the arrival of Nnamdi Azikiwe's *West African Pilot* in 1937. Azikiwe had studied journalism in America and honed his sharp literary skills in the Gold Coast. The sensationalism, picture journalism, human interest stories and organised marketing of the *Pilot* took its circulation to the unprecedented figure of 12,000 by 1940. Success bred success in the shape of the 'Zik' group of newspapers (Azikiwe, 1970).

As noted earlier in discussion of the American press, growth and occupational differentiation in fact *lowered* the status of journalists. From a battlefield surveyed by a few generals the press became a crowded arena of foot-soldiers. The ordinary reporters, often barely literate, poorly paid and frequently exploited, were little respected by other educated Nigerians and saw little future for themselves within journalism. Their patriotism was taken for granted and fully exploited. Abiodun Aloba (Aloba, 1959a, p. 246) has written of the period in which paid professional editors replaced politician-proprietors.

> The Editor, a disgruntled teacher or a dismissed clerk, was nevertheless the respected gentleman with the bowler and the walking stick. No-one knew exactly what his salary was, but everybody knew he drank free whiskey, ate with the greats, and lived on the patronage of his social and political clients. Indeed, when once as Assistant Editor Mr Ernest Ikoli ... asked for his salary he was confronted with the disdainful eyes of an irate editor: 'Salary? Don't you know you are working for the nation?'

Cynical but prophetic, for despite the subsequent commercialisation of the press when European magnates entered the market, the political undercurrent to journalism has never subsided in Nigeria to the same extent as in Europe. IPC, the British newspaper conglomerate, bought the Lagos *Daily Times* in 1947, and Lord Thomson, jointly with the Action Group, the Yoruba-based party, converted two papers into the *Daily Express* in 1958. These papers thrived in the resurgence of party politics in the decade before independence (granted in 1960), but Thomson eventually withdrew in the face of the uncertainties of post-independence politics, and IPC's holding was gradually reduced by the 'Nigerianisation' programme of the military government. The last development has been the proliferation of state government papers as party politics has been, at least ostensibly, proscribed.

Nigerian journalism was thus created by anti-colonial protest, baptised in the waters of nationalist propaganda, and matured in party politics. The separation of politics and journalism has remained incomplete and the dual allegiances of journalists to professional and political goals have created conflicts whose resolution in daily practice underpins much of contemporary Nigerian journalism. The pre-independence ferocity of the press is a living memory for present-day journalists, its success a tribute to the potential power of their craft. Azikiwe, a characteristic example of the journalist-politician to reach high office in African statesmanship (he became Governor-General, and, after independence, President), has written that 'the most potent instrument used in the propagation of nationalist ideas and racial consciousness, has been the African owned nationalist press'. Kenyatta, Nyerere, Mobutu, Nkrumah, Senghor and others all illustrate the fusion of politics and journalism in their own careers.

It would be a mistake to assume this is as true for the journeyman-reporter as for these illustrious leaders. Chick has argued that 'the cosmopolitan atmosphere of Lagos has left its mark upon newspaper-men, and foreign control of a segment of the press ... has also helped to insulate journalists from some of the more dramatic manifestations of intertribal competition'. He also suggests increasing professionalism, rising standards and occupational solidarity have thickened this insulation (Chick, 1971). Nonetheless, the residues of this political saturation of journalism provide interesting material for the analysis of contemporary practice in Nigeria. Their particular forms within broadcast journalism will be examined in Chapters 5 and 7 (see also Golding, 1977).

Broadcast journalism

Broadcasting has normally begun as a technical novelty, been developed commercially by the more opportunist members of the radio and telecommunications industry, and has finally grown into the major entertainment medium of the twentieth century. Somehow it became a news medium at the same time, and although news broadcasting usually begins spasmodically it invariably advances to the front line in the scheduling considerations of television executives. Normally television news is the fixed point in a kaleidoscopic world of dramas, quizzes, soap operas, documentaries and education.

Three problems face broadcast journalism in its evolution as a distinct form of programming.

First, broadcasting organisations are normally sanctioned by law and have their operations and structures defined by statute. Legal requirements have to be translated into routine practice, and it is in the consequent attempts to operationalise the generalities of the law that so much of the friction between broadcasting and the state is generated. Second, broadcast journalism has to establish a degree of autonomy from the press. Initially it has been seen as a competitive threat, particularly to the evening newspapers. The press has usually required limits to be put on the timing and extent of news broadcasting. Broadcasting journalists were usually dependent on the press as a source of news in the early years, and it was only gradually recognised that broadcast news was potentially other than newspaper news distributed in a new way. For many journalists the trend to autonomy became too advanced and threw up a conflict of identity between the role of broadcaster and of journalist (the significance of which will be considered in chapter 7). Third, broadcast journalism has to come to terms with the highly regulated distinction between fact and comment which it was constrained to observe because of its dominant public presence, monopoly, close relationship with government and constitutional position. Newspaper journalism has produced the creed of objectivity. Broadcast journalism had to be more than honest about the debate; it had to be above it. Gradually new creeds of impartiality and balance were developed while the distinction between fact and comment was institutionalised in organisational form by the separation of 'news' and 'current affairs'.

The entry of news into broadcasting has always reflected these problems. As Anthony Smith (1973, Ch. 3) has put it, 'Of all the strands of culture which are fed into the world at present through broadcasting none has had to fight its way with such great difficulty into the processes of broadcasting as that of journalism.' The new medium, never initially conceived as a news medium but always and obviously a medium of considerable power, had no built-in structures or techniques to cope with the problem of news. Charters requiring the avoidance of controversy and opinion were as predictable in their high minded vagueness as they were inapplicable in professional practice. Broadcasting was essentially an entertainment medium, news the icing on the cake. The feedback of entertainment values, now fully part of newspaper journalism, was intensified by journalism's struggle for a respectable and respected slot among the programme types created by broadcasting. In the remainder of this chapter we survey these issues in each of the three countries of our study.

Ireland

There appear to have been three stimuli to the introduction of broadcasting in Ireland. First, there was the need to create an integrating cultural force for the emergent state. This need was heightened by growing awareness of the cultural power of the BBC. As the then Postmaster-General, J. J. Walsh, pointed out in 1924, the 'claim that this nation has set out on a separate existence . . . not only covers its political life but also its social and cultural life' (Gorham, 1967, p. 12). Second, there was considerable pressure from the manufacturers of the equipment required in broadcasting and reception. Third, the successful exploitation of wireless telegraphy in the recent wars of independence was a live memory for many of those involved in the debates of the 1920s.

However, the commercial pressure seems to have been the heaviest and when a speculative government 'White Paper' was issued in 1923 approaches had already been made by Marconi and the London *Daily Express*. The BBC model was the obvious one to follow, despite Walsh's declaration that 'any kind of Irish station is better than no Irish station at all'. Indeed, when a personnel selection committee was established in 1925 several BBC men were invited to assist, including the charismatic managing director, John Reith. Nevertheless, the Dail Committee had recommended financing by advertising as well as licence fees, and this was the form adopted when 'Dublin 2RN' began broadcasting on 1 January 1926.

Economics brought the organisation into immediate conflict with government. 'The greatest difficulty in the early days was fighting the parsimonious civil service bureaucracy . . .' (Fisher, 1978b, p. 21). Advertising was confined to Irish concerns, and coverage was limited, so the organisation had to fight for sustenance. Broadcasting was directly administered by the Ministry of Posts and Telegraphs, yet the Ministry of Finance had a veto over all expenditure and appointments, and much of the infighting was between these two departments.

The twin problems of finance and ministerial responsibility out-weighed discussion of news coverage during the 1930s. An argument more romantically motivated than technologically rational was advanced for the need to provide a short-wave service of news and views from home to expatriate Irishmen, especially in the USA. Although the service was not introduced until 1947 and abandoned a year later, it did provide much needed extra staff and equipment to the benefit of the continuing medium-wave services.

An inquiry into the organisation and control of broadcasting in 1938 evolved into a standing committee comprising representatives of the Ministries of Posts and Telecommunications, and of Finance, plus the Director of Broadcasting. Ministerial control was to remain a contentious feature of Irish radio broadcasting until, in 1973, a Radio Council was established (Comhairle Radio Eireann) which took over much of the day-to-day running of broadcasting without, however, diminishing ultimate ministerial responsibility and control. Staff, of course, were still civil servants, and indeed remained so until 1961. The Council, intended as an intermediate step between independence and government control, had five members; two academics, a businessman, and two representatives of Irish cultural organisations. It was at this time that the first significant moves in political broadcasting were made with the lifting of the ban on broadcasting by TDs (elected members of the Dail) and Senators.

News and current affairs had hitherto been largely dormant. In Gorham's view 'the history of news broadcasting in Ireland was a sorry one right up to and after the Second World War' (Gorham, 1967, pp. 35-6). Concern with the ability of broadcasting to foster an autonomous Irish culture had swamped consideration of its potential as a news medium. The initial staff of twenty included only one staff news man. The news was gathered by a haphazard process of selection from BBC broadcasts, the local newspapers and government releases.

Even the war, or The Emergency as it was officially known in the Republic, which was not a party to the conflict, brought little expansion. The news staff rose to three, a News Officer and two assistants. The war did provoke further active consideration of news neutrality however. All bulletins had to be cleared by the head of the Government Information Bureau, and the problem of impartiality was solved by a scrupulously balanced if dull recital of claims and counter-claims from both sides in the war.

The major problem for the news department was that of sources. Unable to gather its own news, it was forced to passively digest from elsewhere, including, in an attempt at diversification, monitored broadcasts from Vatican Radio. But persistent criticism bore fruit at the end of the war with the appointment of eight domestic news correspondents around the country.

The real development of news came with the arrival of television. By 1959 there were about 30,000 television sets already in use; BBC programmes were variably receivable in the north and east of the country. A commission was set up in 1958 which finally recommended the introduction of television on a fully commercial basis. Its recommendations were ignored and the government announced that television, along with radio, was to be run by a semi-state board in the form of a Broadcasting Authority to be known as Radio Eireann (it became Radio Telefis Eireann in 1966). Although membership of the Authority was not open to members of either parliamentary chamber, political control was at least implicit in the power granted to government to remove any member from office at any time. All members of staff became 'officers and servants of the authority' and thus ceased to be civil servants. The Act became effective in April 1960 and television broadcasting began at the end of 1961.

By this time the initial problems of news broadcasting, autonomy from the press and the acquisition of independent news sources, had been partially tackled. In addition to the domestic correspondents, agreements were reached with Reuters, the Press Association, and Exchange Telegraph in 1946, and three years later with the American United Press. The second stage, the differentiation of news and some form of current affairs, was a much later development. Five minute topical talks had been introduced in 1953 by the News Editor. There had been a Talks Officer since 1939, whose title had become General Features Officer in 1945, and who dealt with a wide range of material from farming talks to the news in Irish (produced by the News Officer and simply translated). By the late 1950s the news department was producing feature programmes but largely of the 'round-up' or news digest type.

The expansion of staff and organisation prompted by television formalised all this, and a separate division (one of five, the others being engineering, programmes, administration and finance, and public relations) for radio and television news was established in 1961. This division proved to be one of the organisation's permanent problems and its history has been punctuated by conflict and contention. The details of these are discussed in Chapter 4. By 1963 the News Division was supplying about five hours of news and news features a week for television. The division was also responsible for a nightly news-feature 'Newsview'. RTE joined the Eurovision news service in 1967 and opened a Belfast office in 1970.

The distinction between news and current affairs has a particularly fraught history in RTE. '7 Days', a weekly current affairs programme introduced in 1966, was moved in 1968 to the News Division. Even this fact is contentious. An alternative reading offered by the then Head of News is that 7 Days was placed under his aegis, though never made an integral part of the News Division. Many observers felt this brought it under closer surveillance by the guardians of the impartiality requirements of the 1960 Act. After three weeks off the air and various alterations, the programme was transferred but remained a separate unit. 7 Days finally disappeared in 1976, and its production team were dispersed to three new current affairs programmes (Broadcast, 1976).

The later development of RTE produced seven divisions, three of which deal with output; radio programmes, television programmes and news. Both programme divisions have within them a features department which includes magazines, and public affairs.

RTE has been prone to periodic organisation shuffling, often prompted by an ambiguity of control between technical and programmes hierarchies. The initial structure was a departmental one, with Heads of Departments directly responsible to the Controller of Programmes. This faltered, possibly because the Heads were either producers, divorced from programme-making or functionless administrators. In 1963 a 'vertical group system' was introduced, in which producers were amalgamated into groups under group Editors. In 1966 an Editorial Board to act as the main planning body was set up. Production facilities were responsible to the Head of Engineering, a link which caused considerable dissatisfaction among some producers (see Dowling and Doolan, 1969). After increasing tensions the system collapsed and in 1968 a departmental system, under programme heads, was reintroduced. In 1970 the seven Divisions were made directly responsible to the Deputy Director-General, and further reorganisation took place in 1972 and 1973, including, in the latter, a new Current Affairs grouping extracted from the existing television, radio and news divisions.[3]

Television news in Ireland has thus developed under both internal and external pressure. The organisational structure of RTE kept the relationship between news and other areas a live issue, while the inevitable proximity to government in the continuing crisis of coverage of the north pushed the production of both into the front line of controversy. In 1971 a Broadcasting Review Committee was established to 'review the progress of television and sound broadcasting since the enactment of the Broadcasting Authority Act, 1960 ...'. It reported in 1974, and was highly critical of news. The illuminating reactions this provoked are discussed in Chapter 4. The Committee also recommended that RTE establish a second channel, and although this was delayed, after a national survey demonstrating a demand for RTE 2 the way was open for construction for the second network to begin. Initial transmissions began in June 1978, being a mix of home-produced programmes and retransmission of British programmes.

Sweden

Radio broadcasting in Sweden began in the early 1920s. Both amateur radio enthusiasts and the state, through the Royal Telegraph Board, experimented with pilot transmissions. In 1925 sole broadcasting rights were ceded to Radiotjänst, a company formed for the purpose by a combination of commercial, political and cultural interest groups. Shares in the company were held by the radio industry, the press and Tidningarnas Telegrambyra (TT), the Swedish news agency owned by and operated for the Swedish press. The first director of Radiotjänst was also head of TT and doubled both roles for 10 years. TT was often designated 'semi-official' despite having no formal links with government. Its involvement in news broadcasting has persistently formed a part of the strategy employed by the Swedish government to supervise broadcast news. Initially Radiotjänst took all its news from TT, and competition with the press was curtailed by prohibiting the TT bulletin before 9.20 p.m. The Second World War greatly stimulated to the demand for radio news, and during the war the '9.20 rule' was relaxed. It was not till 1947 however that broadcasting was allowed by government to produce its own news.

By 1954 there were 2.35 million radio sets in the country, or roughly one for every three inhabitants. There had been some planning for television in the late 1940s and a Commission was set up in 1952 to investigate the future of Swedish broadcasting including television. Its final report in 1954 recommended a non-commercial service, despite considerable pressure from commercial interests and even experimental television transmissions financed by advertising. Television transmissions began in September 1956 and attracted very rapidly growing audiences. Within three years Sweden had the second highest density of set ownership in Europe, and by 1963 90 per cent of the population had access to television.

With television came a general reorganisation of broadcasting, which was placed under the control of Sveriges Radio (SR). SR is effectively a public corporation or semi-state body like the BBC or RTE, but since this is unknown to Swedish law, SR is organised as a private company. Up until 1956 shares in Radiotjänst had been owned by newspapers and radio manufacturers though the government had representatives on the Board of Governors. Sixty per cent of the share capital of SR is owned by what are collectively termed the popular movements – the unions, the co-operative movement, the temperance movement, various adult educational associations and so on. Twenty per cent is owned by industry and commerce and 20 per cent by the press organisations and individual newspapers. The shareholders elect five members of the Board of Governors, while another five and the Chairman, that is an effective majority, are nominated by the government. SR has complete monopoly of all national broadcasting in Sweden, although the National Telecommunications Administration is responsible for the actual transmission of programmes.

In general, SR kept away from news in its early days, partly to avoid becoming itself a subject of political controversy, partly because of the strength of the press interests on the Board, and also because originally producers and departmental heads within the corporation were drawn from various fields of entertainment rather than from journalism. One or two earlier exceptions stand out. For example, in 1938 Ludvig Nordstrom, a well-known author, made a series of reports called 'Lort-Sverige' (Filthy Sweden), based on a tour of the country. This provoked considerable protest in parliament from the Farmers Party. Generally, however, current affairs were little developed apart from short commentary programmes after the TT news bulletin.

Expansion of SR's services really began in the mid-1950s. Two new radio channels were added between 1956 and 1963. News production grew too. Between 1955 and 1965 radio bulletins increased from five per day to 40 per day (still with only five from TT). The press seems initially not to have predicted the importance of television, and remained relatively unconcerned at journalistic developments in the new medium. Most controversies about early television news relate to its location in the schedules. The early realisation that the news slot could to a large extent determine the audience for other programmes brought television news into the first rank of scheduling considerations, a position it has retained. SR's own television news output developed only slowly, but it did not include the offered bulletins from TT. The initial programme, *TV Journalen*, was akin to a film newsreel. With the introduction of *Aktuellt* in 1958 information programming settled into the conventional pattern of regular documentary and current affairs programmes produced by separate departments on radio and television. It was not till 1960, however, that daily television news bulletins were produced, by which time yet another reorganisation of the corporation was under consideration by yet another Commission.

The 1960 Commission reported finally in 1965. As a result of the Commission's deliberations, though not reflecting its conclusions, the government decided to introduce a second television channel intended to compete with the existing service but nonetheless to be controlled by SR. The Government rejected advertising as a source of revenue, despite the now complete saturation of the potential market for receivers, and thus the levelling off of the increase in licence revenue.

The introduction of TV2 meant a major rethinking of the role of the news department. Mainly for economic reasons it was decided to retain a single Joint News Office to provide basic factual news bulletins for all radio and television services, as well as coverage of major events like the opening of parliament or the Nobel prize ceremonies. In addition each service would have its own departments for the production of news commentaries, current affairs and documentaries. Organisationally this strengthened and formalised the distinction between fact and comment, or between 'hard' news and background. Another argument in favour of the Joint News Office was that competition was irrelevant to the reporting of fact. Variety was only necessary in the presentation of comment and opinion. In practice, however, the distinction remains a blurred and contentious one, and the strains of defining and asserting these boundaries continued to place pressure on the news organisation into the 1970s.

Much of the drive for expansion of news services during the 1960s came from the Director-General of SR from 1955 to 1970, Olof Rydbeck. A career diplomat, he was particularly concerned to widen SR's coverage of foreign news, and he increased the number of foreign correspondents to twelve. Rydbeck also took an active interest in news production, presiding over a morning meeting at which the day's news prospects and policy matters were discussed (Rydbeck, 1965). This was initiated because 'at the time of the Soviet Union's atomic bomb tests at Novaya Semlyor and the tense foreign situation in Scandinavia in connection with the Soviet note to Finland in 1961, it was considered especially important that Sveriges Radio should, in its various programme channels, give a similar evaluation of the course of events' (Rydbeck, 1965, p. 41). This concern for a uniform news policy was thrown into focus when the potentially contrary policy of 'internal competition' was introduced with the start of TV2. Resolution of this dilemma was intended to emerge from the formation of a Joint News Office, but separate commentary and current affairs units.

At the start of the decade, Rydbeck identified three organisational changes likely to affect SR in the 1970s; competition, internationalism and regionalism (Sveriges Radio, p. 17). There had been growing criticism of SR's monopoly but only a few commercial interests and representatives of the right politically favoured the introduction of a commercial service. By the time the next Commission sat, commercialism was not even on the agenda. Competition was debated in terms of autonomy for and competition between different public service broadcasting subsidiaries (Swedish Broadcasting Commission, 1977). The Commission took their model from ARD (the federal system of regionalised broadcasting in Germany formed in 1950 to decentralise broadcasting). ARD, however, like the second German channel ZDF, has failed to overcome tendencies to centralisation, a not uncommon feature of such attempts (cf. the intended regionalism of commercial television in England). In Sweden, the then Minister of Communication (later to be Prime Minister), Olof Palme, favoured what he called 'the shining example of the BBC'. Regionalism is one of those universal 'good causes' in broadcasting policy which costs nothing to support in political terms, but which, in economic and organisational terms, would cost a lot to develop. A number of regional centres were set up but so far as news was concerned their activities were limited to the production of film for the Central News Department. Regional news programmes were introduced slowly after 1972. The massive increase in production costs engendered by colour necessitated more compromises on the ideal of regionalism and the amalgamation of smaller regions into larger groupings. By 1975–6 regional news bulletins were available on television in four districts but amounted to no more than 130 broadcast hours annually in total (Swedish Broadcasting Commission, 1977). Regional radio news was more extensive. 4,125 hours were broadcast in the same year but with the foundation of Sveriges Lokalradio as a subsidiary of SR, local radio stations were developed which were expected to take over this function from the regions. The next Commission on Broadcasting which reported in 1977 was also enamoured with the idea of a regional television channel. It used two new sets of initials to identify its proposals, TVS (national) and TVR (regional) in keeping with the custom of three-digit identifications for the Swedish television channels. Nevertheless its proposals are not to be closely followed by the government in the reorganisation proposed for 1979. Once again the intention is simply to increase the regional contribution to the national network.

In Sweden the carefully defined and frequently examined status and organisation of broadcasting have made television news a political football of some importance. The ambiguous relationships with government have prompted the drafting of a series of codes and agreements intended to guide practice in areas of controversy. The ramifications of these will be considered in Chapter 4.

Nigeria

Because of its late development and inevitable dependence on external technical assistance, Nigerian broadcasting was even more closely modelled on BBC antecedents than the Irish or Swedish organisations. The vast size of the country, the heterogeneity of its population and the regionalised political structure have all contributed to the plural nature of Nigerian broadcasting. The Federal Government station, the Nigerian Broadcasting Corporation, covered the whole country on radio, and Lagos and parts of the West on television. After the division of the country into twelve states by the military government in 1966, attempts were made by many of the states to set up their own broadcasting services, in many cases successfully. The two most significant provincial stations, in Ibadan, and in Kaduna in the north, predate this development, and as elsewhere in this report this discussion concentrates on these two and the NBC.

Broadcasting in most African countries began as a service to settler communities, bringing them news of the colonial homeland and establishing valuable links within the communities. In British colonies this developed as an outgrowth of the BBC Empire Service. Kenya was the first British African colony with a regular service, started in 1928, and wired radio services were introduced into several other countries during the 1930s. Aware that external broadcasting services from Moscow were well ahead of Britain's, the Colonial Secretary appointed the Plymouth Committee to 'consider and recommend what steps could be taken to accelerate the provision of broadcasting services in the Colonial Empire, to co-ordinate such services with the work of the BBC, and to make them a more effective instrument for promoting both local and Imperial interests' (Colonial Office, 1937, p. 1). The Committee envisaged a mixture of selected BBC material and local government programming piped into homes via 'wired wireless' to give a service which would be 'controlled, and objectionable wireless propaganda excluded'. At first the service comprised simply retransmissions of the BBC broadcasts, and in Lagos this was introduced almost as soon as the BBC launched its Empire Service at the end of 1932. The relay service, based in principle on the radio relay exchanges established in Britain in the 1920s, probably existed in Lagos before 1935 but was officially launched at the end of that year. As Mackay (1964, p. 1) remarks, 'this new broadcasting service from London was to set a pattern which in time became an integral part of broadcasting development in the Federation'.

By 1939 there were still less than 1,000 subscribers and about 2,000 licensed receivers. Until the 1950s the history of Nigerian broadcasting is essentially the story of the BBC external services. Inevitably this was to settle deep roots of organisation and practice for later developments. Government involvement in the making of programmes was begun unusually early in Nigeria compared to other countries in West Africa, when the Public Relations Office, later to become the Federal Information Department, provided programming for the relay service.

After the war colonial authorities in Britain began to reconsider broadcasting in the light of growing restiveness in some areas. The Colonial Office sent out a BBC engineer and government engineer to examine the situation in West Africa. Their report (Turner and Byron, 1949) set the basic technical pattern for broadcasting throughout Anglophone West Africa, though modified by the political and economic changes to come. The social objectives were set in a report prepared two years later by T. W. Chalmers, seconded from his post as Controller of the BBC's Light Programme. He considered

> that radio is ... the most potent mass disseminator of culture and information that the world possesses, and ... the object of bringing it to Nigeria is to assist in the development of the country in every possible way and in an orderly fashion. Our aim in broadcasting therefore must be to assist those processes that go towards the making of an enlightened democracy. One of the most powerful weapons in the radio armoury is impartial news and information programmes which must develop as rapidly as possible (quoted in Mackay, 1964, p. 14).

The wariness of British colonial administrators was tempered by the readiness of manufacturers to extend their markets for both transmitting and receiving equipment to West Africa. The BBC, as the sole transmitting authority in Britain, supervised the manufacture of its own equipment, and manufacturers were eager to secure export outlets, while hedging their bets by joining the campaign for a commercial second television service in Britain. The Korean War had kept them fully occupied but had at the same time set in motion a rapid rise in prices of electronic equipment. The breakdown of the 1951 constitution in Nigeria and the reassertion of regional autonomy also militated against the full adoption of the Turner–Byron scheme for development based on Lagos. However, Chalmers' recommendation for a broadcasting service was accepted and the Nigerian Broadcasting Service was established in 1951, with Chalmers himself as Director of Broadcasting. In fact broadcasting did not get under way till the following year, and there was some difficulty in getting expatriate staff, particularly after a Marconi engineer was drowned at Bar Beach. In 1952 a Department of Broadcasting took over the functions, plant, and staff hitherto under the Departments of Posts and Telegraphs and of Public Relations.

The size of the service was growing steadily but was still fairly minimal, even allowing for the likely ratio of six or seven listeners per set. In 1949, 9,000 subscribers were wired to the 10 centres around the country. By 1954 there were over 50,000 subscribers, in addition to 4,562 licensed radio sets, almost certainly a gross underestimate of the true total. Through the 1950s the formula that 'organisation of the Nigerian Broadcasting Service is on a regional, not regionalised basis' was gradually eroded by the facts of Nigerian political life. The Colonial Office report for 1952 concedes resignedly that 'it is now clear that the political and social developments of the Regions will mean that regional broadcasting will play an even more important part than was originally anticipated' (Colonial Office, 1954, p. 119). In 1952 the first News Editor was appointed. The three steps on the route from a department of information to a separate government department, finally to a statutory corporation akin to the BBC were the standard turning points in broadcasting in most British African colonies. Before the third stage was reached in Nigeria news broadcasting was already a feature of the service, relying on the BBC for foreign news and government information for local news. Engineering problems often caused problems in the distribution of this news and Mackay recalls that 'expatriate public servants, anxious for the latest cricket scores, could pick up their 'phone and receive a ball by ball account via a leak in the wireless lines'. (Mackay, 1964, p. 26).

BBC news continued to feature prominently in the schedules, though news talks, summaries and commentaries were produced in profusion and, from 1954, even party political broadcasts. Wired rediffusion services, as opposed to broadcasting, were felt to be preferable since they afforded greater control over the programmes available to listeners, in particular preventing exposure to 'subversive' material from overseas.

The movement of political events had lent weight to demands for the separation of broadcasting from government, and in 1957 the Nigerian Broadcasting Corporation replaced the NBS. Inevitably the model was the BBC and the Corporation was run by a Board of Governors supported by a Board of Management. In 1957 all the members of both boards were British, and the members of the Corporation were appointed by the Governor-General. As well as a Chairman, the Corporation included three Chairmen for Regional Boards. After the inception of the military regime in 1966 the Board consisted of officials from the main relevant ministries, together with a military representative, and the Director-General. The establishment side of the Corporation's activities was under the aegis of the Statutory Corporations Services Commission. The difficulty of attracting expatriate staff meant rapid 'Nigerianisation', and all programme departments were Nigerianised by 1960. News was a little backward in this respect, the last BBC-seconded Director of News left in October 1962.

The news and current affairs output of the Corporation expanded rapidly after 1962; the goal of hourly news bulletins was achieved that year. Whereas in 1957 there were 74 weekly bulletins in English and 90 in Nigerian languages, in 1966 there were 236 English news broadcasts and 180 in Nigerian languages. A television service, set up for the Federal government by the American National Broadcasting Company, had commenced broadcasting in 1962. It was managed by this company but its basic policies were determined by the Corporation. In 1967 the television service became integrated as a division of the Corporation. Like radio, it accepted advertising but relied primarily on government subvention.

The regional governments were always ahead of the Federal administration in the prestigious race to establish television. Spurred on by eager European and North American companies, many African states had television services very early in the development of their broadcasting systems. Based in Ibadan, the Western Nigerian government television service proudly bears the motto 'First in Africa'. In fact the television service in that region actually started before the radio service, the former in October 1959, the latter in May 1960. Initially the venture was run in partnership with Overseas Rediffusion Ltd, who had been involved since 1952 in the development of NBC's wired radio service in the region. Increasingly the political objectives set for broadcasting by the regional government conflicted with the aggressive commercial ambitions of Rediffusion, and the government bought out the company in 1961. The Ibadan-based services continued to be more commercially sophisticated than other Nigerian services, employing popular programming, and market research to a far greater degree than elsewhere. As is usual in smaller broadcasting organisations the news department is common to radio and television, and is one of the six departments in the corporation. The relationship to the regional, Western State, government was analogous to that of NBC.

In the north the Broadcasting Company of Northern Nigeria (BCNN), more commonly known by its call-sign Radio Television Kaduna (RTK), was established by a tripartite partnership between the regional government, and two British companies, Granada Television and EMI. Radio and television transmissions began simultaneously in March 1962 (Diamond, 1965). The shareholdings of the British companies were finally sold in 1970, and transferred via the Interim Common Services Agency to the six northern states who owned the

Corporation. News was always an important part of the Corporation's programming, relying heavily on government information services and a scattering of correspondents throughout the northern region.

In February 1976 the state structure was reorganised to increase the number to 19. In 1977 a Decree created a Nigerian Television Authority with all existing state and federal television organisations under its control, in a new six-zoned division of the country (for broadcasting purposes). The Authority was said to be aimed at enhancing 'competition in co-operation, variety in unity, and democracy within national ideals' (Anon, 1977, p. 38).

In terms of the three legacies mentioned at the opening to this chapter, that of constitutional acceptance of a 'fourth estate', the creation of a full-time occupation in journalism, and the emergence of an ideology within this occupation, this historical account suggests that broadcast journalism is heavily indebted to its print forbears for all three. In Chapter 4 we examine the extent to which broadcasting caused particular problems for the political role of journalism and forced a redefinition of its constitutional position. In Chapter 5 we examine whether the processes by which news is produced in a broadcasting organisation cause a similar reassessment of the occupational ideology of journalism, or conversely whether those processes are influenced by beliefs and values derived from journalism outside broadcasting.

Notes

1. Advertising has a long history as a source of newspaper revenue and an influence on press performance. For a persuasive argument about the length and significance of this history in Britain, see Curran (1977).

2. For the importance of this in the contemporary British context see Hirsh and Gordon (1975), and Golding and Murdock (1978).

3. For the most recent account of these shifting patterns see Fisher (1978b), pp. 50–3. There is also a full description of the period 1965–73 in Broadcasting Review Committee (1974).

Chapter 4

The social context of broadcast news

Most of the pressures and constraints on news production we shall consider in this study are informal, and unrecognised. They are to do with the pragmatics of personal and institutional interaction. But at a less subtle level news is produced within structures which are quite distinctly defined; externally by the relationship of the broadcasting organisation to the state, the culture and the market, internally by the relationship of the news department to the remainder of the broadcasting organisation. This chapter briefly considers these relationships.

Broadcasting and the state

Broadcasting was involved with government from its inception. In many countries national monopoly control was taken to be a technical necessity to protect the national interest represented by military and intelligence users, and generally to regulate the air waves. It took some time for the potential of public broadcasting to be realised. Then acceptance was only grudging by authorities whose main concern was to ensure the medium was available to military users. Concern with the content of broadcasting was initially displaced into a concern with the control and development of the system of distribution. Raymond Williams (1974, p. 25) has argued with only slight exaggeration that 'Unlike all previous communications technologies, radio and television were *systems primarily devised for transmission and reception as abstract processes, with little or no definition of preceding content.*' (Original emphasis.) 'In the first era of broadcasting the problem facing the industry,' according to Anthony Smith (1973) 'was simply how to spread to every individual member of society the technical means for receiving new messages.' Nor is this problem entirely a thing of the past. In the countries we studied administrators were still highly concerned with extending (Nigeria) or filling in (Sweden and Ireland) their distribution systems to achieve saturation coverage of the country.

Several writers have attempted to summarise the range of broadcasting systems thrown up by different societies. Two very similar catalogues have been suggested by authors writing from quite different positions, Raymond Williams, and three senior American communication theorists, Siebert, Peterson and Schramm. The Americans, in a report prepared for the National Council of Churches in the cold war years of the mid 1950s, drew up a fourfold set of 'theories of the press' (in which is included broadcasting). The first is the authoritarian; the media are for control of the people by the ruling elite, their purpose to service state power. This theory was developed in sixteenth- and seventeenth-century England. The second theory is the libertarian, derived from the classic writings of Milton, Locke and Mill and based on the idea of a free market place for competitive political information and ideals. Third, comes the social responsibility theory, the hero of the thesis, based on the notion of the freedom of the press, and access to privately owned media over which the state should have no control other than to check excesses and ensure they serve the public interest. The media itself take on the responsibility for quality control to ensure that decision making is based on unprejudiced, neutral information. Finally comes the totalitarian theory; the media are state owned and closely controlled arms of the state apparatus contributing to successful dictatorship by the ruling party. This theory is put into practice in most exemplary fashion by the Soviet Union (Siebert *et al.*, 1956).

Raymond Williams has produced a surprisingly similar list, though based rather more on concrete criteria of organisational form than on imputed guiding philosophies. His four 'kinds of communication system' are the authoritarian, in which communications media are intended to protect and enhance the total power of a ruling minority; the paternal, 'an authoritarian system with a conscience', involving much censorship and deliberate dissemination to the masses of values held to be good for them by a ruling minority; the commercial, in which control over communications is determined by the forces in the market-place; and finally the democratic system, as yet nowhere established, which, whatever its organisational form, would be based on principles of free and universal access to means of transmission and reception.

Alongside such models of broadcasting we can set the major accounts of the role of journalism in the state. Four variants have emerged. First, the classic conception of the fourth estate, in which journalism acts as an independent watchdog of the liberal freedoms in a parliamentary democracy, its independence guaranteed constitutionally, its public responsibility by the exercise of consumer sovereignty in the market-place. Second, the notion of journalism as the public relations wing of totalitarian government. Third, a role independent of government yet with explicit political objectives related to political party or philosophy, and rejecting impartiality yet not objectivity as journalistic ideals. Fourth, the role which broadcast journalism is most inclined to make its own, that of neutral observer of the passing scene. This and relevant elements of one and three are further discussed in Chapter 7.

In this sort of schema Nigeria, like many African countries, would appear to be different from our other cases. Organisationally, as Ainslie (1966, p. 174) puts it,

nearly all changes in African broadcasting ... tend away from the
concept of broadcasting as a function independent of government. ...
The tasks of radio have emerged as so much part of, and essential to, the
policies of Government, that many of the countries that inherited with
independence a statutory corporation in charge of broadcasting, have
legislated to bring radio – and television – back under direct Ministerial
control

The second apparent difference is in objectives, or in journalistic
philosophy. African journalism has produced a clear statement of
alternative approaches in the writings of Kwame Nkrumah. Derived
from Lenin, they extol the virtues of the press as a political weapon in
the struggle to organise the masses in the fight against imperialsim. 'The
drumbeat of the African revolution must throb in the pages of the
newspapers and magazines; it must sound in the voices and feelings of
our news readers. To this end we need a new kind of journalist for the
African revolution' (Nkrumah, 1963). Yet in many African countries
this fervour and clarity of vision have somehow resolved into calls for
the press to 'contribute to national unity', 'foster development' or aid
education. These are real, if inexplicit ideals, but not irreconcilable with
the conventional understandings of journalistic ethics. The results of
such reconciliation by Nigerian journalists are discussed in Chapter 5
(see also Golding, 1977). It is also worth recalling that Lenin was
proposing not a theory of the press (what journalism is) but an
organisational directive.

In practice, two broadcasting systems have proved to be the main
alternatives adopted throughout the Western world. The first is the BBC
model of a single, monopoly organisation organised around the
principle of broadcasting as a public utility, licensed though not directly
controlled by government. Where BBC type institutions are a
department of government (as in most anglophone African countries)
they retain nonetheless the style and ethos of their progenitor (see
Golding, 1977; Katz and Wedell, 1978). The second model is the less
centralised, commercial form of broadcasting developed in North
America. The main organisations in our study all derive from the BBC
model, despite the support of advertising revenue all but Sveriges Radio
receive. These involve different compromises: between 'public service'
and commercial objectives; between government, advertising, or public
subscription revenues; and between varying degrees of state control. In
the account which follows we shall be particularly concerned to discover
what problems these differences raise for the daily practice of journalism,
before turning to the management of these problems in operational
routines and ideologies. So far as the relationship between broadcasting
and the state is concerned this may be conveniently divided into a
consideration of the basic system established for broadcasting, the
continuing process of inquiry and regulation to which this establishment
is subject and finally any specific interventions by the state to which
broadcasters have had to respond. As a result of this analysis three

different types of relationship can be identified – *mediated* in Sweden, *interventionist* in Ireland and *accommodatory* in Nigeria.

Yet for all these differences between the countries in the role of the journalist and the relationship between broadcast journalism and the state, content analysis, as reported in Chapter 6, revealed that the journalism produced was itself not so different. The same institutional areas, illustrated by the same events and the same people, dominate the news. Of course there are differences and it would be misleading to dismiss them. But the important determinants of output are the constraints on the material available to newsrooms and the common beliefs about audience needs and demands. These constraints act on the variable traditions and histories in each country to produce diversity within a pattern. Moreover the autonomy of journalists from government interference, or from objectives and methods set by government is not itself the separation of journalism from the state. As we shall see below, much depends on the overlap between government, politics and the state more broadly defined. To examine the relationship between broadcasting and government is only to open the topic of broadcast journalism and the state. The real intermeshing of these two is in the coincidence of news as a particular account of how the world works, with the ideology of the state as a broader version of this same account. The extent to which these coincide is examined in Chapter 8; the belief systems that produce their coincidence in Chapter 7.

The regulation of broadcasting

Public service utilities run by public corporations have for practical purposes been a novelty of this century. It has taken legislative and administrative ingenuity to devise the forms in which such bodies could be developed within the legal and administrative systems of different countries. In Britain, the BBC has been credited with being a pre-Morrison case of 'Morrisonite' nationalisation (Burns, 1977, Ch. 1). The post-war British Labour government was much impressed by a case in which public control of an industry had been introduced with little controversy. The Swedish legal system could not directly accommodate a public corporation. In that case the BBC model was transposed into a non-profit-making, limited company. But as Edward Ploman has written, the effect was to create in a novel form, a central administrative agency for the implementation of law.

> Sweden has for centuries made a clear distinction between the functions of the ministries and the central administrative agencies (or public service agencies); law is thus not implemented by a ministry but by these agencies which now number about 80. They have a constitutionally-guaranteed independent position in relation to government ... Even if the Swedish Broadcasting Corporation has been formally given the legal

status of a limited company, it in fact resembles one of these independent administrative agencies in the appointment and composition of its Board of Governors. (Ploman, 1976, p. 4.)

Irish broadcasting developed as a department of the government, with aims closely related to cultural objectives defined by the political executive. The Broadcasting Authority Act of 1960 changed all this. It created a public corporation in the form of a state-sponsored body, having monopoly control over broadcasting and 'all such powers as are necessary and incidental to that purpose'. State-sponsored bodies are a usual form of corporation in Ireland and similar authorities control some of the medical professions, social services like the blood service, some industries like peat, steel, electricity supply, the national airline, rail, road and water transport, milk marketing and so on. Their employees are not civil servants, though their respective authorities are responsible to a 'sponsor' minister, in the case of RTE the Minister for Posts and Telegraphs.

Nigerian broadcasting, like that in many developing countries, has become more rather than less closely integrated into government, at both national and regional level. In fact Nigeria was in many ways exceptional among African countries in not introducing broadcasting from the outset as a government institution. Where French colonial territories had spawned highly centralised, closely controlled, metro-politan-orientated broadcasting organisations, British territories developed semi-independent corporations fashioned inevitably on BBC lines. As Ainslie (1966, p. 158) remarks, 'in the early sixties, the BBC could look with some satisfaction on a whole brood of more or less dutiful offspring in East and West Africa, all fashioned in the maternal image, and all schooled in the sacred principles of "balance" and "impartiality" that govern the mother organisation in matters controversial.' Through a series of constitutional and organisational changes the objectives of Nigerian broadcasting have become incorporated in those of the state, though the journalistic principles of impartiality and objectivity have never been threatened or questioned overtly. As elsewhere their extraordinary elasticity has allowed a wide range of practices and beliefs to occupy the position they define.

Broadcasting in Nigeria has been organised at two levels, national (i.e. Federal) and local (i.e. regional, or since 1967, state). The Nigerian Broadcasting Corporation was created by an Ordinance (No. 39) of the colonial federation in 1956, which took effect in April 1957. The Corporation was empowered to provide 'as a public service, independent and impartial broadcasting services'. The BBC rhetoric and philosophy were reproduced in detail, style and substance. The legacy of British organisational style, down to the incomprehensible catalogue of initial letters describing hierarchical positions which pepper corridor conversations, remains as testimony to this attempted reproduction. The Corporation was obliged 'whenever so requested by an authorised officer in the public service of the Federation or an authorised police officer' to broadcast any announcement it was requested to by such people. But, despite the wide range of officers thus given authority this was not very different from the reserve powers held by the government in the BBC Charter.

Independence and increased regional autonomy put the Lagos-based NBC under great pressure. The regional governments were persistently critical, and the reponse was to redefine the obligations to the state of the broadcasting organisation. In 1961 an Act amending the Ordinance was passed giving the Minister power to 'give to the Corporation general or specific directions on matters of policy or matters appearing to the Minister to be of public interest, and the Corporation shall give effect to all such directions'. The Minister defended the clause by pointing to similar Ministerial powers governing such bodies as the Ports Authority, the Electricity Corporation, and the Railway Corporation.

The switch from civilian to military government in 1966 led to the more direct integration of broadcasting with government. The NBC board of 16 governors was replaced by an eight-man board including an army major and officials of the Federal Ministries of Information, Finance, Communications, Education and External Affairs. The onset of the Civil War in 1967 produced an 'emergency' situation, never since declared to be at an end, which completed this process. Henceforth the objectives of the Corporation were entirely those of the Federal Military Government:

> The importance of broadcasting as a medium for the creation of national consciousness came sharply into focus during the year ... not only were rebel lies about the true position of things in Nigeria being effectively debunked, the case for a united Nigeria was also forcefully put across to the world.
>
> (NBC Annual Report 1967-8)

> As the Nigerian crisis continued into its third year, the NBC continued to play a major role in the publicity and propaganda efforts of the Federal Military Government. Specially written newstalks were carried three times every day and the One-Nigeria slogan and civil defence jingles were broadcast every hour after the main news and news summaries. Most of the topical discussion programmes concentrated on explaining the background to the crisis and giving the reasons why the rebellion must be crushed.
>
> (Annual Report 1969-70)

After the end of hostilities in January 1970 the wartime status of broadcasting continued. The Corporation was now committed to the Federal Government's policy of 'reconciliation, reconstruction and rehabilitation'. Two obvious levers of control are financial and administrative. Ostensibly supported by licence fee and advertising revenue the NBC 'depends mainly on subventions from government' (Kolade, 1974, p. 80). The government established a Statutory Corporations Service Commission, and a similar Tenders Board which controlled senior appointments and major budgetary decisions, or as it was wryly put, 'enable the Corporation to concentrate more fully on its operational programme policy-making role'. These two boards were later abolished.

As broadcasting has moved closer to the state in Nigeria so it has adopted many government policies as its own and redefined its own production practices to accommodate them. This process is further discussed below but first it is important to compare the situation in Ireland following the attempt to redefine the relationship between broadcasting and the state in that country through the Broadcasting Act. Rather than clearly defining the constitutional position, the Act, and subsequent interpretations of it have served only to produce ambiguities and tensions between state and authority, and in turn between the Authority and its employees. These have been of two kinds. First, the role of RTE *in the state* has been unclear, that is the extent to which its general policy and purposes should coincide with those of elected governments. Second, the role *of the state* in controlling the activities of RTE has been spasmodically contentious in ways that seriously affected news production. The first of these ambiguities calls into question the nature of the objectivity required of RTE and the political boundaries within which information and ideas about political conflict should be confined. The second concerns the actual organisation of news gathering and production and the extent to which 'professional' considerations outweigh or indeed are distinct from central political direction.

It was in an attempt to reduce these ambiguities after years of nervously coping with the strains of reporting Ulster and the IRA that an Act to amend the 1960 Act was introduced in 1976. This extended requirements for objectivity and impartiality to a wider range of programmes, and also prohibited broadcasting of 'anything which may reasonably be regarded as likely to promote, or incite to, crime or as tending to undermine the authority of the State'. RTE immediately responded by advising its employees that this should not be seen as 'requiring RTE to discontinue or diminish programming which holds society and public policy and administration up to critical scrutiny ...' (see Fisher, 1977, p. 48).

There was less ambiguity in Sweden over this relationship even if continual commissions and reorganisations gave an impression of insecurity. Fundamental stability was to a large extent guaranteed by law. SR discharged its obligations as the monopoly broadcasting corporation in Sweden within a legal framework set by two radio laws, the Radio Act and the Broadcasting Liability Act, a supplementary agreement between the corporation and the state and its own articles of association as a company. Its performance, particularly in meeting the obligations laid on it by the Radio Act and the agreement with the state is checked by Radionämnden, the radio council, which considers complaints against SR's programme output. Its own organisation and operation are governed by regulations set out by the government, and its members are appointed by the government. The versions of all these laws, agreements and regulations current during our study ran from 1966 and 1967, the time when the corporation was being reorganised to accommodate the second television channel. The agreement came into force on 1 July 1967 and was set to run for ten years. This period was extended to allow the committee to report and the government to consider legislation. In May 1978 a parliamentary revolution announced an administrative organisation of SR into a parent company with four independent subsidiaries responsible for national radio, television, local radio and educational radio/television.

This reorganisation will make little difference to the relationship between SR and the state, though it includes a proposal to raise the licence fee. In common with other countries Sweden has found that the saturation of the market for sets has made the licence a less buoyant source of revenue so that government action is continually necessary to raise the rate. Recent commissions and broadcasting legislation have been concerned more with questions of internal autonomy and competition. The new law for example is designed to separate radio and television in the hope that separate development will raise programme quality in both services.

The Swedes and their broadcasting system are prone to recurrent commissions of inquiry and legislation of one kind or another. In exasperation, the Director-General of Sveriges Radio once exclaimed that 'When the last Swede on earth dies, he will do so suffocated by dust from public enquiries into – the last Swede.' In the period after our observation studies were completed, Parliament passed legislation on local radio and stereo broadcasting, set up a Committee of Inquiry to study new basic legislation for all media, and further committees to investigate the future of broadcasting and the financial problems of the press. Sitting during this period was a committee on educational broadcasting, and in the pipeline were government inquiries into commercial concentration in the media and possible reorganisation of the Radio Council. The sheer number of commissions and laws, and the detail into which many of these have gone in terms of type of organisation to be adopted and even the way programme policy should be administered suggest close government interest, if not control.

Nevertheless the independence of broadcasting is guaranteed by the basic law, currently the Radio Act of 1966 as amended in 1972 and 1975, which establishes SR's monopoly in broadcasting including 'wire transmission for direct reception by the public', i.e. cable-casting. The law prescribes that 'the exclusive right shall be exercised impartially and objectively'; that 'no authority or public body may examine in advance or prescribe the advance examination of radio programmes or prohibit radio transmissions or wire transmissions on account of content' with the exception of cases involving national defence; that further obligations may be laid on the corporation by an agreement between itself and the government and that its performance shall be examined by a radio council.

The agreement, which came into effect in 1967 for a ten-year period, covers both further matters of principle and of organisation. The corporation is required to 'uphold the fundamental democratic values in its programme services'; to provide a diversified output and to avoid the simultaneous transmission of similar types of programmes on different radio and TV channels; to reconcile the basic requirements of impartiality and objectivity with the further need for extensive freedom of speech; to verify factual statements prior to transmission; to 'aim at essentials' in the choice of subjects for programmes and their presentation; to respect the privacy of individuals, to correct mistakes in broadcast output, and to offer a right of reply if appropriate in such cases. The Broadcasting Liability Act of 1966 is modelled on the Freedom of the Press Act and defines broadcasters' liabilities in cases of libel. The Act stipulates that 'for every radio programme there shall be a programme supervisor for the purpose of preventing libels. Nothing may be broadcast against his wishes'. The supervisor is to be appointed by the management of the corporation. He and he alone shall be liable for libels committed except that in the case of live programmes the supervisor may decide that those appearing in the programmes should themselves be liable as he may well have little control over their output.

The new Act was introduced to ensure that someone was responsible for programme output as, under Swedish law, only individuals and not organisations are recognised as parties to a law suit. In 1960 a particularly controversial programme about hospital conditions was broadcast which led to questions in parliament and to the demand that someone should be made responsible for broadcasting output, just as in the press the editor is held to be responsible. In effect therefore the Act opened SR's operation to the possibility of another type of legal scrutiny.

The Broadcasting Liability Act also extended to broadcasting a requirement similar to that found in the press that programme makers should not reveal the identity of their sources unless this was required by law. Precedents suggest that even this exception would only be enforced in the case of serious crime. For example, before the enactment of the liability law, the police had asked for the names of some pimps and prostitutes who had been interviewed in a broadcast. Their request was refused. Nevertheless, there has been continuing discussion on whether this anonymity rule should be strengthened to exclude even the legal exception.

Alongside these external regulations SR has developed its own internal Code of Broadcasting Practice. The initial impetus for formulating such a document came from the same controversy over the infringement of individual rights by broadcast material which led eventually to the promulgation of the Broadcasting Liability Act discussed above. This Act was largely the result of work by an academic advisor to SR, Svante Bergström, Professor of Law at Uppsala University, and Gunnar Hansson, then legal adviser to SR. These two, together with a committee appointed within SR, worked on the formulation of the Code as well as drafting the Liabilty Law to bring SR into line with the press and other publishers.

By 1962 a Code had been prepared covering general rules for all broadcasting, setting out in particular the liabilities of SR and broadcasters as they were before the 1966 Act, and then special rules for news broadcasting and inadvertent advertising in SR's programmes; for example, by showing of posters round the ground during the coverage of a sports event. Henrik Hahr, then Chief Assistant to the Director-General at SR but who had himself been a head of news, summarised the sections relevant to news as follows:

> On the subject of broadcast news, the Committee makes it clear that an objective, impartial, independent and prompt news service is in the interests of a democratic society. It should be conducted in principle to conform with *regular journalistic practice* though paying careful attention to the *difference in status* between *Sveriges Radio and the press*. Since the general public is supposed to be able to rely on the news broadcast by SR, staff members are required to make sure that their *news sources are trustworthy*. The editorial staff or department which produces the programme is to be responsible for *the evaluation of news*. Attempts by outsiders to influence the evaluation of news or the wording of a news communication should be disregarded. An item of news shall be made public as soon as possible. *Of particular relevance to SR however, is that speed must not be obtained at the cost of accuracy* [our italic]. (Hahr, 1963, p. 25).

This very special position was further amplified by provisos as to the procedures which editorial staffs should take to check the veracity of the information, to present it in a precise and restrained fashion and in general to 'act so that the public can put its reliance on Sveriges Radio as a communicator of news'. (Ibid.)

In other matters the Committee drew heavily on the code of practice formulated by the Publicists Club (PK), the main social forum for journalists in Stockholm. The club's code was formulated with the Freedom of the Press Act very much in mind so since the passage of the Broadcasting Liability Act brought SR's situation more into line with that of the press, the PK code has become more relevant to SR. In some cases it is its provisions which appear in the act. Examples of requirements now supported by the law are the provision of a right of reply and the need to ensure anonymity of sources.

The PK rules also dealt extensively with the reporting of crimes, in particular setting strict limits on the occasions on which journalists might publish the names of criminals or those involved in criminal proceedings. Further, they warned against the possibility of defamation in general. SR's own code drew particular attention to the care which should be taken in reporting individual complaints against professional or occupational groups. It noted the related danger that 'In dealing with such cases, staff members must not be misled into the kind of cautious behaviour which might be interpreted as submissiveness towards public officials and other persons in public life.' Nevertheless the implications are clear. In assessing the accuracy of statements which, as was seen above, were liable to become the key test of objectivity, due weight should be given to the occupational or public positions held by those involved in the news event. Some sources are more trustworthy than others, and position could be taken as some guide on this point.

Finally some special provisions were made in the code to deal with the picture content of television news. For example, journalists were to avoid pictures of violence which might become upsetting and obtrusive, to avoid suggesting through pictures some point not already made in the commentary and to take care that innocent parties were not negatively implicated in some item because they appeared in the pictures. These latter two provisos suggest a distrust of the picture element in television journalism as adding new dimensions to journalistic performance which were not already covered by the standard procedures of journalistic practice.

When fieldwork for this study began in 1971 journalists at SR, particularly those working in the Central News Department, were quick to point with some pride to these rules. They regarded them as a somewhat unusual attempt, by international comparison, to formulate and codify procedures for the selection, processing and presentation of news. Nevertheless the book of rules appeared to be little consulted in the course of a working day, as indeed one might expect given the length of experience of most of those working in SR. Its primary value seemed to be as a source of reference in occasional planning and policy discussions within Central News. Of particular interest to the study is the emphasis which this code placed on authority and reliability. As we shall see below, this relates both to the stage in the development of broadcast news in Sweden in which it was drawn up and the relationship between the Central News Department and the rest of the organisation. Although broadcast news is usually discussed in terms of the paired criteria, impartiality and objectivity, a third, authority, is never far below the surface.

The broadcasting – state relationship in practice

(a) Mediation

As noted above, Swedish broadcasting has been provided with an intermediary body, Radionämnden, to mediate its relationship to the wider society by interpreting such requirements as impartiality and objectivity which have been placed on it. It has also operated in a country blessed with internal security. In both of the other countries relationships have been changed and problems of ambiguity thrown into sharp relief by the security problems of the state.

Radionämnden is best translated as radio council as in many ways its functions are analagous to that of the British Press Council. It is a review body established to consider complaints. By regulations promulgated in 1967 it was to have a membership of seven, all appointed by the government. Although the government pays some attention to the political allegiances of appointees, the members of the council are not primarily politicians but representatives of culture and the arts. The regulations require members to have extensive legal knowledge and in many ways the function of the council is to turn the abstract principles of the laws and the agreement into a set of case law applicable to particular situations. In the early years of its existence Radionämnden was not regarded as a very important body, either within the corporation or within Swedish society at large. But as public controversy developed about the nature and scope of television coverage in the late 1960s and early 1970s, so more and more use came to be made of the council and its role became politically controversial. In 1970 the number of complaints topped 200 and in recent years there has been a continuing increase. The membership of the council has been increased to eight with four substitutes but the council and its secretariat are still heavily overloaded.

As with the international controversy about bias and partiality in factual television, general accusations tend to be levelled against news broadcasting but most concrete cases of complaint have referred to current affairs and documentaries, not news strictly interpreted. Radionämnden's judgements are interesting however because in general the council has supported the techniques broadcasters have derived to protect their professional independence. Staffan Vängby has provided a thorough review of Radionämnden's decisons in this area up to 1970 (Vängby, 1971). Within Sweden the controversy over bias in television output developed against the background of the Vietnam War abroad and industrial unrest at home. In 1969–70 there was an unofficial strike against the state-owned mining company in the north of Sweden. The strike was so unusual in a Swedish context that in some ways it was the equivalent of an internal security crisis for the country (see Fulcher, 1973). Before this period of controversy Radionämnden had helped to establish such principles as that broadcasters could make their own provisions to compensate for partiality. A refusal to appear by one party to a dispute should not lead to the suppression of all reports of that dispute. This principle arose from a case in 1957. In a time of government crisis the Prime Minister did not wish to comment while the other parties did.

Further, the council had already accepted the general principle that selection decisions were to be taken in terms of news values and that the corporation must have great freedom to assess such news value. For example, asked to consider whether SR should have relayed a Soviet statement on the reason for the invasion of Czechoslovakia which the complainant held to be a direct lie, the council decided:

to sift political statements possessing news value according to whether or not the content of the statement fitted the truth would obviously be a breach of the corporation's duty, as laid down in the agreement, to provide, in suitable form, information on current events. *Great freedom must be given to the corporation in assessing whether or not a statement possesses news value* (Vängby, 1971, p. 80, our italic).

Similarly, a complaint against an interview with a delegation from North Korea was also rejected on the grounds that such an interview 'must be taken to have clear news value'.

Asked to consider whether there was consistent and persistent bias in SR's coverage of the Vietnam War, Radionämnden commissioned a special study by Professor Jörgen Westerståhl of the Department of Political Science, Gothenberg University. Professor Westerståhl attempted to analyse the concepts of impartiality and objectivity in such a way as to reduce their constituent components to variables which could be measured by content analysis. These analyses were subsequently refined in further studies which the Professor undertook of the coverage of the 1968 General Election and the LKAB conflict (the Northern mining strike). The fact that these two subsequent studies were commissioned by SR itself – the first by the Director-General, the second by the board of governors – is itself an interesting commentary on the intermediary function served both by Radionämnden and by this type of content analysis research. Both could be relied on to defuse the immediate controversy with a reasonable chance that they would vindicate the corporation's practices in the end.

The controversy over the 1968 election coverage grew out of relatively conventional charges of political bias made by some politicians involved in it. Both the controversy over the Vietnam War and the LKAB strike however reflected what has been termed 'the rebirth of ideology' which occurred internationally in the late 1960s, in a specifically Swedish context. Controversy over the Vietnam War focussed attention on Sweden's neutrality and internationalism, while the prolonged un-official strike against LKAB called in question Sweden's system of national negotiation for wage awards and the long-term alliance between the unions and the Social Democrats in government. This rebirth took much the same form in Sweden as elsewhere in the Western world. Divisions appeared which were partly expressed in age differences, partly in political differences and the greater prominence given to left wing views outside those represented by the established parties, and partly in a difference between those who were in a general sense part of the establishment and those who felt themselves to be outside it. SR, like the other broadcasting organisations around the world, found itself in the middle of these divisions being accused by each side of being in the other's camp. The fact that the 'rebirth of ideology' coincided with change and expansion at SR appeared to be a justification for those on the right who accused SR of being on the left, or at least of being infiltrated by those on the left.

Professor Westerståhl's studies, however, provided no support for such views or indeed for the opposite. By comparing SR's coverage of the various issues with that of the Swedish metropolitan press, Westerståhl found that SR's coverage generally came in the middle between the varying political viewpoints represented by different newspapers. He subdivided the two goals of objectivity and impartiality into truthfulness and relevance, and balance and neutral presentation, though accepting that his technique primarily dealt with the third aspect, balance (Westerståhl, 1972). In a case like the Vietnam War it was impossible independently to establish truthfulness, while relevance depended on news judgement. To some extent the comparative method provided a check that there was no persistent bias in the news judgements arrived at in SR, that is *they could be shown to be similar to news judgements made elsewhere by other journalists*. Academics and others in Sweden subsequently criticised Westerståhl's studies for reducing the complexities of impartiality and objectivity to a rule of thumb which ignored problems of general media bias.

Westerståhl had made the point in relation to both relevance and balance that news coverage necessarily depended on events. If the events themselves were unbalanced or, as in Vietnam, the available news material was mostly coming from one side in the conflict, SR could not be expected to provide the missing material or to stop coverage of such an important event because it was not available. The Radio Council accepted Westerståhl's general conclusions that there was nothing to criticise in SR's coverage. It also built the last point into its case law. In his view of Radionämnden's pronouncements on impartiality, the sometime secretary of the council, Staffan Vängby (1971, p. 78) quotes Westerståhl as follows:

> the relatively independent nature of the news means that the actual course of events will determine in high degree both how much and what type of news is published, and that different parties can be 'favoured' or 'disfavoured' without the question arising of any lack of impartiality in the medium concerned.

This had been a point of particular significance in the Radio Council's deliberations on another complaint about a slightly different type of programme, the daily reviews of the Swedish press. The complaint was that necessarily such programmes were biased against those parties and views which were under-represented in the press. Because of the predominance of 'bourgeois' papers (Conservative and Liberal) these two parties effectively received much more coverage than the Social Democrats, whose press was limited and ailing. This is one occasion on which the council was divided, apparently on political lines. Nevertheless a majority accepted the argument that SR could not be blamed for simply reproducing 'an existing state of affairs. That this particular state of affairs is not characterised by a balance between different opinions cannot imply that the programme as such is either partial or unobjective'. One member however held that 'Press Chronicle', the programme in question, was not a news programme and so should be balanced. But in a later judgement the council reiterated its opinion that 'it is impossible to base the selection of statements for Press Chronicle on other principles than their news value and general interest'.

From this review it is apparent that Radionämnden has acted as something of a champion of SR's professional independence in the news field. Staffan Vängby concludes from his review of Radionämnden's judgements in the news field that 'Only in a few cases is a certain criticism of the Corporation's news evaluation noticeable in the Council's decisions and even then the Council has never found a breach of either the Radio Act or the Agreement to have occurred.' The title of Vängby's review is itself significant translating into the familiar couplet 'Impartiality and objectivity'. Radionämnden has accepted the twin doctrines of news values and the reflection of the course of events, rejecting such alternative views as that SR should form its own judgement about the truth of news items, in particular of statements quoted as news, or that SR should consider possible effects. In this connection there is a distinction to be made between accuracy and truth. What matters is that any item or statement should have been accurately reported, not that any judgement should be made as to its intrinsic truth. For example, in considering a complaint that SR had taken Eurovision coverage of the European games in Athens in spite of the comfort this might give to the dictatorial regime in Greece at the time, Radionämnden restated these principles.

> The information on current events required of the corporation by the Agreement is to be objective. This means that the main principle of selection must be, in addition to the accuracy of the information given, its importance. Items should thus be selected in the light of the different news value different information can be assumed to have. It is obviously no part of current news assessment to take into account such circumstances as the effect the communication of news can have in creating opinion favourable to an undemocratic regime in a foreign country, or official Swedish attitudes to such a regime ... the obligation of the Corporation, in its programme services, to 'uphold the fundamental democratic values' supports rather the view that such considerations should not influence selection, since fundamental democratic values include a free news service which aims at objectively correct information that will provide a basis for discussion and the formation of opinions. (Vängby, 1971)

(b) Intervention

This Swedish experience is in marked contrast to the Irish. In that case there have been no intermediaries between the broadcaster and the state. The Irish government itself has been responsible for deciding how the broadcasters should interpret their duties. In Sweden there has been a mediated relationship between broadcasting and the state, in Ireland, one of intervention. These interventions have been based on the celebrated Section 31 of the 1960 Broadcasting Act on the government's power not only to appoint but to remove the members of the Authority and to approve the appointment or removal of the Director-General. Section 31 of the 1960 Act includes the following provisions:

1. The Minister may direct the Authority in writing to refrain from broadcasting any particular matter or matter of any particular class, and the Authority shall comply with the direction.

2. The Minister may direct the Authority in writing to allocate broadcasting time for any announcements by or on behalf of any Minister of State in connection with the functions of that Minister of State, and the Authority shall comply with the direction.

The results of the first formal use of these requirements in 1971 will be discussed in a moment. Up till that time no written direction had been issued, but the very requirement that directions be committed to paper for the record increased the likelihood of informal pressure and interference. In 1966 a news bulletin reported a statement by the Minister of Agriculture to farmers, immediately followed by a dissenting response from a spokesman for the National Farmers' Association. This produced an angry telephoned complaint from the Minister of Agriculture and the critical comment was dropped from later bulletins. After widespread criticism of the Minister's action, the then Prime Minister was moved to make the following remarks, often quoted since:

> Radio Telefis Eireann was set up by legislation as an instrument of public policy, and as such is responsible to the Government ... the Government reject the view that Radio Telefis Eireann should be, either generally or in regard to its current affairs and news programmes, completely independent of Government supervision ... It has the duty, while maintaining impartiality between political parties ... to sustain public respect for the institutions of Government ...

The vibrations of this incident shook the organisation and threw into sharp relief the ill-defined position of the Authority and of RTE's constitutional obligations. Press and commentators struck predictably outraged poses, and at the end of a chain of events which are now difficult to reconstruct reliably, the Head of News resigned. Many saw confirmation of the weakening of the RTE Authority and of the Director-General when six months later a proposed news team visit to North Vietnam was cancelled. The decision was made by the Authority after the Prime Minister had 'spoken to the Chairman of RTE and informed him that in the opinion of the Government the best interests of the nation would not be served by sending an RTE team to Vietnam'. (Dail Debates 13 April 1967) Over a hundred members of RTE staff sent a letter of protest to the Prime Minister, an action deplored by the Director-General.

Isolated exceptional incidents of this kind signal the point at which the understandings between news broadcasting and the state become threatened. The tacit exchange of autonomy for responsibility becomes unbalanced when one of the parties to the exchange stretches the rules in its own favour. A variety of constitutional and legislative strictures circumscribe not merely what news operations may be conducted but what form news may take. What becomes apparent in a careful examination of these, however, is their studied vagueness, forcing journalists back on their own definitions of correct practice and professional observance. Article 40 of the Constitution, as well as having the conventional guarantees of freedom of expression, also states that 'the organs of public opinion . . . while preserving their rightful liberty of expression, including criticism of public policy, shall not be used to undermine public order or morality or the authority of the state'. This has been explained by Kevin McCourt, Director-general from 1963 to 1968, to suggest that 'foremost among the aims of broadcasting is that of inculcating an appreciation of the basic values of the social and political order and a respect for the institutions on which this order is based'. This is a very positive expression of programme philosophy, difficult to put into practice in a newsroom but nonetheless a coherent argument to place behind decisions about news coverage and selection.

The most direct expression of journalistic obligation arose from section 18 of the 1960 Act. This provided that 'it shall be the duty of the Authority to secure that, when it broadcasts any information news or feature which relates to matters of public controversy or is the subject of current political debate, the information, news or feature is presented objectively and impartially and without any expression of the Authority's own views'.

The logic-chopping such a demand might provoke is obviously endless. Attempts to turn it into operational rules seem doomed to failure. A circular from the Director-General in 1969 (occasioned by the various rows that led to some senior resignations) noted that 'we have never attempted to define how (Section 18) should be observed through a range of hypothetical situations'. Gradually, however, the statutory and ethical notions of impartiality and objectivity have been transmuted into operational notions of balance and disinterestedness. The same circular goes on: 'The words "objectively" and "impartially" have always been taken at their face value as meaning that the important facts or arguments of a situation should be presented uncoloured by any expression of opinion which might be seen to be an RTE opinion and that the presentation should be fair and unprejudiced.' The same question-begging interpretations appear in a later circular which states:

> The obligation to objectivity is seen as requiring broadcasting staff to apply *normal programming criteria* in their selection and presentation of programmes ... the obligation to impartiality is seen as requiring broadcasting staff to acquire the relevant background knowledge on the subject matter being treated of, to present, either directly or through

participants, the relevant information correctly and to achieve fair
balance in representation (emphasis added).

The point to emerge from all this is the practical impossibility in
normal circumstances of defining journalistic practice by constitutional
or legislative decree. Organisational attempts to distill the crude
expressions of intent into a set of operational instructions remain vague,
inexplicit, indefinite and open to infinite interpretation. At least they do
so up to a limit. That limit is set by the root assumptions about
legitimate political contentions shared by government and broadcasters
alike. One of these was located with subsequent great publicity by the
Chairman of the BBC. '... as between the government and the
opposition, as between the two communities in Northern Ireland, the
BBC has a duty to be impartial no less than in the rest of the United
Kingdom. But as between the British Army and the gunmen the BBC is
not and cannot be impartial' (Hill, 1974, p. 209). The RTE memo stated
that 'No broadcasting service can or should be impartial in all matters: it
is not impartial about crime or racial prejudice or religious intolerance.'
And so back to McCourt's injunction to 'inculcate an appreciation of
the basic values of the social and political order'.

If objectivity in general evaded rigorous definition, its application to
the coverage of the North was rudely solidified by the activation of
Section 31 in October 1971. The Minister then directed the authority in
writing to refrain from broadcasting 'any matter that could be
calculated to promote the aims or activities of any organisation which
engages in, promotes, encourages or advocates the obtaining of any
particular objective by violent means'. The authority thought the
directive difficult to follow when phrased in such general terms, and
indeed, as it stood, it could have proscribed coverage of the army and
police, as well as its intended and obvious target the IRA. The problem
of devising a general rule for a particular case was never so fraught.
Technically, RTE had already frequently contravened Section 18 of the
Offences Against the State Act 1937 which made it an offence to publish
information about organisations deemed unlawful.

From October 1971 coverage of events in the North came to dominate
RTE news, and increasingly preoccupied the Authority and RTE
executives. The Programme Policy Committee, which met twice weekly,
constantly reiterated its conclusion that the best service RTE could
provide for their audience was an unemotional low-key coverage of the
North. Constant reassurance of the partiality of others, notably the
BBC, was sought and found, to be held up as clear evidence of RTE's
successful negotiation of the inevitable pitfalls created by the Section 31
directive. Yet for journalists observance of the directive required the
suppression of material justified by the occupational ethic of newsworthiness and the professional ethic of exposure and 'fully informing
the audience'. During the course of 1972 the authority was recurrently
forced to balance its obligation to the Minister with the pressure from
news staff to exploit the ambiguities in the directive. The initial

intentions were firm. At one of the first meetings of the Programme Policy Committee after the issue of the directive the Head of News repeated the Director-General's view that 'the implications of the direction on news reporting will be marginal, and will not in any way relate to news content'. It was decided that the actions of illegal organisations are a necessary part of the news and must be reported, and thus no departure from usual practice was required. The one clear proscription was against allowing a member of an illegal organisation to put his point of view directly.

In November 1972 an RTE reporter obtained an interview with the then Chief of Staff of the IRA, Sean MacStiofain. Before transmission, he consulted the Head of News, who cleared the interview. In the absence of the Director-General (away in Galway on business connected with the Irish language radio service), the Head of News discussed the matter with the deputy Director-General who approved transmission in principle if it was given in 'a suitable context' and presented in a low-key manner. It proved to be a last straw. MacStiofain was arrested hours after the interview. The government wrote to the authority saying that the broadcast was a breach of the directive and that an explanation was required. No adequate explanation being provided other than to point out again the vagueness of the directive, the entire authority was dismissed and replaced. The reporter who conducted the interview was subsequently jailed for contempt of court for refusing to identify one of the voices on the recording of the interview as MacStiofain's.

We will be looking in more detail in the next chapter at the impact of the Ulster situation and the directive on the journalists and news production, but one or two conclusions emerge from this account so far. It forced executives to consider the definitions of practice contained in relevant legislation, but without great embarrassment or hardship. Indeed, advantage was sometimes discerned in the midst of adversity as when the Controller of Television observed that RTE coverage of the North was superior to that of the BBC because the directive had removed emotion from the reports by concentrating on indirect statements rather than filmed histrionic speeches. As he put it, 'in these difficult times, irrespective of a direction, this is obviously the correct policy for RTE'. In response to this remark the Deputy Director-General noted that this policy coincided with RTE's responsibility under the constitution not to disrupt public order or the institutions of government.

Rather than a serious imposition of governmental control over programming, the directive was a re-emphasis of the relationship between broadcasting and the state. The ramifications for the authority and its executives were clearly troublesome at best, unbearable at worst, but they were largely contained at this level. For newsmen it produced a different kind of problem, underlined by the imprisonment of Mac-Stiofain's interviewer, a threat to professional autonomy normally left tacit. We shall examine in the next chapter how far this seriously disturbed or confirmed the application of normal news values and practices.

In 1971 the Minister appointed a Broadcasting Review Committee to review the progress of radio and television and consider possible further developments. Its main deliberations concerned the establishment of a Broadcasting Commission with some degree of supervision over the RTE executive, and the opening of a second television channel. The committee, which reported in 1974, did in addition examine news and current affairs, and its pungent comments drew an angry reaction from the Head of News. The committee's report made various charges; that there was an excess of 'instant' news, lack of supervision, inadequate provincial news and other minor undeveloped charges. Oddly, it devoted little space to coverage of the North other than to accuse the news of not 'having conformed to an adequate standard of objectivity and impartiality' (p. 94). The accusation fails to be specific and is predictably unable to translate these statutory requirements into specific recommendations for journalistic practice. The reaction from the Head of News was particularly scathing about the failure of the committee to take note of the effects of the ministerial direction. If the charge was failure to be impartial, the defence was the traditional one – the criticism had come from both sides – the solution predictably unspecific; 'For our part we believed the greatest aid and comfort we could bring all the people was as far as possible to report accurately and truthfully all that happened.' Yet the situation was extreme, the violence, while not without precedent, extraordinary in post-war Ireland. 'There was no received wisdom to help cope with it.' Except, that is, for the traditional hierarchy of news values and the professional ideologies created by the situation and routine of news production. In October 1976 a further directive under section 31 made prohibition of interviews or reports of interviews with the IRA more explicit. The Amendment Act passed at the end of 1976 extended the authority of the state, as noted earlier, and also set up a potentially influential Broadcasting Complaints Commission.

In looking at the Irish situation in some detail it is apparent how the relationship between state and broadcasting can fluctuate from considerable liberal licence to direct constraint, yet still fail to produce definitions of journalistic practice. The formulae used by statutory instruments are totally incapable of ready translation into practice, while the problems of observing them serve only to make journalists defensive and uneasy. The solution is always to let the incidentally evolved norms of journalism, fairness, accuracy and comprehensiveness, take their usual form while more broadly to fall back, not on news values but on social values that underpin the vision of society shared by broadcasters and the state alike.

(c) Accommodation

Nigerian broadcasters had gone further down the road than their Irish or Swedish colleagues. In their case it was not just that moments of social stress had shown fundamental agreement over the social value of the state in its existing form. Rather it was that they were prepared to accept specific social values embodied in particular government policies. In a military dictatorship the distinction between government and the state is much less clear than in liberal, Western democracies, further restricting the broadcasters' room for independent manoeuvre. The relationship between broadcasting and the state may be typified as *accommodation* rather than *mediation* or *intervention* as in the other two cases. News values and judgements of importance in particular come to be interpreted in such a way so that there is much closer agreement between broadcasters and the government on the whole range of priorities. The day to day effect of this relation to government is examined in the next chapter. Accommodation to governmental objectives meant, at one level, deliberate assistance with the promotion of government-sponsored campaigns; for example, campaigns for decimal currency, the switch to right-hand traffic, or the elimination of armed robbery. All these in turn were given repetitive exposure both in and out of news bulletins. Similar support for and dissemination of the government's foreign policies was demanded and expected. At another level it involved a conscious redefinition of the objectives of broadcast journalism.

A nine-point statement of NBC objectives was issued in April 1973 by the Director-General. It included the aims of providing 'efficient broadcasting to the whole Federation of Nigeria, based on national objectives and aspirations', of contributing 'to the development of Nigerian society, (promoting) national unity by ensuring a balanced presentation of views from all parts of Nigeria', and of ensuring 'the prompt delivery of accurate information to the people'. The Head of News elaborated on this last objective in some detail to a Management Seminar in 1974. He pointed out that, 'In a developing country like Nigeria, broadcasting must offer a continuous flow of information to the people in order to sustain their right to know about Government intentions and actions as well as what is going on in the world around them. The replenishment of their knowledge in this way facilitates mass mobilisation for national development programmes.'

The 'Operational Guide for News Staff', a style-book seldom used and frequently misplaced, enlarged on the aims of the News Division. Style-books of this kind, codifying operational procedures in detail – when to use figures in words, which colloquialisms to avoid, the correct use of the present-perfect tense – are common in newspaper offices where the intention is to ensure uniform presentation and style. There too they fall a long way behind, in authority, the case law quoted by senior figures in the newsroom and the discretionary powers of sub-editors. However, here again the statement of aims was enshrined: 'We aim to provide news of which the people ought to know if they are to take their place as intelligent members of the community. We must be factual, objective, impartial, and balanced, and always in good taste.' These were laudable objectives but with two problems. First, they were only with some difficulty translated into operational procedures for news production. Second, they had to be reconciled with the practical requirements of those procedures.

Very similar situations obtain in the state stations, whose legal constitution and obligations were very close, if not identical to the BBC-influenced model of the NBC. There were differences of emphasis, however, which came, in practice, to give both the stations we studied greater freedom from government in many respects. The Western Nigeria Government Broadcasting Corporation, and its operating services WNBS and WNTV, were established in 1959 by a law passed in the then Western Regional Legislature. The operation was initially a joint venture with Overseas Rediffusion, the London-based commercial television company. The official line was that the public service aspirations of the regional government could not be reconciled with the commercial aims of the company, and the former bought out the latter in 1961, after which it was the sole owner. In fact a desire for greater control in the politically turbulent years after independence in the region was complemented by an optimistic assessment of the revenue-generating potential of broadcasting. The station has never been profitable overall, though the radio service alone has been making a profit since 1966.

The legislation governing WNBS contained the usual requirements to 'maintain a proper balance', 'that any news given in the programmes (in whatever form) is presented with due accuracy, impartiality and objectivity' and 'that due impartiality is preserved as respect matters of political or industrial controversy or relating to current public policy'. In the political crises in the west, following the contentious census of 1963 and the 1964 elections, government took an active interest in broadcasting. As elsewhere in Nigeria many journalists compare unfavourably the bad old political days with the firm, but largely predictable dictates of working with a military regime. After 1968 the General Manager was responsible to the Western State Statutory Services Commission for staff matters and directly to the Military Governor's Office for establishment matters generally. The station pursued a politically cautious policy based on avowedly commercial programming and organisational survival.

The northern station, the Broadcasting Corporation of Northern Nigeria, achieved a measure of independence in a rather different way. Though it had considerable advertising revenue, BCNN was not commercially profitable, and it did not pursue solely commercial success in its programming policies. But as the child of the former Northern Region, it now found itself with six parents in the state structure instituted in 1967. Only two of the states, Kano and North Central, contributed to the finance of the television service pending the extension of television to the rest of the region. Journalists within BCNN felt their independence from government to be much greater than the rather despised subservience of their colleagues in the NBC.

They saw it as resulting from the shrewd ability of management to play off the contending claims of the six controlling states. The undoubted vigour and boldness of the Kaduna-based *New Nigerian* newspaper was felt to result from the same strategy.[1]

In addition the problem of government intervention was to an extent displaced by an identity of interests between state government and broadcasters in their common suspicion of the federal government. Accommodation worked at regional rather than national level. The north versus south version of Nigerian politics was an important element in the social vision of BCNN journalists and tempered their concern with local political interference. The reality and importance of this will be explored in the next chapter. The station established itself during the civil war when its support for and advocacy of Federal Government policy was total. Its success established its aspirations to be a national station, and this ambition continued to guide its policies.

At this time the Nigerian military government considered itself to be administering a country in crisis. Broadcasting was seen as an essential tool of national development, defined as the achievement of government policy. The 1970–4 National Development Plan stated the two main objectives of information services (i.e. government supported media) to be 'the fostering of national harmony and the promotion of the spirit of national reconciliation particularly in the circumstances of post-war Nigeria. Another main objective is the mobilisation of public support for the national development effort through the dissemination of appropriate information . . .' (Federal Ministry of Information, 1970, p. 255).

The creation of 12 states was intended to mute regional antagonisms and promote local, but not sectional or fractionalised administration. Many observers judged this to have been largely successful, though dispute continues about the exact structure of the states and the adequacy with which minority group interests are promoted. The number of states was increased to 19 from February 1976. Return to civilian government had been promised for 1976, but scepticism and ostensibly a concern about the extent of corruption in national administration, produced a bloodless coup in July 1975. In February 1976 the new head of state, General Muhammed, was assassinated in an attempted coup. In these circumstances mass media clearly do not expect to retain the same relative freedom of action implicit in the separation of state and media guaranteed by the liberal constitutions of many western industrialised societies. The question is whether control by government and the setting of objectives by the state explain broadcast journalism in a country like Nigeria.

Formally Nigerian broadcasting media had functional independence, defined in terms identical to those governing their British progenitors.[2] The informal pressures were often enormous, the hazards of miscalculation frequently severe. The title of novelist and playwright Wole Soyinka's book *The Man Died* recalls a telegram he received in reply to an enquiry about the outcome of an incident involving a WNBS journalist. The journalist, Segun Sowemimo, had been beaten on the orders of the then Military Governor of the Western State after taking photos of the Governor's wife dancing with another man at an official function. Sowemimo died after long hospitalisation and suffering from gangrene (Soyinka, 1972; 303–5). In 1970 an NBC drama production used simulated news bulletins in a play about a military coup. The government's reaction was swift and uncompromising, leading to the arrest and temporary imprisonment of four senior executives. As the NBC annual report dryly puts it, 'regrettably some of the artistes who participated also suffered this inconvenience'. A more recent case of a newspaperman aroused considerable dissent among journalists. A *Nigerian Observer* journalist called Amakiri published a report on the threatened mass resignation of teachers in Rivers State. The report coincided with the then State Governor's 31st birthday celebrations and its 'embarrassing' impact prompted the arrest of Amakiri who was subsequently stripped, caned and had his head shaved. The journalistic community was outraged and calls for the Governor's resignation and a full enquiry continued for a long period. Eventually Amakiri was awarded substantial damages in court.

Such incidents were extreme and unusual, and their widespread publicity has been some measure of this. But harrassment, intimidation, threatening phone calls, arbitrary arrest, abuse of office, corruption and dictatorial requests were the common currency of relationships between a military regime and journalists. That such methods were less exploited in the 'benevolent dictatorship' of the Nigerian military than by rulers in many other countries should not disguise their importance. But we shall be arguing in the next chapter that they are outweighed in their impact on news production by the kinds of constraints found as much in Sweden and Ireland as in Nigeria.

Broadcasting and the national culture

One of the examples cited above of agreement between Nigerian broadcast journalists and the government on policy objectives, that of the change to driving on the right, could also have been cited for Sweden. Swedish broadcasters were closely involved in the public education campaign mounted prior to the introduction of the change in Sweden. Indeed the Nigerians, whose change came later, made some use of the campaign expertise the Swedes had acquired. The example serves to underline the point that though the mechanisms and practices involved in the relationship between broadcasting and government may differ from country to country, in practice the effects may be quite similar. Much depends on the extent to which basic social values are shared by broadcasters, politicians, rulers and others in the society.

Comparing the three countries therefore we would expect to find some variation in the priorities given to particular values and so to the importance attached to the people and events who represent them. Relatively unique characteristics such as the Swedish preoccupation with union leaders and industrial relations news, the Irish concern about the north and Nigerian interest in development could be traced to the particular historical and political experience of each country. Other policies current in the different newsrooms, some explicit, others more covert but generally recognised, could similarly be traced to journalists' sense of what was acceptable in their society. Not that this sense was based on a general sampling of national opinion. The sample, such as it was, came filtered both through the journalists' personal experience as members of a particular educated elite and through their occupational experience of working in broadcasting organisations whose major constituencies, government, politicians and interest groups, had clear ideas not so much on what public opinion was as what it ought to be.

Most newsrooms have rules of thumb about topics they will and won't deal with and ways of treating particular issues. In Nigeria, awareness of government foreign policy created just such guiding principles. RTK, for example, serving a large Moslem audience, was avowedly pro-Pakistan in the disputes with India, and gave prominent coverage to Moslem religious festivals. As the voice of Northern Nigeria journalists in RTK were aware of and willing to illustrate the tension between north and south. In Sweden a similar amalgam of influences including organisational policy, an awareness of government policy and unspoken assessments of the national mood produced consistent tendencies to play up some issues and play down others. The clearest example of organisational policy was the rule not to report crime news unless it raised issues of wider legal and political significance. This was organisational policy in the sense that it was written into the formal rules of the central news department and had a long history in the corporation. It was also almost universally accepted by staff. Journalists on Rapport, for example, reported it as being *their* policy, as if it did not have a wider history and currency in other departments.

Swedish internationalism showed itself both in general support for foreign news and in particular understandings on the treatment of specific countries and issues. Many journalists recognised that in taking this line as with their policy on crime they were adopting a paternalist attitude to their audience. It was a paternalism which they shared with many in Sweden's political and social elite. Olof Rydbeck, the Director-General mainly responsible for building up SR's team of foreign correspondents and its intake of foreign news, was a diplomat whose career was only briefly interrupted by his excursion into broadcasting. On the treatment of specific issues government policy was a particularly important clue to the national mood. Thus for example, when reporting Vietnam, journalists felt that since the Swedish government had openly opposed American policy, there was less reason to accept at face value western news agency versions of events there. Another theme which seemed unconsciously to reflect the journalists' assessment of national mood as reflected in government policy was an interest in stories which showed the policies and practices of right-wing governments overseas in a bad light. Much of this material did not come through the regular channels supplying news. Special arrangements had to be made for example to get film out of Spain about industrial unrest on May Day or to use freelance material from South America, as Rapport had done on occasions. Within the periods we studied, developments in Rhodesia provided an example where this type of story did come through the conventional channels. Like Northern Ireland it was a story which showed foreign regimes in a bad light when compared with the Swedes' own sense of international social justice. This sense, which is often recognised by foreigners, is a realistic assessment of the mood among Sweden's business, professional and political elites, rather than among the general population. Indeed there was a feeling that journalism in general and SR in particular had helped to make ordinary Swedes less insular than they had been.

Apart from the embargo on crime these policies and emphases were implicit rather than explicit, unconsciously reflected in practice rather than clearly stated at any level within the organisation. They serve to make the point that even exceptional cases in the sense that they show some variation in the interpretation of the standard rubrics of importance, impartiality and objectivity, were not exceptional in that they happened within the specific context of the relationship between broadcasting and the state, as experienced in the different national cultures.

A second important point of comparison between the three countries is the extent to which they shared the social value that broadcast journalism should be free and independent of government. This in spite of differences in the experience and practice of the broadcasting–state relationship discussed above and in Chapter 5. In all countries contravention of this norm could be put to arbitration. Government intervention in broadcasting was a 'good story' for the press and likely to provoke a reaction from other intellectuals. The cue for publicity and the effect of it on future government policy were of quite a different order in each case. The reported contact between the Swedish finance minister and the Director-General which prompted the so-called Malta crisis (see Chapter 5), the sacking of the Irish broadcasting authority and the imprisonment of Nigerian broadcasters are only comparable to the extent that they prompted other groups in the society outside the government to respond in the same terms. The difference in the relative power of those other groups in each country was one factor which accounted for the different significance of those and other similar incidents. Another was the extent to which liberal democracies as compared to military dictatorships can be regarded as multiplex states. So far as there are contrasts rather than comparisons to be drawn between our three countries the source of such contrasts is to be found as much outside broadcasting in the state, culture and economy of each country, as inside the broadcasting organisations.

News departments and broadcasting organisations – the institutionalisation of objectivity

Broadcasting has three functions: to educate, inform and entertain. With tedious and predictable repetitiveness this formula has decorated statute books and organisational charters since the medium was a twinkle in Lord Reith's eye. For a sociologist the intended distinctions between these functions are unworkable. A whole tradition of research has developed around the principle of discovering the various ways – educational, social, psychological – people use different media material. Many entertainment programmes inform; many information programmes educate; the gratifications provided by a programme can only be guessed at from its notional genre. The social functions of broadcasting are far wider, and more complex, than the pithy and familiar phrase would suggest.

Yet the organisational form of broadcasting is, for the most part, based on these distinctions. The departmental and programming structures of most broadcasting organisations reproduce the boundaries entailed by the separation of information, education and entertainment. In turn they attempt to complement the requirements of legislation by separating information and comment, fact and opinion or background into different departments. By contrast we shall argue that the urge to entertain, in the broadest sense, is an important determinant of information provision, and that the separation of information and comment is hazardous and, ultimately, false.

In the first part of this chapter we have looked at the external context of news broadcasting. We now turn to the internal context within the broadcasting organisations. Organisational differentiation is of two kinds; by technology – radio separated from television – and by the product, which can be either of a specific type – news, light entertainment – or for a specific target audience – women, children, farmers, adult students. (For what follows see organisation charts in appendix.)

Separation by medium was little advanced in Nigeria. NBC television was a division within the corporation, and has a separate building some two or three miles from the main Broadcasting House. Prestigious but expensive, television is seen as a necessary development despite its very limited audience socially and geographically. The television service had a director like radio, but there was also a director of news and current affairs. Much was made of the consequent dual hierarchical structure in which the head of television news was responsible functionally to the director of television, but editorially to the director of news and current affairs. In fact, in a comparatively small organisation personalities tend to dwarf their formal positions and editorial and functional responsibilities become confused. Nonetheless, the distinction was frequently discussed and cited in occasional inter-departmental sniping. In 1975 a new departmental structure was approved, in which Programmes Services was one of four groups. Within Programmes Services were six departments, including one for television, one for radio, and one for news and current affairs (Nigerian Broadcasting Corporation, 1977).

In the other two Nigerian stations radio and television were much closer, and roles were mostly defined without reference to a particular medium. In WNRS there were two operating companies, the radio service WNBS, and WNTV. News was a division of WNRS, like programmes and engineering. The news staff were common to both services with just three or four staff allocated exclusively to television. With television news very much an appendage to radio news the significant organisational fissures were between news and programmes rather than radio and television. RTK was yet another step down the ladder of media differentiation. The company had the usual divisions: news, radio and television being the output divisions. In a newsroom in which, at most, two men specialise in television, the distinction is unimportant, and the news department is completely encapsulated vis-a-vis the rest of the station.

In the bigger operations controlled by RTE and SR, the sound/television distinction has become more advanced. The reorganisation of SR planned for 1979 will make radio and television autonomous companies within an umbrella corporation. But even here significant differences and disputes have arisen inter-departmentally. The four programme producing divisions of RTE were television, radio, news and current affairs. Thus both news and current affairs, though separate from each other, were not split internally into radio and television, other than by the temporary or permanent assignment of reporters or production staff. The complexities of organisation within SR will be elaborated shortly. However, SR again had news as one of its seven programme divisions, the others being the two television channels, radio, regional, educational and external broadcasting.

Thus in all the organisations news finds itself defined as a major strut in the structure, equivalent in a formal sense to all other programmes, and embracing an output category wider than the distinction between radio and television, though naturally implementing the distinction to a greater or lesser extent internally.

The relationship between news departments and other programme departments is an important one, because it is both a cause and a result of the extent to which news broadcasters define themselves and their jobs in professional terms; that is as journalists or as broadcasters. The relationship meets its first problem in the confrontation over resources and facilities, both in the inter-departmental share-out of budgets and in the day to day struggle over shared facilities.

Where resources are minimal this problem can be acute. In Nigeria the film crews were invariably over-stretched by competing demands from news and programmes, and only a few were allocated exclusively to a news department. It was a common complaint that cameramen had been poached by a programmes producer or had their services unduly monopolised by other television departments. Studio facilities were also a subject of contention. No separate news studio was available at NBC TV, while the radio studios were in constant demand for rehearsal and programme preparation. Film editing and processing, viewing rooms, the use of graphic artists all have to be fought for competitively with the inevitable consolidation of a 'news versus the rest' view of inter-departmental relations.

This view is exacerbated by the rather different use made of facilities by journalists in broadcasting. Journalists like to stress the unpredict-ability of their material, the need for them 'to be prepared'. But if they are to be manned and equipped as though every day would bring a Kennedy assassination many expensive resources would be idle for long periods. Reluctant to concede the essential regularity of their work journalists are thus permanently asking for more than the organisation is willing to devote to news broadcasting, in a way that can only seem avaricious and senseless to non-journalists. To the journalists such a judgement is the result of total ignorance of journalism and the nature of news production.

All the organisations had been or were going through discussions as to which kinds of facilities could be commandeered by news departments, and which of necessity should be shared. In Nigeria film crews and transport were the main stumbling block. Comments were often bitter: 'The cameras lean to Programmes, we just don't get maximum co-operation. There's no news studio for television, there's only one car in the whole department.' (Editor, WNBC.)

In RTE a film team of reporter, cameraman, sound man and lighting man could not operate easily, being controlled from different departments. The lack of technical staff attached permanently to the newsroom was seen as the result of limited resources, and efforts were being made to attach more sound men to the newsroom. There was widespread concern that cameramen should not be organisational footballs, that being a news cameraman was a specialised skill requiring permanent association with the newsroom. Presentation staff present a similar difficulty. In Nigeria they were under the control of programmes divisions. Newsmen resented their lack of co-operation and frequent scorn for the prose produced with such care by the newsroom.

The overall budgetary allocation to news departments is summarised in Table 4.1. As a proportion of station budget in most cases, this figure seems low when compared to the proportion of broadcasting hours prepared by news departments. On the other hand news costs more per hour than the average production, though of course less than original drama and variety productions. It is possible to present figures in a variety of ways supporting or disproving the news 'cause'. The important point is that the cause exists, and represents a grievance contributing much to the sense of journalistic isolation from other broadcasting functions.

Lack of resources is very much a matter of relative deprivation. One junior journalist at WNBS expressed himself happy with transport

Table 4.1 News costs relative to programme costs*

		News costs per hr as ratio of all programme costs per hour	News Dept. budget as % total station budget
SR		1.4	4.2
RTE	TV	1.6	5.5 (combined)
	Radio	1.2	
NBC	TV	2.6	8.2
	Radio	1.1	4.4

*Calculated from annual reports and other documentation current at time of observation studies.

facilities: 'yes, that's OK here, they have their own van'. Nigerian journalists looked to newspapers or, if at WNBS or RTK, to NBC for comparison. At RTE and at SR the reference point was the BBC or ITN in England. Whereas in Nigeria the most common cause of complaint concerned general office facilities – lack of and unpredictable efficiency of telephones, shortage of typewriters, tape recorders, even note pads – in RTE greatest discontent was directed at the unavailability of videotape recording at crucial times. Inadequate provincial coverage in Ireland would, it was felt, be improved by the acquisition of portable video recorders and the development of local injection points and link networks, possibly with a proliferation of small unattended studios. In Sweden disputes over the availability of video recording facilities for news and sport were very similar to the disputes over cameras in Nigeria.

Deferring for a moment the complex developments in SR, we can expand on the place of news in the organisation. First, news occupies a central place in scheduling, it has an assured claim to air-time and usually a fixed time-slot. Programmers may resent the impact of this immovable fulcrum upon which their material has to be articulated. At RTE the experimental shifting of news to 10 p.m. posed a threat to producers of subsequent programmes, wary that their audience would be extinguished by the natural conclusion to an evenings viewing provided by a news bulletin ending at 10.20. For the newsroom a later bulletin left more time for preparation and greater elbow room to handle late developments in foreign and provincial news.

Second, because of its divisional status, news has a closeness to organisational centres of power. Yet within news departments there was considerable scepticism as to the importance given to news within the organisation. In Nigeria 46 per cent and in Ireland 41 per cent of journalists felt not enough importance was given to the department. Particularly galling was what was seen as undue criticism and lack of recognition despite a difficult job well done, amplified in Nigeria by common complaints about relatively poor pay and conditions. On the other hand, news was seen as the shop window of the organisation. It was at once the most sensitive and vulnerable of the outputs, and one of the most popular. 'RTE attaches sufficient importance to the newsroom. It's aware that we are one of the big local draws ... but as an organisation it has a low opinion of news.' (Sub-Editor, RTE)

This common evaluation, that news was treated with more concern than the department that produced it, was repeated elsewhere. In the face of organisational opposition status is asserted on the only grounds left, the incontrovertible importance of the ultimate product, whether justified by audience size, political or social significance, or intrinsic merit.

Third, journalists and other programmers would use different criteria in different ways to evaluate competence. This brings the news department into conflict with engineering. The journalists were seen as technological innocents; 'those people in the newsroom who just do not understand and apparently do not wish to understand the technical and engineering aspects of broadcasting – they do not understand the nature of the medium they are using', as the situation was described by a senior RTE engineering man. The most common complaint was that the journalists had not learnt to wean themselves from newspaper styles and techniques. A senior executive in RTE described these problems: 'The people in news ... haven't integrated themselves in RTE as a television organisation with a result that they are not able to utilise facilities such as sound, cameras, etc. with anything like the expertise that the programme makers will utilise....' On the other hand the journalists felt that technical provision took little account of specifically journalistic needs:

There's been a terrible mistake in allowing new telecine facilities; telecine is unsuitable for news because you need a long warm-up ... The management's at fault – it doesn't know anything about telecines. It's a system which suits non-news departments. The new processing plant takes an hour for colour – we use Agfa – everybody else (i.e. BBC, ITN) uses Kodachrome. Kodachrome is ideal for news ... Because news people didn't have anything to say RTE instituted a colour film processing which suits all other departments save news. (Sub-Editor, RTE)

This is just one aspect of the dual identity enjoyed, or endured by broadcasting journalists. Loyal to a creed and belief system developed in another industry their occupational distinctiveness raises acute organisational problems. Administrators were often inclined to view the complaints of news staff as evidence of their limited understanding of broadcasting practices. 'News is about five to six years behind the rest of the organisation ... we still have too much of the traditional newspaper, too much of rosters, and looking to procedures, actual structures and procedures of people who feel insecure at a lot of the moves on and start to hang on for dear life ...' (Senior Executive, RTE)

In Nigeria scorn for the technical naivety of news staff was often soured to bitterness by the evident rapid promotion of young, inexperienced staff in the newsroom caused by the rapid turnover and loss of senior men to more lucrative fields. Yet the newsmen merely felt even more vulnerable because of this, aware of their lack of political weight in organisational infighting. A cut in news bulletin lengths at WNBC was assumed to result from pressure by the commercial department to carry more advertising, raising an inevitable 'why are we always the ones to get cut?' riposte.

In many ways the most important organisational split is that between news and current affairs, representing as it does an attempt to turn a concept of news into institutional form. The Swedish case is particularly interesting because of the changes being undertaken and put to the test during our research period.

The two-channel system was intended to avoid unnecessary duplication by having a Central News Department, leaving commentary and current affairs to the separate production teams within each channel. The two channels came to acquire distinct identities. TV 1 attracted most of the experienced staff from the prior organisation, redubbed 'TVO'. TV 1 was also similar to TVO in much of its output, and broadcast on the same channel, thus appearing to be a natural successor. The channel was organised on a system of project groups rather than in conventional departments (see Appendix). A project group was intended to be a self-sufficient unit comprising all the technical and production specialists required for programme making. The loose structure led to frequent adaptations and recurrent disputes over roles and responsibilities.

In TV 2 a simpler structure of a more conventional kind was intended to produce equivalent flexibility and openness to ideas. TV 2 came to acquire a radical reputation, both inside and outside SR, assumed to be the result of personnel policies instigated by the channel head, a former editor of a weekly general magazine published by the Co-operative Movement. In general TV 2 seemed to exhibit greater organisational flexibility and higher morale than TV 1.

The Central News Department (CND) as a third programme production unit was built on the already established central organisation, directly responsible to the Director-General. Both physically and organisationally separate from the two new channels, the Department was responsible for the main news bulletin transmitted by them, TV Nytt, which succeeded the earlier Aktuellt of TVO. The CND also handled sports and special events, and dealt with Eurovision and Nordvision exchanges in news and sports. In addition, foreign correspondents and foreign coverage were co-ordinated from the CND. Thus the CND acted as an intake service for news and current affairs output on both channels. As the pivotal news service for the corporation, TV Nytt was seen by its producers and its audience to have a particular duty to be comprehensive, credible, and responsible.

The potential difficulties of this structure were suspected early on. At its conception the Deputy Director-General noted some of the likely problems:

The prescribed news organisation has been criticised. If variation and competition are aimed at, the argument goes, then this should certainly apply to the news service. Another objection is that the borderline between news reports and commentaries is not clear and that therefore there will be overlapping in any case, with increased costs as a result. (Sveriges Radio, n.d., p. 28)

The actual prescription for the news organisation around whose interpretation controversy raged was contained in parliamentary proposition No. 133 of 1966. This restated the argument that costs precluded competing news departments. A common news department was to collect and process information in order to broadcast 'short news programmes of only a fact-giving character in radio and television'. The different programmes were to be free to search out their own news, but were to concentrate their efforts on 'commentary, analysis and reportage'.

The disputes within the corporation were rooted in this parliamentary proposition. Many working in the CND felt that Rapport, the TV 2 news programme, was making an unjustifiable bid to become an alternative news organisation within SR. On the other hand, those working for Rapport felt the 25-minute TV Nytt produced by the CND for TV 1 was usurping the commentary functions of Rapport. As the CND was supposed to act as a service agency it put Rapport at a competitive disadvantage, particularly as Rapport was sandwiched in the schedules between a 10-minute TV Nytt on its own TV 2 and the later, longer TV Nytt on TV 1. By and large Rapport based its case on the need for diversity and freedom of choice, while the CND reiterated the principle of economy and rationalisation.

The controversy became public as a result of coverage of an unofficial strike in the state-owned mines in the north, which seemed to produce just the duplication the new organisation had been intended to avoid. The CND argued that the scope for different approaches in news coverage was limited; Rapport staff argued that their own methods treated subjects differently from the rather traditional style of the CND. This was mainly exhibited by the lengthier treatment of four stories a night on Rapport, and the more routine proliferation of agency or telegram-style reports on TV Nytt.

The conflict and its resolution is further discussed in the next chapter. What is important for our present purpose is that the resolution, though it fitted the letter of the parliamentary proposition administratively, presented the newsmen with a new set of problems based on the distinction between news and current affairs. A much reduced CND was to produce short 'telegram' bulletins with no moving pictures for both channels. This meant that far from being liberated, the staff of Rapport, which could formerly be regarded as a current affairs programme, now felt themselves obliged to fill the gaps left by the depletion of CND bulletins, and to dovetail their more innovatory criteria of selection with traditional news values of importance. In 1973 both Rapport and

Aktuellt were extended to a full half-hour, while the number of TV Nytt bulletins was further cut, adding to the pressure on the commentary programmes to become more topical, to deal in news rather than current affairs. As one Rapport reporter put it, referring to British programmes, 'Rapport was always more like 24 Hours, now it's more like News at 10'. To a lesser extent Aktuellt staff felt the advantages of being in the opposite position, having more time to deal with fewer stories. Nevertheless concern was expressed on both sides that the opportunity to differentiate the two programmes had not really been grasped, that they were coming to look like each other with the attendant implication that the other criticisms, double coverage and lack of diversity, would be applied.

Diversity had been increased in the sense that the new short TV Nytt bulletins were a very different way of presenting the news. Barred from using film, the bulletins were read by a newsreader to camera with some stills, particularly maps, interspersed. The content of the bulletins was simply agency telegrams. The style of presentation and content harked back to the early days of news in SR when only agency reports had been carried. Television journalists regarded it with contempt as a waste of the medium, no more than radio news with pictures. Altogether the compromise reached in 1973 seemed designed to satisfy everyone in the short run and no one in the long term.

This attempt to introduce diversity into broadcast news stands as a striking testament to the impossibility of achieving variety, in the sense of a diversity of voices. Two news staffs are better than one in the sense that there are two outlets for material. In the Swedish case some freelance and regional reporters were able to build up a relationship with the editors of one or other programme which ensured a showing for their stories. But the style and content of the material was largely set by the factors discussed earlier in this chapter, the relationship between broadcasting, and the state and the national culture.

Current affairs programming at RTE has been a constant source of organisational strife. The separate divisions for news and for current affairs were the end product of a series of metamorphoses. Before 1967 television current affairs was jointly controlled by the Controller of Television Programmes and the News Division. In 1967 television current affairs became the responsibility solely of the Programmes Division. The main television current affairs effort was a twice weekly programme, 7 Days. Controversial and ambitious, its producers felt themselves to be testing the boundaries of licenced independence in broadcasting. In their own view, and to some observers they were creative young Turks pricking the hides of an overbearing administration and an anxious government. The News Division was itself experimenting with news commentary programmes at this time, and one explanation of the ensuing organisational explosion was the view of many in the hierarchy of the News Division that they were too constrained, that 'News got the scoops. Programmes Division got the comment' (Dowling and Doolan, 1969, p. 115).

After a series of rumours, accusations of interference and harassment, the Director-General, in early 1968, moved 7 Days to the jurisdiction of the Head of News. Interpretations of this move vary: empire-building by the Head of News; an attempt to politically neuter the programme; naive mismanagement by the Controller of Programmes; a sensible rationalisation of unnecessarily duplicated efforts. Whatever the reality, it was widely interpreted as intended to bring an outspoken programme into the stifling ambit of the impartiality requirements attached to news programmes. This view is supported by the Director-General's remark in a Newsletter circulated to staff at the time, that he 'had frequent concern about 7 Days programmes which at times tended to lack impartiality' (Dowling and Doolan, 1969, p. 131). The Director-General, due to retire soon after, left the station fairly quickly.

The programme 7 Days returned to public attention in 1969 when it transmitted a programme on illegal money-lending in Dublin. Concern over the conclusions drawn and the methods used by the programme led to the setting up of a Judicial Tribunal of Inquiry by the Prime Minister. The Tribunal report was unflattering; the programme had used unreliable sources, not checked its facts and most wounding of all, the journalists had failed to make every effort to ensure that the facts were true and accurate. In sum, as a deputy in the Dail debates put it, 'the main lesson to be learned from the inquiry is that newsmen should always be objective' (Dail, 4 March 1971). The programme staff had been weighed in the balance and found wanting, and the punishment was to have their noses rubbed in their own professional creed.

The organisational contortions continued. In 1973 a new Current Affairs group was set up to co-ordinate all current affairs work in radio and television, including 7 Days, and the weekly radio news comment programme, This Week. The Broadcasting Review Committee Report welcomed this move of current affairs 'out of news'. The news department was less happy to see its ambitions to develop more adventurous and expansive journalistic skills frustrated, though the loss of 7 Days was less regretted, it having always preserved a high degree of autonomy and reserve from the rest of the News Division. The department, and particularly the Head of News, were most sad to lose This Week, a favoured and much admired child of the department.

This paradox, that the more news appropriates the provision of explanation and background the less like news it becomes, runs through the attitudes of journalists in all the departments we studied. For the traditional journalists in RTE the over-elaborated versions of news required by news executives were simply evidence of the effete, intellectual approach developed by those with no instinct for news, no hard news sense. This divergence of philosophy is important, and will be looked at more closely in the next chapter.

The constant confrontation of a desire to expand the horizons of news production with the constraints of traditional news values and imposed definitions of impartiality have taken place with acute organisational consequences in both SR and RTE. In Nigeria organisational differentiation has not yet evolved to the same degree, though it is ubiquitously assumed to be inevitable and desirable. Current affairs are usually produced as an appendage of news, often by the same staff. The programmes take two forms, either as compilations of news items on a particular theme – the local area, foreign news, a state visit – or as discussion programmes in the European style of current affairs programmes.

At NBC a Current Affairs Unit within the News Division was developed in 1970 to produce all current affairs output on radio. Previously handled by a section modelled on BBC Talks, with its connotations of ponderous lectures on worthy topics, the unit represented the demand by graduate news staff to do more than process agency and government releases. The work of the unit was nonetheless closely articulated around news – Newsreel, covering news events throughout the country; Newstalk, providing five-minute backgrounds to items in the news; and news magazines, providing mostly foreign news stories in miscellanies or as subjects for discussions.

In television current affairs were handled largely by a Public Affairs section within the Programmes Division. This section handled sports, a schools debating programme, discussion programmes, interview programmes and a whole range of material variably labelled elsewhere as features, public affairs or just non-fiction. Within the news department was a special events section, rarely more than one overworked, but dedicated individual, left with the task of putting together news commentary programmes. These were very largely news miscellanies or interviews and were heavily based on other news department work. There was little in the work of either Special Events or Public Affairs that forced the issue of distinguishing current affairs and news, and the greatest problems were described as 'money and red tape'. Through lack of time and resources current affairs did not stray far from the confines of news, though panel discussions were a popular format for this kind of programming. But the subject matter was defined by news output. Caution abounds in the face of governmental concern.

This was even more true at WNBC. Current Affairs here was entirely separate from news, but organisational differentiation was purely notional. In practice the current affairs unit, which also produced sports programmes, worked physically and creatively within the news department. Its output was again based on news, comprising miscellanies and interviews. Caution was well to the fore and all programmes had to be pre-recorded to facilitate clearance, if required, by the Military Governor's office. Part of the unit's output was accounted for by the transmission of old World in Action tapes acquired from the British commercial television company, Granada.

The Northern station, BCNN, with its more developed tradition of 'critical' journalism had introduced a current affairs unit of growing distinctiveness. However, much of the impetus was lost when the Head of the Unit, a graduate with an academic background and a reputation for sharp administrative acumen, left in 1973. He had deliberately developed the unit as an aggressive alternative to news, asserting that 'in current affairs we don't have to be bound by news objectivity'. Stories of refusals to bow to government demands abounded in the department, and the unit as a whole had obvious high morale and confidence. Most of the staff in the department were graduates, in marked distinction to those in the news department.

Summary

The distinction between news and current affairs is an important one in defining the character of news itself. The school of thought which regards news as 'the facts and nothing but the facts' is concerned to resist the encroachment of current affairs into their domain. On the other hand, journalists eager to extend their task and favourable to more explanatory and discursive forms of news see the distinction as artificial and unnecessary. In Sweden this latter approach came into conflict with the organisational imperatives ensuing from the implementation of a parliamentary proposition, and in the subsequent conflict it appeared to be the needs of the organisation that emerged victorious. In Ireland any attempt to circumvent the conventional journalistic restraint entailed by demands for objectivity and impartiality only served to re-emphasise how little these concepts could be stretched in the direction of comment and criticism. In the recurrent organisational reshuffling the distinction between current affairs and news was always reasserted to point up the definition of news itself. In Nigeria current affairs remains very largely a news by-product. The organisational form distinguishing current affairs has emerged, and is seen as fundamental, but has not yet sufficiently evolved to the point where the licence implicit in current affairs either seduces or threatens conventional journalism.

'Current affairs' is a label unique to broadcasting. It implies an approach to the presentation of news which is more expatiatory than the central tenets of the journalistic credo can allow. It is, therefore, as we have suggested, both seducer and threat – a lure to those anxious to inflate the journalist's role, a warning of the irresponsible directions journalism might take if losing regard for its traditional disciplines. The next chapter examines how these disciplines affect and are used in the daily routine of news production.

Notes

1. Here as elsewhere we have not included recent changes, e.g. the as yet undetermined effect of the takeover of the *New Nigerian* by the Federal Government (it has also effectively taken control of the *Daily Times*).

2. The Nigerian Television Authority, created by Decree in 1977, has functions defined, in part, as follows:

> It shall be the duty of the Authority to provide as a public service in the interest of Nigeria independent and impartial television broadcasting for general reception within Nigeria.

Chapter 5

The production of broadcast news

Anyone who has been in a television newsroom for just a day must have been struck by its apparent disorder and confusion. The day has a rhythm, an ebb and flow, as peaks of frenzied activity give way to somnolence and relaxation. But this rhythm seems to relate only tenuously to the emergence of the final product. The stereotypical newsroom of the Hollywood imagination is hysterically bustling, coping on the edge of chaotic breakdown with a commodity that is unpredictable, fast-moving, elusive and protean. The stereotype, like all stereotypes, is born of a half-truth. It is less true of television newsrooms than of newspapers, and tells much less than the full story of either.

In this chapter we outline the structure of news production as we found it in the newsrooms we studied. The general picture that emerges is of a strongly patterned, repetitive and predictable work routine, essentially passive in character and varying only in detail from country to country. Before extracting this pattern we describe a day in a newsroom, giving one European and one Nigerian example. These are artificial constructs from many weeks field notes, but they give a feel of the surface appearance of daily life in the broadcast newsroom.

A day in two newsrooms

The RTE newsroom: the Deputy News Editor arrives at about 8 a.m. and shuffles through the notes and papers left for him by the night man who's been on duty since midnight. As ever Northern Ireland is the crux of the day's work. The DNE knows that the Compton Report (an official inquiry about treatment of detainees in Ulster) is the main news of the day, and Prime Minister Wilson is in Belfast, so that must be followed. There's a note on his desk about a border incident in which a Northern Member of Parliament is involved but 'it's not worth following, although it would have been not so very long ago'.

After a cursory glance at the diary, the events list and then through the pile of newspapers (he's already heard the early morning radio news; there are no surprises anywhere) it's time to have a meeting with the Deputy Head of News. Not everyone who should come to the meeting seems to be around. The Duty Editor TV is ill, Duty Editor Intake is off, their functions become confused and taken over by whoever is available.

The reporters have not shown up yet, and when the DNE goes to his meeting with the Deputy Head of News he is still the only TV newsman in the building. He has to start thinking about facilities; some phone calls to Belfast have to be made, the crews up there will be busy following Wilson around.

The Head of News is away so the meeting is in the Deputy Head of News' room. It starts at 9.15 and today's meeting is a little more formal than usual. By now the Press Association release on Compton is available (embargoed till 4 p.m.) and it confirms expectations – 'should make a good story, this' – though our man has reservations from another angle. 'Is that all – they need to do better than that – weak language, vague and poor excuses.'

The Deputy Head of News takes the chair. He is a serious man, considered by some of the traditionalists as too remote and intellectual in his approach to news, and as lacking what they regard as the flair and instinct of the 'born journalist'. Others welcome this deliberate and considered approach to news as more appropriate to the broadcasting organisation. A similar divergence of views is personalised in every newsroom. After the meeting one of the staff confides 'I shall forget most of what he says anyway – most of it isn't relevant to the news job I have to do.' But the ritual celebration of decision-making goes ahead. There are details to be worked out, vision links to be booked, facilities to be arranged. Sometimes simple and apparently obvious things like booking a line are forgotten, with disastrous consequences. The DHN emphasises that reactions to Compton must be obtained from all parties in the North, but most of that could be left in the safe hands of the Belfast correspondent. The London man should get something from that end. Other items are covered very quickly. It's not clear whether decisions are being taken or just mooted, but the air of getting through the business at hand is sustained. It's confirmed that there would be no film on the border incident; it would probably be dropped. One of yesterday's leftovers, an arms find at Ballymena, seems worth keeping an eye on. Someone mentions an item in the *Irish Press* about professional Catholics leaving public boards in the North. This should be followed, and of course events in the Dail, it goes almost without saying, will be noted – there's talk of a meeting between the Irish Prime Minister and the British opposition leader.

Residually the meeting turns to other matters. It's too soon in the day to take foreign news seriously. The first Eurovision conference is at 10.45 a.m., sometimes a list of possibles is available, sometimes not. Today other things predominate. Mrs Ghandi's problems with Bangladesh are mentioned with little enthusiasm, but there are some domestic matters still to be sorted out. Of course 'we'll take anything on the North (ITN have something on Wilson) just to be on the safe side'.

The Deputy Head of News mentions one or two worthy items; a reopened factory (the close-down had been covered), and the fisheries talks in Brussels. He is uninterested in counter-suggestions about a housewives strike, or a barmaids' union. However, new techniques announced by a cheese-making plant in the Limerick area look more promising, with hints of interesting film to come. It's agreed to keep an eye on talks going on in Washington which could affect transatlantic flights via Dublin – shots of Shannon and Dublin Airports are ordered. But 'Compton is the story – no room for fantasies – let's get on with the main job – all hell will be let loose.'

At the Eurovision 10 a.m. link the 'EVN girl' is exchanging multilingual greetings with journalists in capitals around the continent. The technology is awesome but the results slim.

At 11 a.m. the main morning news conference begins. The discussion continues to focus on Compton. The Assistant News Editor has checked with London and refers joyfully to 'the obvious differences in interpretation on different sides of the water'. The Duty Editor Intake stresses the need to do 'a really good job on this one'. In the past the record has been sullied on big stories by slipshod reportage. There is some dispute about the afternoon Compton embargo, but Deputy Editor Intake refuses to bend this; there had been trouble from the government about previous indiscretions. The political correspondent is to deal with Dublin reactions direct from the Dail, and it is agreed to play Wilson by ear. Discussion of the EVN offers is brief, people often mutter 'that's not our kind of news' and heads nod in concurrence.

The conference ends and somehow the hazy deliberations are shaped into instructions and task definitions. Reporters have been arriving; there are now four. There are meant to be four cameramen, but only three are around, on occasions there are only two. The newsroom empties as reporters go off to catch the news, while the newsroom subsides into the midday interlude. At 13.30 the Eurovision confirmations come through, a complete sales list of offers based on an estimate of likely demand from the morning exchange. The list includes the United States winning the World Golf Cup in Florida, Castro touring in Chile, Sir Alec Douglas-Home in Rhodesia (there's film of a crowd applauding his arrival at the airport, then shots of the building in which talks will take place), the SALT talks in Vienna (shots of US ambassador arriving), and the leader of the Chinese delegation talks to the UN. From Moscow TSS offer the signing of a trade agreement with Algeria, while in Bonn President Heinemann meets the Danish Premier, and the moment is promptly offered to the world by ZDF. In Rome Presidents Saragat of Italy and Jonas of Austria toast each other. ITN and BBC are scampering round after Mr Wilson, while from Belgium there appears to be no EEC news. The French let the side down by confessing that despite a fine demonstration by striking steelworkers they would not have their film on time for even EVN-2, the evening exchange.

By 3.30 it's time for the afternoon conference. The Compton items are shaping up but there's not much film to help them along. One of the radio subs has been given the job of writing a long summary of Compton, and this will be passed on and edited for TV. There was some support for showing 'the whitewashing aspect of the Report', but eyebrows are raised and a cautious 'let it speak for itself – its stupidities are obvious' line seems to win the day. Wilson looks to have been upstaged. The industrial correspondent is at work on the firemen and the barmaids. The latter draw some support, 'there's good TV in that'. The cheese story should yield some film, as should the firemen. There's a new development, though. There's been a major escape from a Belfast jail. Mutes (silent film) should be in on the train from Belfast by 4.45. There's nothing to worry about in foreign news. 'Bangladesh is up again' and 'there's something on Rhodesia but nothing much'. As the meeting breaks up nothing seems to have been decided about these. As usual there's been much dissent and some acrimonious discussion about presentation, but it's been left inconclusive; decisions will be made by the chiefs and the fires are left to smoulder.

The News desk starts to tidy up loose ends. Compton reactions are gradually being netted. From around 5 p.m. the centre of activity moves to the sub's desk and from 'can we get it?' to 'can we use it and if so how?'. In addition to the Chief Sub of the day there are four subs on duty. Another sub in discussion with Chief Sub looks after Wilson (ITN/EVN), the prison escape and a garage explosion in Belfast. His material is ready by 8.30, although there have been technical problems with the Wilson material. Another sub writes a Compton report based on the six-minute radio piece. An opinion is voiced by two of the subs that normally they are concerned with fitting words to pictures but with Compton the process is reversed and their problem is to find pictures to fit to the words. There is a general recognition of the paucity of visuals and this is regarded as regrettable. Belfast and London correspondents will both have fairly long passages to camera. There's initial dismay when a film interview with a Northern opposition MP comes in. It's full of static, but this is no rarity and is accepted stoically.

Between 8 and 9 there's a rush as a climax is approached. Some very quick writing is required after 8.45 for recently arrived visual material. A late story on Paisley is included. At 9.07 a Lynch statement in the Dail becomes available (political correspondent) and it was decided (Chief Sub) to include it. The problem is one of timing – would they be in trouble again for going over? It's an important news day, but there's been trouble often enough with Controller TV. The bulletin often over-runs, sometimes with prior permission, sometimes not. It seems to have got a little out of hand. If only the programmes people would realise that serious news is more important than an inflexible programme schedule. Still, it's not very professional to keep over-running. In the event, the main bulletin is extended for 2 to 3 minutes, although permission has been obtained for 6 to 8 minutes.

The day looks not so very different in Nigeria. At NBC television the resources are minimal by RTE standards, pitiful by the side of SR. Yet again an impression, not of over-stretching but of much effort to limited ends is obtained. The coat is cut to the limited cloth available, but the end result is roughly the same.

By 8 a.m. when the first television shift starts the radio news day is already well under way. In an hour they will be having their first editorial conference. But in the less formal, delayed, schedule at Television House, 8 a.m. is a long way from the evening's bulletin. The general duty 'messenger' is laboriously tidying up endless streamers of Reuters print-out and throwing them in the cardboard bin. As yet he's alone in the newsroom. The Editor, the only post between the Head of Television News and sub-editor level, is at the radio conference. He doesn't go regularly but it's useful to keep in touch with goings on at Broadcasting House, the organisation's headquarters and site of the radio studios.

The news information officer (NIO) comes in to sift through the miscellany of invitations, press releases, advertising free-sheets and decorative hand-outs that drop like confetti on newsrooms everywhere. These are sorted fairly randomly into totally irrelevant and others. The others are booked into the diary and form the basic universe of human drama from which local news coverage is selected. Three or four reporters are out on local assignments having taken their instructions the previous day from the assignment sheets compiled from the diary. One is at the Mainland Hotel for the second annual general meeting of the Nigerian Bottling Company. A second has gone with a cameraman to record the reception of a team of FAO consultants by the Federal Commissioner for Agriculture. The airport man (one of two fixed news points; the other is Dodan Barracks, HQ of the Head of State) is waiting for the arrival of a visiting Soviet military delegation. One of the younger reporters is due to go with a cameraman to a school sports day just outside Lagos. NBC TV domestic film news is local news; reduced both in scale and catchment area by the problems of physical communications. There is frequent talk of exchanges with WNTV and RTK but this hardly ever comes to anything. It is being planned and like many imminent improvements its imminence has been celebrated for years.

The newsroom stays quiet till 2. The special events officer sorts through recent news films for his weekly news round-up but otherwise it's inhabited only by lizards and the Head of News, in his office locked in combat with the telephone 'doing administrative jobs'. The Nigerian working day ends at 3, and it's a convenient break-point in the TV news day. At 3 all senior men present plus the news information officer convene in the Head of News' room for the conference. The agenda is the same every day; post-mortem on yesterday, prescription for tonight, prognosis for tomorrow. The NIO reads out today's assignments and assurance is sought that someone has been sent to cover each of them. It turns out that one reporter has failed to get to his appointed observation post. No car was available. This introduces the regular wailing over scarce resources and the iniquitous and monopolistic practices of programme producers. The discussion begins to lurch into that contentious area of cars, allowances, quarters and work schedules that regularly provokes outrage among the journalists in the face of what seems obvious hostility and exploitation by the Corporation. The Head of News draws the group back to the agenda and promises to 'take the matter up'. This vague allusion to the Head of News' contacts higher up in the Corporation fools no one, but it is a formula that has a suitably palliative effect on heated tempers and symbolises the claims of the department on an unheeding bureaucracy.

The list of assignments for tomorrow's locals is intoned. No one listens too carefully; one day is much like another. Two envoys are presenting their credentials to the Head of State; a fifty-man Nigerian delegation to a Ghana commerce conference returns tomorrow; a church service to mark World Red Cross Day. There's some haggling over who goes to what. Receptions are always pleasant but travelling across Lagos at that time of day is a nightmare. The Lagos 'go-slow' – a literal and entirely accurate parochialism for the island-city's notorious rush hours – is a genuine and much-used alibi for the late arrival or disappearance of reporters. It vies with 'X is on sick-leave today', invariably understood to indicate that the fortunate X is being interviewed for a lucrative post as a PRO with a European cement importing company.

Tomorrow's locals having been allocated, a critique of yesterday's bulletins is launched. The editor passes on some remarks from the morning conference at Broadcasting House. There has been some concern at the amount of eating and drinking filmed at a reception. 'That's not the way to do it, it's not dignified, just the speeches, that's all you want.' Knowing smiles are exchanged at this. There is no sound-on-film camera so the filming of speeches is an empty gesture, but undignified film produces indignant sources. Part of the function of editorial conference is to consolidate external pressures into professional practice, to mediate the inevitable into the desirable. The government had let it be known that too many aid stories were creeping into bulletins, 'we don't want to be portrayed as a beggar nation'. A slightly pathetic tone creeps in as one reporter complains about their inability to cover a machine export exhibition put on by the Soviet Embassy: 'they usually send a car but there wasn't one'. There's little sympathy for this, but the story was logged in the diary and the authority of the diary is immense, a clear and reliable chart of news landmarks ahead. Rare moments of serendipitous news are treasured. Someone now recalls the recent incident in which a news crew en route by car to Ibadan had crashed (no rarity on the Lagos–Ibadan road) and with remarkable presence of mind had filmed their own misfortune for a dramatic two-minute news film the following day. By contrast, however, on another occasion a film crew had arrived to cover the prize-giving at a tennis tournament only to leave in disgust when they discovered there was no story because the prizes had been stolen.

The conference turns to today's headlines, culled by the NIO from the morning radio bulletins and the BBC World News. These are not discussed, partly from relief that the end of the meeting is approaching, partly because they invite little discussion. The relative merits of news items are self-evident, and the appearance of an item in this section of the agenda is an indication of its guaranteed importance. It has already entered the news cycle via NBC radio or the BBC; it is unquestionably on the day's news agenda.

From now on the newsroom moves from decision to production. The senior sub-editor assumes central importance, the immediate target the short 6 o'clock bulletin. It's only two items, usually the major foreign items. Read by a presentation announcer over stills the bulletin is a formality, not much more than a recognition of the convention that the evening's broadcasting begins with news. It's an affirmation of the seriousness of television. The Chief Sub writes the stories; an AP item on a statement by Egypt's President Sadat about the Middle East 'situation', and the latest on a Nigerian professor found guilty of murder in Liberia. In a compendious drawer he fishes among the stock slides supplied by Visnews and produces one of President Sadat and another of the Liberian capital, Monrovia. All is ready by 4.45, and attention turns to the later bulletins. By now the reporters are back and tussling over typewriters. The noise is dampened to hear the 5 o'clock BBC World News and the sub hastily takes notes of whatever he can catch through the scratchy fade and boom of the short-wave bulletin. He waves someone to switch off the agency wires; their intrusive chatter is often shut off at moments like this. Today, as frequently, nobody remembers to switch them on again and later a phone call to the local AP man brings him dashing to Television House clutching a duplicate roll of AP copy. He does this frequently unasked; AP were selling hard in West Africa at this time (though they had been in Nigeria since 1961) and he is anxious to help out and establish himself, unaware of the cynicism with which his efforts are observed by journalists who, almost to a man, prefer Reuters.

A phone call from the Dodan Barracks press office provides a sharp reminder that tomorrow is the General's son's birthday. A rapidly written item is added to the 7 o'clock bulletin ahead of the FAO and the bottling company. (Such interventions, as we shall discuss later, are resented more often for their inconvenience than their abrupt violation of journalistic autonomy. They are a more or less expected hazard in the professional environment, too regular to be fought anew on each occasion, too obviously intrusive ever to be fully accepted.) The 7 o'clock bulletin is a brief local affair, with just these three stories.

Work on the 9 o'clock bulletin is almost finished. The main task for the sub-editor in charge has been to review available Visnews films; the latest daily batch came in from the airport about 5. There's one from the

Middle East, a conference of foreign ministers in Beirut, so that can be linked to the Sadat speech. There's no time to preview the film; the supplied script is altered a little to link it to Sadat. A left-over local story on the coronation of the Oba of Ikere can be linked to a Visnews piece on a similar ceremony in Swaziland. Some film of riots in Tokyo; a reporter is sent to search the convoluted coils of Reuters tape for any Japanese news on which to peg the film – some swift and familiar calculations of linage, conversion to seconds, and a check to see that the fifteen-minute package is complete. The sub sits back and sends off the copies of the logs, one to master control, one to the director, one to the man looking after the telecine machine. It is 8 o'clock. At 8.30 the newsreader and Chief Sub retire upstairs to the film-editing room for a hasty rehearsal. At 9, while the bulletin is on, the brief late night news is prepared. By 9.30 lights are going out and lifts are being sought for the long drive across Lagos to homes on the mainland. The Chief Sub and editor have now been working, on and off, for over 13 hours.

It is easy to caricature the often crude and necessarily primitive production of television news in a small station. Yet the process and routine are but skeletal and more easily discernible versions of what occurs in television newsrooms elsewhere. Nigerian journalists often expressed anxiety that our research would arrive at a league table which they would prop up with the lowest score for competence and achievements. If anything a handicap would leave them way ahead of the field. More significant is the convergence in production and product entailed in common definitions of news and journalism. At the end of the day in each newsroom there's an air of satisfaction. A neat, tidy bulletin with an unequivocally important main story, well prepared and presented. Again and again one is struck by the instant rewards of news production, the daily satisfaction of an identifiable end-product meeting well-defined criteria of excellence. It's team craftsmanship, the very division of labour producing tight job definitions which minimise the ambiguities of achievement and success. There's never time for the development of doubt or reassessment. In a real sense decisions are rarely made, the production routine is its own monitor. To establish this we tried to move beyond initial, surface impressions.

The structure of news production

As in any industry news production is a sequence of gathering raw material, processing it into the required product, and distributing the product to an intended market. The major formal distinction among journalists therefore is between the gatherers and processors. Distribution is important as a determinant of the way the product is made, but it concerns us less here since it is not carried out by journalists.

Because of the sheer technology and productive capacity required by television news it tends to be a more passive, more production-orientated medium than newspapers. The departments were divided into executives, gatherers and processors with the results shown in Table 5.1. This understates the allocation of personnel to processing, since many reporters in fact spend much, in some cases all, of their time in the newsroom. The general structures within each news department are shown in the appendix.

Table 5.1 Basic functions of news staff*

	Executive	Gatherers †	Processors ‡
SR total	5	36	17
RTE TV	4	21	14
NBC TV§	1	18	2
NBC radio§	3	14	14
WNBC	1	13	8
RTK	1	9	6

Notes:
*These figures represent the situation as we observed it in 1973. They are not establishment post figures. Not included are technical, clerical, presentation staff, or current affairs staff, except those primarily working as newsroom journalists.
† i.e. reporters and correspondents, who may serve both radio and TV on more than one programme.
‡ i.e. sub-editors, editors. TV/radio combined.
§All general reporters at NBC were notionally reporter/sub-editors, though in fact the extent to which they process their own or other people's domestic material is very limited except for senior staff.

The basic similarities between departments are apparent at this formal level. In the larger organisations processing is further split into intake and output, or initial reception and sorting. On Rapport in Sweden intake and output were not separate jobs, but separate functions undertaken at different times in the day. Rotating editors between the two was intended to develop a shared sense of news values among the programme staff and the esprit de corps associated with it. In the early part of the day intake editors had the main control over the selection of stories and the allocation of resources to their coverage. In the latter part of the day overall control switched to the output editor.

Almost all the departments changed their organisational shape during or between our observation periods. In many cases this seemed like housewives moving furniture; aimed to revitalise by its very novelty rather than to provide real functional change. Very often within the bewildering shift of lines of responsibility and job specifications individuals would continue to work much as they always had, seeking advice and authority from their usual sources. Doubtless this is true of many work groups, people being less malleable than organisation charts. It is exceptionally true of a work situation determined so much by a daily routine and the exigencies of collecting material from outside the organisation. The formalities of these changes are illustrated in the organisation charts in appendix 2.

At RTE the main changes were at editor level resulting in a slightly sharper split between radio and television, and a reinforced intake section for television news, in preparation for the proposed longer bulletin. In fact many reporters, though notionally radio or television only, would move fairly randomly from one medium to the other, or service both when covering a story.

All the Nigerian departments at this time were evolving with the prospect of great technical resources and added manpower in the coming years. This usually meant the appointment of correspondents round the country, and more specialisation, by medium and by subject areas within the department. Particularly this was aimed at separating current affairs from news. One further aim was to plug the gap between executives and juniors. Because of career structures in Nigerian broadcasting (see Chapter 7) this gap was often wide. In NBC TV, for example, in our first observation period the next man down from the Head of TV News was some four rungs down the ladder. By our third period an editor had been appointed to bridge this gap. WNBC undertook a major reorganisation of its news division in 1973, citing four reasons for so doing. First, inadequate geographical coverage locally and nationally; second, over-hasty news production due to overwork; third, lack of balance and judgement and thus a need for more senior men; and fourth, more staff to aid presentation. The aims of specialisation, increased responsibility, and wider geographical distribution of staff were shared by all Nigerian departments.

Moving from the formal to the informal structure of news making we find that the production cycle consists essentially of four elements:

1. Planning. In the long term fixed predictable events are selected for coverage and resources allocated. Overall policy is to a greater or lesser extent discussed. In the short term daily news coverage is arranged and men and machines matched to events.
2. Gathering. News material is actively collected by reporters and correspondents, and brought into the newsroom.
3. Selection. Material is collated from reporters, and correspondents, culled from agencies and sifted down to a select number of items for final transmission.
4. Production. The selected items are put in order, treated for suitable presentation and a package prepared to make up a programme or bulletin for broadcasting.

Planning

Central among journalistic beliefs is the idea of news as random and unpredictable events tracked down by the skills of journalistic anticipation and circumspection. In fact much time is spent in the newsroom reducing the uncertainty of the task by plotting events in advance and determining which are to become news. Long-term planning considers general themes and policies to be included in news coverage and, often, its relationship to other broadcasting. More important, because closer to and more a determinant of daily news production is short-term planning. Two mechanisms achieve this: the diary and the editorial conference.

The diary is a key document in any news office. It records predictable events that automatically merit coverage by their unquestionable public importance. It is also a register of less significant events vying for inclusion in the 'automatic' category. In a sense production of the diary is news production in advance, except that it is based on the mere knowledge that events will occur not on observation of them unfolding. The diary is the implicit script of news. The contents range from the formalities of politics (planned visits by politicians, coronations, elections, expected legislation, official reports and the like) to cultural, religious, social or sporting occasions (the Spring Show in Dublin, the end of Ramaddan, the Nobel prize-giving, and so on).

The diary is written from the press releases and invitations which flow into the newsroom, and from the past record of routine coverage. It is a newspaper practice much scorned for the 'soft' nature of the news it promotes, and because it stifles initiative, inventiveness and journalistic enterprise.

> We do mostly diary stories – that's the way we work here. I think it's bad. Any time I have contact with newspapermen I suggest they phone in unscheduled stories. RTE doesn't seem to want to disrupt its day. RTE commits itself to covering too many innocuous diary stories. When an unscheduled story breaks everybody's committed. (Reporter, RTE)

On the other hand there's something about the special nature of broadcasting, its monopoly situation and quasi-official status, that makes the recording of such events a matter of duty. Television news becomes a broadcast 'journalism of record'. Many Nigerian journalists took pride in the diary as evidence of the professionalism with which their work was conducted, and took it as a sign of the improved status of the occupation that they were invited to such events. However, many were sceptical of its value, and voiced the conventional dislike of diary stories as dull, repetitive and undemanding. This distaste for diary stories is universal, suggesting that their persistence is due to organisational imperatives more powerful than the taste or choice of journalists. These imperatives are the unchanging definitions of newsworthy events and the need for pre-planning in an essentially cumbersome operation.

The daily routine of planning is conducted at editorial conferences; gatherings of variable formality which ritually celebrate the limited discretion involved in news selection. Editorial conferences signify on the one hand the degree to which news is arranged and selected *a priori*, while on the other hand their repetitiveness from day to day and limited outcome point up the unchanging nature of these *a priori* choices.

In SR there was some contrast between the departments, and also between our observation periods. The television section of the Central News Department held daily meetings at 9.30, followed at 11.45 by a full CND meeting including people working on commentary programmes and management representatives who were linked in electronically, though not actually present. The hierarchical and specialised structure of TV Nytt was reflected in the detailed and personalised remarks on particular items. On Rapport the self-consciously innovative ideals of the team were built into the daily 11.00 meeting of all staff, technicians, journalists and executives. By this time the intake and output editors had already conferred and the outline of the day's coverage was clear. In the early days of Rapport these 11.00 meetings were lively and wide-ranging, a post-mortem in some depth, including a videotape replay of the previous night's programme and review of the day's plans. Frequent references were made to first principles ('Is it important to people?').

At this time TV Nytt was seen to represent an old style of journalism from which Rapport was escaping. The CND was concerned to be reliable and comprehensive, as it was central to the Corporation's news output. Attitudes formed in the old one-channel system carried over most strongly to TV Nytt on TV 1 in the new two-channel system. Over time, however, the production of Rapport became more in the nature of a routine, less a topic for continual scrutiny and debate. TV Nytt was reorganised, then replaced by Aktuellt which became more like Rapport. The final periods of observation followed a period of intense news activity in Sweden and time for reflection was attenuated. Where the 11.00 Rapport meetings once ran naturally into lunch breaks and canteen conferences, they now were limited in time and scope. Discussion moved from content (news philosophy, choice) to presentation (technicalities, means not ends). Inevitably processing emphasizes the latter rather than the former, and the emphasis on processing in the revised CND made concern with content a very secondary consideration given the dominant agenda-setting by news agencies and Eurovision.

In all SR news departments there were regular weekly meetings to assess news prospects and policy. At the CND these mainly revolved round the preparation and presentation of the 'Wilson list' – so-called after the man who prepared it. This was a weekly news diary of predictable events to which advance commitments could be made. There were also other sectional meetings of foreign and domestic groups.

Similar weekly schedules were prepared at RTE. These 'fixtures' as they are termed, and the analogy with the planned schedule of a sporting season is a revealing one, summarise the likely nodal points in the coming week's news. A fixtures summary for one week reads:

Northern stories will probably continue to provide the main news stories of the week. The fixtures are mostly routine but one of the most important is the opening in Washington on Tuesday of new negotiations in regard to the air agreement. There is at the moment a lull on the political front following the expulsion of Messrs Blaney and Paudge Brennon from the Fianna Fail Party in the Dail, but the debates in the Dail may provide some minor stories.

The week's list then follows, including for example:

Sunday: Clune commemoration, Dublin Castle. Minister for Education at dinner, Bardon.
Monday: Minister for Local Government visits housing site at Tallaght.

And so on through the regular round of ministerial speeches, formal openings and receptions. Interesting is the definition of politics and political action. It has been a busy week; a major row, a personality clash and finally expulsions from the ruling party. Now 'there is a lull on the political front', no power struggles, no major legislation, no parliamentary drama, and so, in the conventions of news terminology and observance, no politics.

At RTE there were two daily meetings, at 11.00 and at 3.30. Attendance continually varied from day to day and from morning to afternoon. This led to difficulties. Decisions about stories taken earlier in the week, by X but in the absence of Y and Z, would be revised or reversed when Y and Z returned in ignorance of X's conclusions. Sometimes the meeting was chaired by Head of News, sometimes by his deputy, sometimes by a Duty Editor. Decisions often seemed to be taken which bore little or no relation to resources available, and therefore to the possibility that these decisions would be put into effect. In part there was uncertainty about the role of news conferences. Some executives wanted to get the desk to make decisions independently of the conference so that the production cycle could get moving earlier. On the desk there was some reluctance to act this way, being wary of the extra responsibility entailed. Yet in reality the editorial conference dealt only marginally with considerations of policy or direction. There is no need when news is so clearly defined and unproblematic:

> There's almost daily discussion about news, but I feel that all newsmen are the converted talking to the converted ... There's a broad agreement among reporters as to what should be done. (Reporter, RTE)

> There's plenty of discussion – choice of stories, efficiency in pursuing them, and technical presentation – but it never seems to achieve very much. Three years ago I could have talked more having come recently from an efficient organisation. Now my mind is coloured by experience, established patterns and the personalities involved. The mind is geared to how one can get things done within this context. (Reporter, RTE)

Schlesinger, in his study of news production in the BBC, has described how conferences were essentially preoccupied with technical detail.

Radio did not have post-mortems while TV was mainly concerned with the next programme (Schlesinger, 1978, Ch. 3).

At NBC there was some difference between the 9 a.m. radio conference and the afternoon television conference. At Broadcasting House the presence of senior news executives lent the proceeding a weight and solemnity lacking at the smaller TV conference, an impression heightened by the legal training and style of the Head of News. As radio staffing was less bottom-heavy than TV, discussion was more horizontal, less hierarchical, though ultimately no more effective in actually altering news collection or selection rather than merely arranging and confirming it. The radio conference at 9 was at the overlap of two shifts (4–10, 9–5) so that several editors could attend, usually about six, plus the senior news executives. The agenda is prepared by the Chief Reporter. Discussion is very largely on problems of presentation ('the story on the Church conference was used in too many bulletins, we must keep news fresh'; 'the Security Council story should have been higher in the bulletin'; 'on that loan to farmers story we didn't clearly distinguish the loan being arranged and it actually having been received'). Unlike television, radio produces national news, and a regular feature of conference discussion is the adequacy of news from the states. Because of the continuous production line of radio news, 'news every hour on the hour', the conference merely slots in as a reviewing body rather than having a central place in the daily schedule. It is inevitably most concerned with retrospective judgement of technical proficiency and the minutiae of factual detail which universally represent sound journalistic practice (pronounciation, ages, currency equivalents, dates, amounts, titles).

The television conference is attended by more or less anyone in the newsroom above junior levels, usually about seven or eight people. We have already outlined its agenda. The limited exercise of choice when selecting stories for local coverage is based on three criteria. First, convenience, in the shape of the availability of someone to do the job, a cameraman to film it, and the physical accessibility of the event. Second, its intrinsic news value, and third, external encouragement, that is, pressure from news sources, the government or the corporation to cover it. As we shall see, this third factor has become incorporated into news values, and thus criteria two and three receive little active consideration at editorial conferences as they are unchanging and well understood. Discussion tends to concentrate on the more immediately apparent source of difficulty – lack of resources. Some news items raise problems – a beauty contest was considered frivolous, and resentment at interference by minor government officials is occasionally channelled into discussion of general principles of autonomy. But foreign stories, with such a limited selection of film material to choose from, are rarely discussed. The conference is for the most part an organisation and methods meeting.

At WNBC editorial conferences were scheduled to be held three times a week, but in fact had fallen into desuetude. Bulletins were highly routinised and often ready two or three hours before transmission. This contrasted with RTK, where a looser structure and higher morale kept the editorial conference alive. Recognised to be a ritual, and in many ways empty gesture, the conference was nonetheless zealously preserved as central to the working day. Attended by all newsroom staff it had the usual agenda of review and prospects. The underlying policy of news was kept well to the fore, not in terms of what kinds of events make news but in terms of how news would affect social process. This was conceived particularly in terms of jolting government into action over things it was felt to have neglected. This 'watchdog' or fourth estate plank in news ideology was well developed at RTK, an aspiration fed by ambitions to match the muscle-flexing of the current affairs department. Nonetheless decisions taken by the editorial conference could play little part in news selection given the very limited range of available material to choose from.

If news is about the unpredictable, its production is about prediction. Both the diary and the editorial conference are aimed at plotting the flow of events in the world and marking them for manufacture into 'stories'. Of course there is a strong awareness that the excitement and more exotic skills of the craft are about the indeterminate. But this comes to be defined in limited ways. Thus one Nigerian sports reporter indignantly pointed out that: 'we do have unexpected stories. Like this afternoon there's the launching of the Western States Racquets Association at Governor's House. We only got the press release this morning. Mind you, we'll have to drop the Ibadan v. Legon game to cover it.' While another observed that: 'we don't do many diary stories really. Like today we had two accidents and one surprise arrival at the airport.'

Of course airport arrivals are a standard source of news film, so an unexpected passenger is a surprise variation on an established theme, just as the accidents are rude shocks to their victims, but not to the news audience. The point of emphasising the planned and unchanging nature of news production is not to imply the potential superiority of a sensational journalism of accidents, shock deaths, and bizarre intrusions into the calm order of life. It is intended to illustrate the ordered routine of broadcast journalism and its focussed attention on those kinds of events and institutional areas which have come to occupy the centre of the social world it portrays.

Gathering

Among the most common of sentiments in the newspaper world is the 'pride in being a reporter', a pride often articulated in deliberate reaction to the lowly status of the news-gatherer by the side of the leader-writer or bylined correspondent. The sentiment lives on in broadcasting, but is stunted by the limited opportunities for active foot-in-the-door sleuth journalism offered by the medium. First, broadcast journalism actually produces far fewer stories per day than newspaper journalism; there is just not the space for a large volume of reportage. Secondly, the demand for film or tape accessories to a story puts a premium on swift, individual reporting, and at its most cumbersome involves a full team of reporter, cameraman, sound-man, lighting man and associated equipment which cannot possibly be as mobile or flexible as one man and a note pad. Third, as we have argued, broadcast journalism is inherently passive because of the labour and resources required for processing, as opposed to gathering news. Only a minority of stories can be covered by newsroom-based reporters or correspondents. The number of reporter-assignments each day varied from three or four in the Nigerian newsrooms to one or two in Sweden; bulletins contained between 10 and 16 items on average (Rapport's policy of news in depth produced the exceptional average figures of seven items per programme).

Many journalists were well aware that compared to newspapermen they had limited scope for news-gathering.

> On a newspaper you're exposed to more things, you go out more. Here we're tied down. (News assistant, NBC r)

> I prefer newspapers. I am a reporter, radio is too tight, I feel I need more scope. A newspaper's more demanding, there's more scope to go out and report. That's what I love. (Sub-editor, NBC r)

The distinction was less severe in the better manned newsrooms in Europe, and, as we shall see, other differences between newspapers and broadcasting were apparent. At RTE passivity was more likely to be blamed on the slow news reflexes of management.

> They tend to be slower off the mark than most reporters would like. There's too much discussion of stories rather than getting moving. The system a few years ago – two morning news conferences before anything got done – those days the real work of news-gathering didn't begin until well after midday – no movement in stories until about 11. (Reporter, RTE)

> The main point in a general way is that not enough news is covered ... On a newspaper you assume the desk will be ahead of you and you will have something to do before long – not on television. On a newspaper you're productively idle, not idle idle on a slack day. (Reporter, RTE)

News-gathering in fact revolves around fixed points of news-making, covered first by correspondents concerned with particular geographical areas or specific subjects, second by 'stringers', especially for provincial and foreign news, and third by regular contact with reliable and productive sources of news or news 'beats'.

Specialisation of correspondents is the highest level of job differentiation in the newsroom and attracts the highest prestige both to the correspondents themselves and to the newsroom with the largest array of specialists at its command. One of the most frequently-voiced concerns in Nigeria was the lack of such men. None of the Nigerian newsrooms had a foreign correspondent, and apart from sports there was no subject specialisation. In SR there were 14 foreign correspondents who worked for the CND and primarily responded to requests from them. They were located in Beirut, Washington, Bonn, Geneva, Moscow, Rome and Vienna, with two in each of New York, London and Paris. In other words, in the usual news capitals. Within the CND seven people ran the foreign news section to co-ordinate material for these correspondents. The news programmes had their own area specialists. Of the 62 journalists we interviewed in Aktuellt, Rapport and the CND, 10 dealt only with foreign news, 23 only with domestic news. RTE had correspondents in London and Belfast, but no other foreign postings.

Newsrooms in all three countries used a system of home-based reporters travelling to cover stories as they arose. This is cheaper than permanent foreign postings, though still very expensive, and inevitably a great rarity in Nigeria, infrequent at RTE, rather more common at SR. Foreign coverage has to depend almost entirely upon the news agencies either for complete information, or as a guide and warning system about stories in their initial stages which might warrant the outlay of travel and subsistence funds for newsroom staff to go themselves. Thus having an area specialist in the newsroom enlarges the capability of the organisation to react to news of a foreign event by mobilising his expertise and background knowledge. But it does not change the surveillance techniques which discover those events or evaluate their newsworthiness to begin with. Such surveillance is left, by default, to the agencies whose primary *raison d'etre* is, after all, to spread costs in the collection and distribution of foreign news.

Subject specialisation is an interesting index of the way news values are translated into organisational practice. The traditional specialisations in foreign, diplomatic and political news have been extended in recent years to include a shifting range of subjects seen to require the expertise and undivided attention of a 'correspondent'. In the context of British journalism Tunstall has shown how this reflects changing notions of audience requirements and, in commercial media, of subject areas likely to attract large audiences and therefore advertising (Tunstall, 1971, Ch. 3). In as much as media not supported by advertising nonetheless share the assumptions about news of those that are, they will reproduce in their staffing arrangements an ability to cope with these subject areas.

In turn news will tend to reflect this staffing structure; specialists cannot be left idle, and just as news from news capitals flows steadily because there is someone there to produce it, so subjects graced with a specialist will be guaranteed a regular place in bulletins. An Aktuellt reporter had established himself, at least informally, as a specialist in traffic and road safety, and a regular supply of stories on this subject appeared in Aktuellt programmes. In SR general reporters were consistently disadvantaged in getting material into bulletins. In all departments they lacked any leadership or organisation. They were not identified with any major area of news which would find its way into the programme as of right. They were left to plough their own individual furrows, with more or less success in getting their material on to air. Any attempt to produce carefully prepared pieces on a relatively timeless topic was very often doomed to frustration by its displacement by a more immediately topical or important item.

Here, as elsewhere, staff often felt they were missing vital areas of news because of the lack of an appropriate specialist. In SR aspiring specialists were much irritated by this assumption. The same feeling in RTE was buttressed by the well-known proliferation of specialists 'across the water'.

> The BBC have used existing staff to fill some of their needs. For example Biddulph on diplomatic affairs, Hosken on their industrial staff, Brian Curtois, Brian Saxton – it's possible for them to be drawn into a specialist area and be given a title. In the RTE context you're excluded. They could set people up here in areas like health and medicine, local government – economics might require a graduate. (Reporter, RTE)

> We must be the only newsroom in the world to have only one political correspondent at the moment. Our national industry is agriculture and we don't have an agricultural correspondent. I was down at a ploughing match in the country and intelligent farmers were having a hilarious time discussing the boobs we've pulled – for example with harvest stories, farmers and rain. In many fields we have nobody. We don't really have an industrial correspondent ... We have no economics correspondent, nor one to cover military affairs, aviation, transport, diplomatic, home affairs, local government, health ... (Reporter, RTE)

Of course once set on this course it's just a question of thinking of new subject areas in which to specialise. The actual specialisation was as follows. RTE had five correspondents working to the news desk; Belfast, London, Politics (often from the Dail), Economics and Industrial. At SR specialisation was well advanced; of our 62 interviewees, 40 specialised in some subject area; 7 in parliament or domestic politics, 6 in economics or financial news, 4 in industrial and labour news, 3 in international politics, 8 in specific foreign areas and 12 in miscellaneous subjects like science, education, the environment, housing and medicine.

These subjects provide the main supply of news and can be expected to generate events of reliable newsworthiness. For this, relationships are often established between reporters and news sources. The sources can be trusted to provide information, statements and background when events surface, and are also available to keep the reporter posted on ongoing developments in the field. The relationship is an exchange, the source providing candour, perhaps exclusively to just one reporter, as well as privy information, in return for reliable coverage and discretion. It is a system most highly developed in political journalism, at its most elaborate in such parliamentary exchanges as the British 'Lobby' (Tunstall, 1970). Such exchange relationships are generally more extensive in newspaper than broadcast journalism.

Regular 'beats' are also much more a feature of newspaper journalism. Since broadcast news contains only the major stories of the day it is little concerned with nurturing unexpected, perhaps half-hidden, stories that regular contact might throw up. In addition, often being a monopoly, broadcast journalism is less concerned with the 'scoop', the triumphant capture of an exclusive story ahead of rivals. Of course the 'scoop' mentality is not absent but the production process and market situation dampen its significance.

Despite this, regular exchange relationships do develop. Industrial correspondents aware of the delicacy of negotiations in a strike, and anxious not to lose the confidence of either union leader or captain of industry, may hold back a report or trim it. Many journalists feared that the ultimate logic of this was pernicious. In both RTE and SR there was a feeling that 'this is a small country' and everybody knows what's going on. One RTE journalist feared that 'the leak system is creeping in here on diplomatic or government stories – "well informed sources" – If a man says something he should be prepared to say it publicly or not at all'.

In fact a code develops in these exchange relationships. A source will speak 'on the record' – for broadcasting, or 'off the record' – for the reporters' ears only, or 'not for attribution' – allusive use only, by reference to the conventional ghost 'informed sources' or 'reliable sources close to X'. For this to advance to the stage of tacit suppression requires a more evolved group of senior specialists than any but the largest broadcasting organisations can deploy.

Any such abuses are seen as a hazard of the job, their minimisation one of the skills experience provides. In Sweden older journalists, particularly, felt that relations with sources were a good deal better than they used to be in that newsmen and sources understood each other's needs better now. One case, admittedly mentioned because it was unusual, was a leak by the Swedish defence ministry of secret documents to an SR journalist in the hope that he could create public interest, and thus help build up public antagonism to proposed defence cuts. The journalist resented being used, but felt it was a fair bargain, information for influence.

A few regular beats are created which do not require specialised knowledge or expertise, but are the result of the need for routine and predictability. NBC, for example, had two fixed news collection points – at the Lagos airport, and at Dodan Barracks, the official residence of the Head of State. In addition a beat is created by the regular round of what one journalist neatly termed 'call-upons'. These are the interminable courtesy visits paid by visiting economic and political dignitaries to commissioners and other government figures.

News gathering, then, taps some of the core elements of journalism's occupational ideology; the journalist as newshound, the outward orientation of journalism as an active collector of information, the independence of journalist from source. In practice broadcast journalism is relatively limited in the gathering it can do, and the production of television news is, in large part, the passive processing of news the newsroom cannot avoid. Gathering is possible in proportion to resources available, but remains the icing on the cake. Even in highly equipped and financed news organisations there is enormous reliance on the news gathering of agencies and on a few prominent institutional sources, most notably government.

Selection

Before looking at the criteria which are used in the selection of news stories we can describe the actual process of compilation. The sifting and moulding of material coming into the newsroom is the process of converting observed events into stories. The skills involved are largely those of 'sub-editing'; that is editing, but with less power of discretion than a newspaper editor. In practice these skills range from the correction of style and grammar to conform with standard practice, to complete responsibility for the final product.

First among eligible stories for selection are those produced by reporters and correspondents working for the newsroom. The fact that these are normally produced in response to a desk request adds to the likelihood that they will be used. In Nigeria it was common to hear the complaint that there was just not enough news, and it was rare for a reporter to have his story spiked unless it was totally unusable. In practice it was usual for whole bulletins to be written by one man, usually the duty editor or chief sub.

Traditionally reporters and sub-editors are in permanent conflict. To the reporter the sub is an unfeeling butcher hacking fine prose for unworthy ends. To the sub the reporter is callow and undisciplined, unaware of the overall needs of the product. Like many mythologies created in the newspaper world this carries over into broadcasting but is much muted. The opportunities for conflict are few; there is little chance for extensive writing on which to wield the axe, most stories prepared are used, and many other restraints apart from the sub-editor are apparent to the reporter, including technical ones. In Nigeria the staff structure was such that there was often a considerable gap in experience and seniority between reporter and sub-editor, and the authority of the latter was therefore seldom questioned from below. Indeed reporters often complained not of excessive control but of insufficient guidance and supervision. The same complaint was mentioned by many of the general reporters in SR.

At RTE reportorial discontent grew out of the common assessment that desk men and executives did not understand the medium:

> a television reporter's work cannot be supervised unless the supervisor goes out too ... When I'm in the office there's very little supervision because the bosses don't know about television techniques. (Reporter, RTE)

> No reporter's work is supervised by anybody who has *been* a broadcasting reporter. Duty editors ... lack understanding of what broadcasting is about. (Reporter, RTE)

Thus a traditional dispute was updated into the different technical competences and backgrounds of news staff. On the other hand some reporters had the opposite view:

> There's not enough attention given by the chiefs to the problems of reporters. When a problem arises it should be gone into with the film crew. There should be regular talk-ins with camera crews on mutual problems. Reporters and perhaps cameramen should be given more information about the technical side of the work – for quite some time I didn't know what cutaways were for. (Reporter, RTE)

In general, however, processing is so routine that the problems are not acute. In Nigeria although most junior staff were 'reporter/sub-editors', effectively sub-editing was done by one or two senior men. The sub-editing done by junior staff is limited to foreign news – that is rewriting of wire agency reports. In Sweden there were conscious efforts to avoid rigid task differentiation, particularly on Rapport. Most people subscribed to the prevailing orthodoxy that supervision was unnecessary and not a problem. Control was expected to emerge from collective criticism after the event rather than in a collision of intentions during production. The orthodoxy survived despite the very obvious presence of intake and output editors issuing instructions on length and angle during editing. A taken-for-granted process becomes an invisible one.

The second source of material for selection is the news agencies, the international wire agencies, Eurovision and the news film agencies. We have already hinted at the enormous influence of the agencies on selection and the wire agencies in particular are an example of a supply which creates and shapes its own demand. The newsrooms took the international wire agencies at this time as shown in Table 5.2.

Table 5.2 News agency subscriptions

	RTE	SR	NBCTV	NBCr	WNBC	RTK
Reuters	X	X	X	X	X	X
AP		X	X	X		
UPI	X	X				
AFP				X	X	X

Reuters is the British-based agency, AP (Associated Press) and UPI (United Press International) are American, AFP (Agence France Presse) is French. The table shows less than the whole story. At SR agency material came to the CND which in fact subscribed to AP, UPI and Tidningarnas Telegrambyro (TT), the Swedish domestic news agency. Through TT it received Reuters and to a limited extent material from AFP and the Russian agency TASS. The Nigerian stations occasionally altered their subscriptions, especially between AP and AFP, though Reuters was considered indispensable. At RTK however Reuters had been dispensed with at one point because of a lack of African stories. There was no domestic agency in Ireland but RTE took the Press Association service which supplies domestic news within the British Isles. Nigeria also had no domestic agency, but a decree establishing a Nigerian News Agency was promulgated in 1976, and the agency became operational in late 1978.

Reuters is widely regarded as the best of the agencies (by 56 per cent of the Swedish journalists including those who nominated TT, 46 per cent of the Irish and 48 per cent of the Nigerians). The quality that earns it this support is reliability. This is defined as dependable accuracy in marked contrast to what were seen as the exaggerations or rash, impulsive jumping to conclusions indulged in by the American agencies in their desire to be competitive. One Swedish journalist cited a typical story saying that if there was an air crash Reuters would put the casualties at 100 dead, UPI at 150, and AP at 200. Swedish and Nigerian journalists were concerned, in different ways, at pro-western bias in the wire agencies, particularly the American agencies. Even Reuters was regarded with suspicion and it was a house rule at NBC that no Reuters stories about Nigeria were to be used. Western reporting of Nigeria is still looked on with general mistrust since the Civil War, in which world media by and large supported the secessionist Biafran cause by emotional reporting of Federal military excesses and 'genocide' (see Davis, 1977).

There are three significant aspects of the use of the wire agencies in news compilation. First, despite reservations about the suitability of their material, the agencies are essential sources of foreign news. Indeed, they are quite literally irreplaceable. The cost of foreign correspondents is infinitely greater than agency subscriptions. For example, in SR in 1970–71 subscriptions to AP and UPI cost 150,000 kr (about £12,500) and 162,000 kr (about £13,500) respectively. This is nothing compared to the 2,908,000 kr (about £242,000) spent that year on foreign correspondents. The BBC's television budget for foreign news in 1976 was £$1/2$ million (Schlesinger, 1978, p. 71). By contrast the Ghana News Agency's subscription to Reuters in the same year cost £24,000 (Harris, 1977). For less well off organisations support of foreign correspondents is beyond their budgets. For them the regionalised services of the agencies, often at scaled-down subscription rates, are the only feasible source of foreign news. For example, WNBC's subscriptions to AFP and Reuters jointly cost about £11,000 in 1973. This of course is precisely the economic logic from which news agencies derive. Harris has shown how such regionalised services are expanding rapidly, still leaving their subscribers unhappy with the content of the news supplied (Harris, 1977).

The second feature of agency use is the global uniformity of news definitions their use imposes on newsrooms. Selections can only be made from the material available, and clear guidance is given as to the importance and relative significance of news items. 'Nightleads', mid-day summaries, 'splashes', 'snaps' are provided as cues for copy- and sub-editors. In remoter stories for which the newsroom cannot supply its own expertise agency interpretation is not lacking. We are not examining here the values implicit in agency journalism, but suggesting that such values do exist and are influential in news production. We will expand on this in Chapter 6. Uniformity is inevitable since three or four agencies are providing the basis for foreign news coverage in every newsroom in the world. The tyranny of supply is nowhere clearer than in this dependence.

This leads to the third aspect of agency significance. Although newsrooms clearly have an autonomy, to a greater or lesser extent, in their choice and treatment of foreign stories, these choices tend to be influenced by the sheer authority of the agencies (Harris, 1976). One agency may be despised for providing Hollywood gossip and baseball scores, but the subscription continues. Another is derided for its lingering British imperial undertones, but again it remains. Agency coverage alerts the newsrooms to world news events, and it is around this knowledge that newsrooms build their own coverage. So even those newsrooms able to send out teams to foreign stories will depend on agency selection for notice of which stories to consider. The agencies are thus an early warning service for newsrooms whose actions are determined by the observations in agency wires.

A second source of material for compilation in the European newsrooms in Eurovision. This is enormously important in a visual medium as it is a source of news film. Eurovision itself was set up in 1954, though the news exchanges did not begin until 1961. The growth of the system has been rapid and it plays a central part in the foreign coverage of European newsrooms. In 1962 1,106 items were exchanged through the EVN news exchanges; this rose to 3,601 items in 1970 and 6,353 items in 1976. Steadily EVN items came to assume a vital place in the planning and production of television news. By 1972 the number of services accepting news items from the exchanges had steadily risen to an average of 11.4 per item, another index of the uniformity induced by agency journalism. Of course, EVN is not a separate news agency but merely an exchange for items produced by the individual member organisations. However, since the news film agencies (UPITN, Visnews, CBS) began to inject their material into the EVN network in 1963, their contribution has rapidly increased, and they now provide over half the total number of items, Visnews alone providing 27 per cent by 1976. In effect this has changed EVN from a news exchange into just the technical infrastructure by which the major news film agencies distribute their products to European customers. As a foreign editor of the British ITN has written:

> We all turn to them [the agencies] for the first coverage at least of the big non-European breaking story, while many services rely solely on their continuing output right through to the end. If the story is big enough other services might send their own film crews and reporters to cover it in their own particular style, but even when this happens they still welcome the assurance of being covered on routine developments by agency cameramen. (Mahoney, 1975)

The daily Eurovision news schedule is fairly straightforward. At 11 a.m. Central European Time, contributing organisations offer stories they have in hand which they think will be of general interest. Newsrooms then have to indicate an initial interest by 1.45. An afternoon editorial conference takes place at 4.30 to confirm which stories are wanted by whom, and the first actual exchange then occurs at 5 p.m. Since 1968 there has been a later exchange (EVN-2) at 6.55 p.m. and since 1974 a third earlier exchange at midday.

Unlike wire agencies, Eurovision news exchanges are not paid for by annual subscription but by a complicated system based on payment for items accepted. Each organisation is charged differentially according to the size of their audience and their location on the Eurovision circuit. To be included in the exchange an item must be accepted at the morning conference by at least three countries. Such items are then listed in a telex together with any late offers and marginal acceptances for final consideration and confirmation at the lunch-time conference. In making acceptances the EVN editor has the chance to keep his options open and help his colleagues in other organisations who may have more interest in an item than he. Confirmations however cost money, and by that stage the EVN editor has had an opportunity to consult with those responsible for the day's programme to get a more definite idea of their requirements. EVN charges for exchanges between members are basically transport costs, worked out in proportion to the size of the receiving organisation's audience, so that items which have to come by satellite are considerably more expensive than exchanges within Europe. Smaller organisations like SR and RTE may well wait, therefore, in considering a satellite offer to see if the larger organisations jump first. In that case they will carry much of the cost. RTE also has a special relationship with the BBC to allow it access to their material. SR, a small fish in the context of Europe, is herself the big fish in the context of Scandinavia. There is a special arrangement for exchanges between the Scandinavian countries themselves, Nordvision, and within Eurovision SR may find the other Scandinavian organisations waiting on her say so.

Cost is also an important consideration in the use of another Eurovision facility – the possibility of making 'unilaterally' a recording from some other country in the exchange. SR's foreign correspondents regularly reported in from their bases in Europe and America by booking a studio in the country and transmitting their report as a 'unilateral'. As the name implies, the country receiving a unilateral carries the costs. In the case of a satellite transmission from the United States costs were extremely high. Use of such an item therefore was some index of the importance attached to that subject.

Aside from satellite items and unilaterals, at SR considerations of cost were not uppermost in the minds of the journalists selecting the Eurovision material. In the SR newsrooms financial control was separated from journalistic control. There were special staff in each department responsible for keeping a record of expenditure, checking this against the budget and reporting to the head of department. He then made what adjustments were necessary or possible either to the budget or journalistic practice.

However, cost is not the only or even the major factor in routine decisions about EVN items. They are subjected to the same evaluations as other foreign coverage. They have the advantages of immediacy, propinquity (European news is more useful than remoter news), they are visual and can be pre-selected. Nonetheless there were many reservations about the utility of the service. Many Swedish journalists found the items too conventional; too many airport arrivals and departures, conferences and conventions. An Irish journalist talked of 'the same old mug-shots of people walking through doors'. Those who had worked with EVN for some time felt it was getting better but was still too 'old-fashioned'. In Sweden this was partly by contrast with what were seen as the more progressive and innovative journalistic styles in Swedish broadcasting. Particular countries became labelled as notably poor sources of stories. Spain was a favourite butt, since repression there prevented easy access to stories on political dissent or industrial conflict. Other Mediterranean countries were disliked for offering too many items on religion. Representatives of SR and other Scandinavian corporations would torment those countries' representatives in the conference link-ups by asking for material they knew could not be supplied. Irish newsmen too were scathing about the technical proficiency of certain organisations.

Yet as with the wire agencies, reluctance has to be overcome because of the sheer accessibility of Eurovision news items. The general tenor of acclaim was usually along the lines of 'for all its faults it's too useful to dismiss'. This is especially true in smaller stations, and both SR and RTE consider themselves small (this self-image seems to be widespread among all but the three or four largest European broadcasting organisations).

It could be better, but it's very useful. It means we are using today's film over today's news. (Chief Sub-editor, RTE)

From the visual point of view very, very, good. It makes the physical operation of sub-editing a lot easier in that it's strongly visual. (Sub-editor, RTE)

It's an excellent system – a great idea and a worthy one. Otherwise we would depend on flying stuff in by plane a day late. However the system as it comes to us tends to be a load of rubbish. This is very understandable. For example, when we have a story to send out we can't judge for every other station in Europe what use they want to make of it ... (Chief Sub-editor, RTE)

The complaints ranged from sloppy filmwork and film too brief to re-edit, to the unadventurous selection and technique of some newsrooms. Yet Eurovision news goes from strength to strength, its prime virtue of ready availability over-riding all reservations.

Because of the development of the Eurovision exchanges, the third source of foreign material for selection, air freighted agency news films, has declined in importance for the European stations. By and large it is kept for archival use or the occasional emergency. Outside Europe, however, such material is enormously significant. For the vast majority of non-European television newsrooms it is their only source of foreign news film. This was the case in Nigeria, discounting the embassy handouts and commercial publicity films which occasionally come in.

As with Eurovision, unavoidable use of the agency film is tempered by reservations about its quality. Nigerian journalists are sceptical of the western orientation of both the selection of items they receive and the tone and language of the commentaries that accompany them. A subscription to a news film agency brings a daily package of about half a dozen news films, ranging in length from a minute to perhaps four or five minutes. A common contract would be for 2,000 feet (about 53 minutes) a week. These are either mute or with sound-on-film sound effects. With each film there is a shot-list and a commentary written by an agency sub-editor. This is the source of most discontent about the agency products. The agencies are western and produce mainly for audiences in Europe and North America. There are two film agencies of significance in Africa. UPITN grew out of the American United Press Movietone Television formed in 1952, first as UPIN and later as UPITN when joined by the London-based ITN commercial television news service. The other agency, Visnews, was formed in 1957 (originally as British Commonwealth International Newsfilm Agency) to counter the monopoly of UPIN. The third major world newsfilm agency is CBS Newsfilm, which started its syndicated service in 1953, but is of less significance in Africa than the other two. The agencies are news film producers not news story producers; their work is done by a world-wide network of cameramen, and scripts are added in London or New York. In theory the sub-editor in Lagos or Nairobi or wherever can then recut and rewrite commentaries to suit his own audience. In practice this is difficult. The films are fairly brief and thus not easily edited. It is a temptation to leave the careful and highly professional scripts supplied with the films. They are accurately timed and cued to match the film sequences, and for an overworked Nigerian sub-editor with limited facilities altering the total package is courting disaster.

Nigerian journalists were well aware of the failings of the film agencies. The films are often delayed, and film stories commonly deal with events seven or ten days old. It can be a problem getting the material from the airport – the Lagos traffic, the lack of a van (RTK borrowed that of the *New Nigerian* newspaper), perhaps a stubborn and mildly corrupt airport freight manager. Much of the material is irrelevant (see Chapter 6) and too out of date. The agencies cover this problem by supplying many 'soft' stories where loss of immediacy is unimportant. Generally there is dismay about the dearth of African stories. Most of all there is concern about the language. African sub-editors tire of substituting 'freedom fighters' for 'guerillas', 'racist regime' for 'South African government', crossing out 'tribesmen' and so on. Gradually the Nigerian journalist finds himself seeing his own world as an outsider, the journalist's view of Africa becomes coincident with the western view. Resentment is often intense. 'They send us pictures of starving children. We know Africa is poor!' Occasionally the service is cut, WNBC for example stopped taking Visnews in 1971. But the gap has to be filled, and three years later a new contract was signed, this time with UPITN in an attempt to be different from other Nigerian stations.

The economic logic of film agencies is even more compelling than that of wire agencies. To take one end of the scale, the 2,000 feet a week service RTK were receiving from Visnews in 1973 cost £3,000 a year, including a supply of standard transparencies of major world figures. NBC were receiving a greater footage which, in 1971, was costing £7,200 a year. This is little to pay for a complete supply of foreign news film, but of course the real price is more than the economic cost. Total dependence on one or two western agencies means total dependence on a style and approach determined in London or New York by the needs of more important customers in Europe and North America. As in world television marketing generally, Third World countries become hooked on to cheap spillovers from production in Europe and North America, whose economies of scale they are unable to match. In turn these products become the standard by which broadcasting is judged. Visnews and UPITN were much admired for their professionalism and technical quality. In time their selection of news items comes to influence the Nigerian journalist's sense of news values as well as his style of treating news stories.

In the course of production this happens very directly. In the NBC TV newsroom behind the chief sub-editor's chair was a row of seven wall hooks. Dangling from each was a clipboard holding one day's wad of Visnews dope-sheets (the sheets which accompany the films and which contain a summary of the story, details of shots and a cued commentary text). Every day as the new packet came in the dope-sheets of seven days previously were consigned to oblivion and replaced. The new set remained there through the week, a reservoir of news films to be tapped whenever needed, a permanent reminder of the priorities in television news production.

The routine was to select a likely-looking Visnews film, then see if there was a wire agency item on which to peg it. Thus the day's news is sifted for material to accompany the film, and the availability of the film is the prime determinant of the story's selection. The result is often the awkward conflation of distinct events. The President of Sudan was in Bonn, and Visnews were there to capture his appearance. Film of African statesmen about their business is prized, and the dope-sheet is slipped off the board. But the only news-peg available was a brief AP report that the President was in Abu Dhabi, so the two are welded into a 2-minute 30-second item, one of the longest stories in the bulletin, and one of the five film items. Even greater confusions can ensue. On another occasion Visnews had film (two weeks old) of student strikes in the Congo. No Congo news was apparent on the wires but there was a student demonstration in Dahomey. The two were integrated although the Congo strike was anti-government, the Dahomey demonstration pro-government. Nigerian journalists are as socially and politically aware as any others. The point is that production needs, and the exigencies of meeting programme requirements, override news value or social significance in selecting and compiling. To a large extent these needs and exigencies can only be met by leaning heavily on the services of film agencies.

The final, and probably least important sources of materials in compilation are the press releases and hand-outs delivered to the newsrooms. The occupational attitude to this is well-defined; they must be treated with mistrust as an attempt to manipulate the journalist and sway his professional judgement. Official and governmental releases are mistrusted because they interfere with the established journalistic task of teasing out the political truth. Commercial releases are despised as pure advertisement, beneath the contempt of true journalism. Most press releases are derided for their poor technical quality, for not having the information a journalist needs in the crisp well-ordered style and language he prefers. In addition, press releases attract the same weary antagonism as diary stories; they lack the topicality, excitement, unpredictability or depth of the best news stories. Finally they confirm tangibly a dependence on sources which is quite antipathetic to professional self-respect. For all these reasons press releases are very seldom used, except as a starting point. They are used much more, however, than the occupational belief system would suggest.

There are sometimes particular reasons for this. The producers of press releases are usually journalists, and often former colleagues of those to whom their work is addressed. The journalist and PRO know each other's problems and are willing to scratch each other's backs where possible. Often a press release is better than no information at all.

We tend to give press releases greater importance than we should. From organisations, which in this country have been more dog-in-the-manger in the past, half a loaf is better than no bread. People don't mind getting fobbed off by X [ex RTE reporter who became a ministerial PRO] because before him there was nobody they could talk to. (Reporter, RTE)

Where time is short and information is difficult to obtain, judicious and sceptical use of a press release may be prudent, even essential. This is more often the case in Nigeria where shortage of staff and poor telephone and road communications make the collection of information very difficult. The more or less obligatory reporting of press conferences given by senior government figures can put great pressure on junior staff, aware of the possible price of failure.

We don't have tape-recorders, so press releases can be very helpful. There's always the danger of misquotes. You're only a small person and it's difficult to convince a man he didn't say something. This way you're fully covered. (Senior Sub-editor, NBC r)

Others, perhaps less matured in the ways and beliefs of the job, accept the logic of their difficult situations, and welcome the relief of press releases: 'They're very useful, it means you don't need to go out at all.' (Reporter, RTK)

Commercial press releases are far less important than governmental ones, and we shall discuss these below in the context of general governmental influence, after looking at the final stage in the production cycle.

Presentation

Simply stated, news gathering is most concerned with news sources, news processing with the audience. This is an over-simplification, but the presentation of news is, of all the production processes, the most hedged around with trade lore about what audiences will and will not accept, comprehend or enjoy. We are interested here in the way this lore is called upon in the daily production of news bulletins. The more general perspectives with which journalists view their audience are discussed in Chapter 7.

Consideration of the audience affects production first by influencing the selection of items which become news, second in suggesting ways in which those items may be presented. There are many ways in which journalists can discover the views and demands of audiences, the most formalised being to read the information available to them in audience research reports. No such reports were available in Nigeria except at WNBC, where they were almost never seen by journalists. At RTE and SR audience research reports were seen 'regularly' by 36 per cent and 60 per cent of the journalists in the respective organisations, while only 11 per cent (at RTE) and 2 per cent (at SR) never saw them. Seeing is not necessarily believing, however, and there was widespread scepticism about the intrinsic accuracy and merits, as well as about the utility to journalists, of the services provided by audience research departments. At RTE 43 per cent found them 'not very useful' and a further 32 per cent no use at all. Swedish journalists were less damning but less than half found them very or even fairly useful. Criticisms ranged from distrust of sampling and other statistical procedures to complaint about the lack of material directly relevant to news.

The kind of research journalists see as most useful is on comprehension; examining whether audiences can cope with the vocabulary of bulletins, or have a sufficient general knowledge of people and organisations to understand stories. Such research tends to confirm their worst fears that audience abilities are generally over-estimated. This only reaffirms that strain in the occupational ideology which sees journalism as educative; simplifying and explaining the complexities of life for an audience inadequately equipped to understand them. In this lies the professional skill of journalism.

Any other response to knowledge about the audience is felt to be potentially dangerous, since this would compromise professional autonomy to the demand of the market place. Apparent distaste for the sordid realities of marketing the product is of course common in monopoly broadcasting. A considerable amount of research has described professional broadcasters' distance from and ignorance of their audience (McQuail, 1969, Golding, 1974b, pp. 68–73). The broadcast journalist has an awkward dilemma to resolve. Journalistic responsibility is held to entail detailed knowledge of the needs and interests of the audience. On the other hand professional integrity and autonomy prohibit pandering to these needs and interests. The solution tends to be an assertion that audience requirements are well understood by the journalist by virtue of his wide-ranging experience and daily contacts with a wide selection of audience members. For some this means a cynical contempt, perhaps tinged with regret, for their audience.

> The public just want Lil Babs [a popular female entertainer] and they get Lars Orup [a famous reporter with a face like a bulldog]. It's not our business to give them what they want. (Reporter, SR)

> They want more spectacular things like kings' funerals, soft news and entertainment. If the aim was to get as many viewers as possible then we would do that but we don't have those sorts of values. (Reporter, SR)

One Swedish journalist was quite adamant about the need not to be influenced by these imputed requirements. 'They want more soft news. But SR and its news are part of a Swedish tradition of educating the people. Respect for government and authority would increase if we gave more soft news and there would be less criticism of society.'

Despite the obvious monopoly situation of national broadcasting systems journalists are competition conscious for two reasons. First in many cases there remains real competition. RTE journalists were only too aware of the forest of aerials all over Dublin turned towards BBC and ITV transmissions from the UK; it was this that led to the creation of RTE 2. Sweden's two-channel system introduced an element of internal competition, and many Swedish journalists could readily recite viewing figures. 'They used to put a movie opposite Rapport on Tuesdays, this killed us.' In Nigeria, the main news medium, radio, is not localised in the way that television is, and in the states there was widespread awareness of what NBC was doing. Second, broadcast journalists perpetuate many newspaper traits and practices, prominent among which is the search for speed and attractiveness, which newspaper commercial competition promotes. Most journalists were aware that news is a popular item in broadcast output, in the sense that it regularly attracted large audiences, though many were aware that this might indicate a habit rather than a daily acclaim for their work.

> They probably get all they want, but that could be because they've got used to what they're getting. (Chief Sub-editor, RTE)

> I don't know what the public wants from television news. The collection of reaction feedback is very bad. I know what my family think, I can look at TAM – but it's just an electronic figure. As long as they keep watching I must assume they're getting part of what they want. The average guy turns on the news as an insurance and stays with it until it's finished to find out that nothing has happened since the last bulletin. (Editor, RTE)

The only audience research journalists can commonly quote is that showing their rating in a competition with alternative programmes or organisations (see similarly Schlesinger, 1978, pp. 111–15; Epstein, 1973, pp. 91–100). Audience views could be called upon to support any approach to production. Demands for more background and explanation could be supported by pointing out the lack of knowledge amongst the public. The same 'ignorance' could be used as evidence that the news should stick to a bald narrative of facts, rather than risk going over the heads of viewers.

These kinds of concern about audiences involve social values. But day-to-day production has no time to consider social values, and relies on news values to guide selection and presentation. Presentation is the skill of turning taken-for-granted news values into rules of production. We will enlarge on this in the discussion of news values below. In assessing audience response journalists have to rely on accepted definitions of news, what makes a good or a not so good story. Journalistic notions of what is and is not news have been forged in the workshops of a commercial press serving historically particular needs and interests. It is in this process that news values are created.

News values and news production   *conclusion*

Discussions of news values usually suggest they are surrounded by a mystique, an impenetrable cloud of verbal imprecision and conceptual obscurity. Many academic reports concentrate on this nebulous aspect of news values and imbue them with far greater importance and allure than they merit. We have stressed that news production is rarely the active application of decisions of rejection or promotion to highly varied and extensive material. On the contrary, it is for the most part the passive exercise of routine and highly regulated procedures in the task of selecting from already limited supplies of information. News values exist and are, of course, significant. But they are as much the resultant explanation or justification of necessary procedures as their source.

News values are used in two ways. They are criteria of selection from material available to the newsroom of those items worthy of inclusion in the final product. Second, they are guidelines for the presentation of items, suggesting what to emphasise, what to omit, and where to give priority in the preparation of the items for presentation to the audience. News values are thus working rules, comprising a corpus of occupational lore which implicitly and often expressly explains and guides newsroom practice. It is not as true as often suggested that they are beyond the ken of the newsman, himself unable and unwilling to articulate them. Indeed, they pepper the daily exchanges between journalists in collaborative production procedures. Far more they are terse shorthand references to shared understandings about the nature and purpose of news which can be used to ease the rapid and difficult manufacture of bulletins and news programmes. News values are qualities of events or of their journalistic construction, whose relative absence or presence recommends them for inclusion in the news product. The more of such qualities a story exhibits, the greater its chances of inclusion. Alternatively, the more different news values a story contains, the greater its chances of inclusion (see Galtung and Ruge, 1965). News values derive from unstated or implicit assumptions or judgements about three things:

1. The audience. Is this important to the audience or will it hold their attention? Is it of known interest, will it be understood, enjoyed, registered, perceived as relevant?
2. Accessibility – in two senses, prominence and ease of capture. Prominence: to what extent is the event known to the news organisation, how obvious is it, has it made itself apparent. Ease of capture: how available to journalists is the event, is it physically accessible, manageable technically, in a form amenable to journalism, is it ready-prepared for easy coverage, will it require great resources to obtain?
3. Fit. Is the item consonant with the pragmatics of production routines, is it commensurate with technical and organisational possibilities, is it homologous with the exigencies and constraints in

programme making and the limitations of the medium? Does it make sense in terms of what is already known about the subject.

In other words, news values themselves derive from the two immediate determinants of news making, perceptions of the audience and the availability of material. Historically news values come to imbue the necessities of journalism with the lustre of good practice. They represent a classic case of making a virtue of necessity. This particularly applies to the broader values we have subsumed under the title of the occupational ideology – impartiality, objectivity, accuracy and so on. These concern the role and function of journalism and we shall return to them in Chapter 7. News values are attached to the practice of the job, they are story values. Some of the more important are as follows. The first four derive from considerations of the audience, the remainder from a mixture of the three factors described above.

Drama

News stories are, as the term suggests, stories as well as news. Good ones exhibit a narrative structure akin to the root elements in human drama. To recall Reuven Frank, former President of NBC news in America, 'joy, sorrow, shock, fear, these are the stuff of news'. The good news story tells its tale with a beginning, a middle and an end, in that order. In Sweden one of the most prominent news stories in the period of our study was of a bank hold-up in which an escaped convict took hostage four bank employees into the vaults and settled in for a seige for several days, finally succumbing to police gas. The story was rich in human drama; the pretty girl hostage, 'the bandit who couldn't kill', the dilemmas facing the police. The story kept going for a long time after the initial denouement, the criminal was eventually married to a woman who had been touched at seeing his arrest on television, and a strange camaraderie grew up between the victims and their captor.

Dramatic structure is often achieved by the presentation of conflict, most commonly by the matching of opposed viewpoints drawn from spokesmen of 'both sides of the question'. The audience is here felt to be served by being given the full picture as well as an interesting confrontation (cf. Epstein, 1973, pp. 168-9). Because of the limited resources for film interviews this technique is less available to poorer newsrooms, and in Nigeria it is almost entirely absent because of the severe authority of government departments.

Visual attractiveness

Television is a visual medium and the special power of television news is its ability to exploit this advantage. Television journalists are not obsessed by notions of 'good television' or 'good film'. They can't be, given the limited number of stories for which film is available. But the temptation to screen visually arresting material and to reject stories unadorned with good film is ever present and sometimes irresistible. In turn judgements about newsworthiness will be shaped by aesthetic judgements about film. A former editor-in-chief of the British Independent Television News has written that 'the key to putting more hard news on to the air effectively lies, I am sure, in putting more pictures and less talk into news programmes'. The resultant emphasis can be seen in his review of recent events at the time of writing (Cox, 1965).

> The challenge is to turn hard factual important news into pictures ... It has proved an excellent technique on a number of occasions, particularly from Selma when we ran nine minutes of action film ... and in a report from Ireland of a street fight between IRA supporters and the police, which was one of the best punch-ups ever seen on the screen – westerns and Goldfinger not excepted ... [the election coverage] aimed at bringing over on film the essence of the day's campaigning. It provided some memorable television, particularly of the rowdier meetings of Mr Wilson and Sir Alec Douglas-Home.

Great importance is attached to visual presentation. At RTE at the beginning of 1971 presentation was pepped up. A new front projection unit to go behind reporters doing pieces into camera was produced, and a new animated opening and closing sequence developed. As stories develop during the day the likelihood that they will produce good film is kept well to the fore in discussion of their merits. An Irish story on an escapee who had been seen in Clonmel met little enthusiasm until a message came through that film of the chase would be coming. It was then acclaimed as 'the best story of the day'. Time and again television journalists referred to this special advantage of television when asked to describe stories they thought particularly effective.

> Anything which has imaginative filming ... a few pieces during the local elections in the North – not the vote counting but campaigning – showed good use of television – camera crews followed the candidates around knocking on doors. (Sub-editor, RTE)

> Television is excellent ... for handling the story where you need a lot of pictures. This is where you score all the time over other media. (Chief Sub-editor, RTE)

Just as audiences often justify their trust in the veracity of television news by reference to its use of film: 'you can actually see it happening', so newsmen refer to this quality in their favourite stories. 'Another good one was a building disaster. Three people died when it collapsed. We were the first station there and you could actually see people being rescued on camera.' (Head of News, WNBC)

A story may be included simply because film is available or because of the dramatic qualities of the film. A story narrated several days previously will be resurrected as film arrives simply to show the film.

Film can also provide concrete evidence of the global surveillance of electronic journalism by demonstrating visually the journalist's presence at an event.

Entertainment

News programmes seek, and usually find, large audiences. To do so they must take account of entertainment values in the literal sense of providing captivating, humorous, titillating, amusing or generally diverting material. The 'human interest' story was invented for just this purpose. Broadcast news is generally sober and serious, taking its social responsibility and constitutional position as demanding less frivolity than might be licensed in the popular press. Helen Hughes, who over 30 years ago wrote a book on the human interest story, considered that human interest was a dimension added to other types of story. '. . . the news signalises [sic] a deviation from the expected, the normal and the traditional, which, when told with human interest is made human and comprehensible' (Hughes, 1942; see also Hughes, 1940). Although she was writing of the press this is especially true of broadcast news. The whimsical or bizarre events that are the currency of human interest stories, or the celebrities, children and animals that are their stars, are frequently too frivolous for broadcast news. But the human interest angle is an important way of making events palatable or comprehensible to audiences of broadcast news.

For some broadcast journalists there is a tension between the desire to ensure audience attentiveness and interest by following entertainment values, and a concern to maintain standards of seriousness and the plain honest narration of facts; between information and entertainment. This debate was alive in most newsrooms and linked back to arguments about how 'hard' or 'soft' news should be. It stems again from the dilemma of the journalist as producer of a marketable commodity, whose presentation and dressing up for the audience may cut across some of the professional ideals of the journalist *qua* journalist. The solution is normally the co-option of one ideal by the other, in the argument that to inform an audience you must first have its attention, and that there's no point preparing serious, well-intentioned, high-minded journalism if the audience registers its boredom by switching off. Thus entertainment is high on the list of news values both as an end in itself and as a means to other journalistic ideals.

Importance

The most frequently cited reason for including a particular item in news bulletins is its importance. This is usually taken to mean that the reported event has considerable significance for large numbers of people in the audience. Most often importance is cited to explain the inclusion of items which might be omitted on the criteria of other audience-based news values. That is, items which may be boring, repetitive or non-visual must still be included despite audience disinterest. The item refers to something the audience needs to know. This news value is rooted in theories of the social role of journalism as tribune of the people. In broadcasting it has the further support that state-authorised corporations are expected to behave responsibly, informatively and educatively. Importance is often applied to political and foreign news. Both are assumed to be of greater interest to journalists than to their audience. Both are included however because of their unquestioned importance.

The meaning of 'importance' was a live issue in SR, where Rapport staff frequently raised it as a reason for including the kinds of stories they felt traditional approaches (which in the early days they identified with TV Nytt) would ignore. Swedish journalists often felt that because domestic stories lacked elements of drama, entertainment or surprise, they had to be justified as important. The emphasis put on foreign stories contrasted with the view offered by many that news was about things important to many Swedes. The two strands of thought to some extent conflict. On the one hand effective stories were described in terms of the standard currency of international journalism. Big stories were the stories that were flashed round the world by the wire and film agencies. Occasional a Swedish story made it into this league, as for example the bank drama, whose international rating was registered by its widespread acceptance in Eurovision exchanges. Domestic stories rarely met this success. Importance, in the sense of affecting many people in the audience, implicitly suggested domestic stories, although it was sometimes argued that because the big, important events happened overseas and Sweden had little control over her own destiny, importance was to be found in foreign news. The result was a disjunction between the principles that journalists thought should apply to stories and those actually cited as effective, big and important. Domestic stories were occasionally upgraded by their relevance to international stories. One story began as an item in a small left-wing magazine about Swedish secret service activities overseas and in checking on left-wing organisations and activities in Sweden. The story soon became the government's attempts to suppress it and prosecute those involved. The story offended treasured Swedish self-images, suggesting not only that the government had been involved in secret activities akin to those of the CIA, but that it was prepared to infringe free speech. The affair was hailed as the 'Swedish Watergate'. Many journalists were sceptical about the real importance of this affair, but in the end 'real importance' gave way to these other factors.

In Nigeria 'importance' took on a special meaning in the evolution of a category of news called 'development' news. This comprised items which were included deliberately for their utility in promoting social goals associated with development. This unusual absorption of social values into news values will be discussed in Chapter 6. It had the added effect of promoting domestic news which was otherwise dwarfed by the more easily collected and technically superior foreign news.

Size

The bigger the story the greater the likelihood of its inclusion, and the greater the prominence with which it will be presented. This simple rule of course begs the question of just how events are measured and which dimensions are relevant. The most common considerations are the numbers or type of people involved, or the scale of the event as an instance of a type. Thus the more people involved in a disaster or the presence of 'big names' at a formal occasion, enhance the initial visibility of such events and hence their consequent news value. Size as a news value normally qualifies other news values. That is, subsequent to the selection of events in the world as news, the criterion of size is applied to decide which are the most important news events. Less commonly events not normally registered as news become eligible by the sheer scale on which they occur.

Proximity

Like size, the criterion of proximity derives partly from considerations of the audience, partly from problems of accessibility. Proximity has two senses, cultural and geographical. Stories are culturally proximate if they refer to events within the normal experience of journalists and their audience. They are the kinds of events which require a wide range of common language and shared cultural assumptions. For this reason they are normally, but not necessarily, domestic stories. Thus in Ireland the importance of the Church in secular life provides a background for stories on church or religion in other countries which might be ignored in more secularised nations. Cultural proximity can be applied to stories by, for example, putting foreign news into a domestic context to explain its importance or significance.

Geographical proximity refers to the simple rules of thumb that suggest the primacy of domestic news and the allocation of news from the rest of the world according to their nearness to the audience (see Schlesinger, 1978, p. 117). Here geography is distorted by the mechanics of news collection. As we have seen, the distribution of news gatherers is far from random, and in journalistic terms Lagos is far closer to London than to, say, Accra. Nonetheless the criterion is applied, and several Nigerian sub-editors adopted a three-tier news geography: Nigeria, Africa, the world. In the other countries, too, there was a sense of concentric spheres of influence. This design was of course totally disrupted by the availability of material. The geographical criterion thus moderates to two rules. Either, the further away an event the bigger it has to be, or, nearby events take precedence over similar events at a distance.

Brevity

A story which is closely packed with facts and little padding is preferred to loose 'soft' news. Partly this relates to the journalistic role of informing rather than explaining, partly to concerns for what are seen as audience requirements and limitations. Audiences want just the facts and nothing but the facts. Since they also require comprehensiveness clearly no single item can be allowed to drag on too long. This rule was memorably expressed by the dictum printed on one news editor's notice board: 'news should be like a woman's skirt – long enough to cover the essentials but brief enough to hold attention'. News bulletins are normally between 15 and 30 minutes, and contain less than a couple of dozen items. Limiting news stories to their apparently more obvious elements is essential if there is to be room for even a minimal selection of the day's events. This limit seems to emphasise the necessary objectivity of broadcast news while in fact merely disguising the vast edifice of assumptions and cultural packaging which allow such brief items to make sense at all.

Negativity

Bad news is good news. As is often observed there is little mileage in reporting the safe arrival of aircraft, the continued health of a film star, or the smooth untroubled negotiations of a wage settlement. News is about disruptions in the normal current of events. In the literal sense it is not concerned with the uneventful. The concentration on negative events, that is events perceived or presented as damaging to social institutions, is not the result of a mischievous obsession with misery or discontent among journalists, but the outcome of the history of their occupation. News began as a service to groups directly concerned for the uninterrupted flow of commercial life. Interruptions included loss of merchandise at sea, financial upheavals in mercantile centres or, of course, war. These events remain paradigm instances of bad news, and as a result of news per se.

It is for this reason that news is described as a social surveillance, registering threats to the normal fabric of society and explaining their significance. The news value of negativity is therefore an important contributor to the social values in news, defining by default both the status quo and the sources and nature of threats to it. We re-examine this in Chapter 6. It is worth noting that negativity is not a universal primary news value. What western journalists often see as the tediousness and irrelevance of broadcast news in eastern Europe has much to do with the conventions in many of these countries of presenting positive news (industrial production achievements, the award of honours, etc.) while excluding accidents, violence, crime and other negative categories prominent in news elsewhere (Varis, 1974; Lansipuro, 1975).

Some categories of negative news are disliked in broadcasting for their lack of other values. Crime was deliberately under-reported in all three countries in deference to the view that its presentation was pandering to the sensational news values more appropriate to the popular press. In Sweden this view was widely shared at all levels and there were considerable misgivings over the amount of time which had been devoted to the 'bank drama', even allowing it was an unusual crime. Elsewhere many broadcast journalists regretted this tendency to play down crime, and it was more often an executive than a 'shopfloor' view. Many journalists also subscribed to the view that showing too much violence was irresponsible. However, this view was frequently swamped by the power of news values such as drama and visual attractiveness. Again this is defined by reference to the audience. The point is made by Brucker (1973, p. 175):

> It is, of course, a basic principle of journalism that the bigger, the more off-beat, or the more bloody the spectacle, the greater the news value. This is not because newspapermen are more ghoulish or less sensitive to the finer things of life than their fellow men. It merely reflects the ineluctable fact that readers will flock to a story that has shock value but ignore one that is routine.

Or, as a journalist once pointed out, given a choice of two calamities news editors choose both, in the belief that the audience will be held by the dramatic power of tragic narrative.

Recency

The next three news values are derived more from production requirements than the perceived demands of the audience. Recency, the requirement that news be up to date and refer to events as close to transmission time as possible, derives from two factors. First, traditional journalistic competition puts a premium on the supply of 'earliest intelligencies' ahead of rivals. At its most successful this aim produces the 'scoop', an exclusive capture of a news event ahead of all competition. Second, the periodicity of news production itself sets the frame within which events in the world will be perceived. Thus daily production sets a daily frame, and news events must have occurred in the twenty-four hours between bulletins to merit inclusion. Although this is often impossible, especially for newsrooms dependent on air-freighted news film, the dictum that 'it's news when the audience first sees it' was only offered rather sheepishly, in the certain knowledge that it was an unhappy transgression of a root news value. The main point, however, is that processes which do not fit this daily cycle do not register as news by producing news events. Since daily reports are required the necessity of filling a daily quota becomes a laudable goal, and recency emerges as a journalistic virtue. Speed in collection and processing becomes paramount and is often cited as the particular merit of individual journalists or newsrooms. Conversely it is one of the main complaints against non-journalist broadcasters that they do not understand the need for speed and that technical and other facilities are inadequate for journalistic demands. The favourite accolade for Eurovision was that it permitted same-day film of European events. One of the most frequently cited problems was late arrival of unprocessed film and the inadequacy of film processing facilities.

The broadcasting equivalent of newspaper editions is the sequence of bulletins through the day, or evening on television. Journalists were acutely aware of the need to 'keep the picture changing'. In Sweden this was spurred by an urge to beat the internal opposition. In Nigeria it was more to do with the frequency of radio bulletins, 'news on the hour every hour', where failure to provide variety was often criticised. Journalists were fond of the fast-breaking story where the rapid movement of events pre-empted any need for the artificial injection of pace or change. Recency emphasises the task of news in topping up information on those events and institutions already defined as the substance of news.

Elites

As a value within 'bigness' news values emphasise that big names are better news than nobodies, major personalities of more interest than ordinary folk. There is an obvious circularity in this in that well-known personalities become so by their exposure in news media. It is this that leads us to root this news value in production rather than in audience interests. Clearly audiences are interested in major rather than minor figures, people they all know about rather than the acquaintances of a few. But as we shall show in Chapter 6, elites are only partially exposed, and concentration on powerful or ruling groups is neither uniform nor comprehensive.

G. K. Chesterton once said that 'journalism largely consists of saying Lord Jones is dead to people who never even knew he was alive'. Elites are covered to the extent that their activities are accessible and to the extent that these activities match other news values. Thus the political circus is a prime focus of attention, while economic and financial elites remain shrouded. As Chapter 6 shows, the consequent picture of power and social influence is one which emphasises the legislative and constitutional and masks the economic and financial. It is those elites whose activities fit, or who choose to be accessible and visible which make news.

Personalities

News is about people, and mostly about individuals. This news value emphasises the need to make stories comprehensible by reducing complex processes and institutions to the actions of individuals. This aim is, like many news values, a virtue born of necessity. Brief, and especially visual, journalism cannot deal with abstractions and has to narrate in the concrete. Thus it becomes a news value to 'seek the personal angle' or to 'personalise' the news. The effect of this is to treat institutional and international relations either as the interaction of individuals, or as being analogous to inter-personal relations. For example, international political news deals almost entirely with the diplomatic globe-trotting of major politicians, and international relations are seen to depend on how well political leaders get on. The analogies appear in the terminology of the emotions which characterises institutional or national relations. Governments become 'angry', unions are 'hot-headed', nations are 'anxious' or 'eager'. This is most easily portrayed by personalising such acts in the presentation of individuals.

This list may not exhaust all news values but it includes the main ones. Their obviousness can be illustrated by compiling a list of antonyms. It is hard to imagine broadcast journalists anywhere seeking news which dealt with small events, the long term, dull, distant, visually boring, unimportant people, and so on. Yet many of these labels describe events and processes which may well have significance for news audiences, but which are not news. The application of news values is part of the process by which this labelling occurs.

Perceived constraints on news production

One British editor has written that of all the pressures operating on the editor of a morning or evening newspaper the heaviest is the 'shortage of time' (Wintour, 1972, p. 3). Broadcast journalists have an even heavier burden in that not only do they have limited time to prepare their material, but the product itself has to be tightly packed and trimmed to size. They are very aware that a bulletin may only contain roughly the same number of words as a single page of a newspaper. Of course 'a picture is worth a thousand words', though that is of little comfort to radio journalists. But when a broadcast journalist prepares a story he sits at a typewriter, and it is the shortage of word-space that stares him in the face.

Many of the journalists who believed in more background and explanation in news saw time as the main enemy of their hopes. 'If only there was time to prepare material and do the necessary reading and research.' In Nigeria this was aggravated by the desperate lack of library resources. 'The library' tended to be a dusty shelf in the Head of News' office housing an unenticing row of out-of-date *Who's Who*'s UNESCO handbooks and possibly an incomplete *Keesing's Contemporary Archives*. There are no staff to collate news clippings or back files, nor facilities for indexing or storing of materials. Nigerian journalists were often acutely aware of this and cited it as an indication of relative organisational poverty. SR had a comprehensive and efficient but under-utilised library service. It is interesting that in

Epstein's study of American television news production he was struck by the lack of records and poor filing system, indeed there was 'no house respect for it as a source of background information' (Epstein, 1973, p. 140). The point being that it is lack of time to do research and lack of space for the fully researched story, rather than lack of research materials, which hinder the kind of analytical journalism that might require them.

Most journalists subscribe to the 'more means better' theory and attribute many of the defects of broadcast journalism to the paucity of air-time allocated to it. In discussing news programmes they admired, the half-hour news of the British commercial network was frequently cited. The time at its disposal was one among many envied characteristics. In addition, as we shall see in Chapter 7, many broadcasters with newspaper experience saw the lack of space in which to expand their writing as a major loss in the change of medium. In practice the shortage of time accentuates the application of news values; there is only room for stories with the greatest aggregate of news values. Despite the normal lack of time for longer stories all the newsrooms occasionally did longer pieces of anywhere between 3 and 10 minutes. These were responses to unusually significant news items or summary accounts in a long running story. Examples of the former were a series of Swedish stories on the admission of China to the UN, or NBC's coverage of the death of Nkrumah. An example of the extended summary piece was one by an RTE reporter on Vietnam. These are exceptional luxuries seldom allowed for want of time. They are often resented for the problems they cause. For example, at SR output editors tended to dislike these lengthier inserts because they pre-empted so much of the programme, were boring and prevented them being able to pace the programme as they wished. Only executive backing ensured that in the end there was space for them in the programme.

A second most apparent hindrance to news collection is the scarcity of resources of which every newsroom sees itself a victim. A major gap in coverage perceived by journalists in all three countries was news from the provinces, away from the capital or the conurbation in which the newsroom was situated. All three Nigerian stations had plans to recruit stringers or set up offices in each of the state capitals. NBC in particular took its role as the national station very seriously, and 'not enough from the states' was a common diagnosis at editorial post-mortems. WNBS and RTK also saw themselves as national but in practice were slightly less anxious about the national coverage in their bulletins. Since they were bound to include a certain amount of Lagos news about the Head of State or Federal Government they avoided obvious parochiality automatically. The three television services served local audiences only, so that despite lip service to the ideal of national comprehensiveness there was no despair over its unattainability.

Concern about lack of provincial items was greatest in Ireland where the verdict that there was too little such news was recognised at all levels.

It's easier to cover the world, give a precis of world events, but a housing scandal in a large town 70 miles from Dublin doesn't get covered. We might give some coverage to the death of a Japanese Prime Minister whom the people don't know about. It's easier and cheaper because we're linked into the infrastructure of world communication. One of the reasons why we cover the North so well now is that it is now a world event. (Reporter, RTE)

One thing strikes me. There's a bus strike on in Limerick – that's the third largest city after all – this made the bulletin almost as an afterthought, yet to me it's a good provincial home story and could have made much more. A minor strike in Dublin gets well in there, we do it lavishly with film, etc. (Sub-editor, RTE)

In fact, although most Irish journalists agreed there was too little provincial news, many felt this was an unfortunate necessity, since provincial news was difficult to collect:

It's possible for something to be happening in Galway and not to be able to get stuff in until very late in the evening. (Sub-editor, RTE)

It also gave the bulletin too parochial a flavour:

As we don't have another channel or a local opt out, we have the problem of producing an authoritative national bulletin and looking after the provinces as well ... There's a kind of tendency to regard provincial items as provincial unless they refer to your own area, and a tendency to criticise the station on the grounds of provincialism if there are too many items from Cork. If the bulletin is followed by a string of provincial items it does lower the tone. (Sub-editor, RTE)

Because there are no local stations RTE has to cover local stories ... You shouldn't spend resources on local stories like school openings etc. I've just got weary of cutting film of Bishops sprinkling water on the oddest things. (Sub-editor, RTE)

In Sweden inattention to provincial news was related to newsroom organisation. A majority of journalists were unable to hazard any estimate of the proportion of provincial news, whereas almost all could produce some figure for foreign news. Provincial news is as readily identifiable as foreign, as it is nearly always made by one of the district production centres. The reason for the hesitancy seemed to be because journalists in Sweden did not think in these terms. The proportion of foreign news was a continual source of interest because it was an index of the relative strengths of the foreign and domestic news staff. This was a matter of continuing concern and occasional friction in all the newsrooms. By contrast the districts had no representative. Their material was accepted or rejected by the output editors when offered, or occasionally ordered when an event of particular significance was known to be imminent in a district.

Lack of manpower was especially blamed for low foreign coverage. The idea of the big foreign story as 'real news' was seen in the general tendency in all three countries for journalists to underestimate the proportion of foreign news in their bulletins. This is probably also because they forget how much news is passively collated from agencies. Thus in assessing the reasons for different gaps in coverage, journalists think in terms of news gathering, while the gaps are mostly created in news processing. Oddly, while lack of manpower was mentioned as the main cause of gaps in coverage by four-fifths of Irish journalists and two-thirds of Swedish journalists, only a quarter of Nigerian journalists thought this their main problem. Clearly it is a bigger problem in Nigeria than in the other two countries, and just as clearly Nigerian journalists are well aware of the manpower problem. Possibly where news production is necessarily so passive this comes to be accepted as inevitable and therefore not immediately problematic. Nigerian journalists underestimated the proportion of foreign news in their bulletins by a wider margin than journalists elsewhere, again because of the tendency to think of news gathering (primarily domestic) rather than news processing.

Lack of time and lack of manpower or other resources are by far the most obvious of the limitations on broadcast news perceived by journalists. Problems such as the difficulty of obtaining access to certain news sources or types of information loom far less. It is generally felt that these are inevitable and expected hazards of the job whose negotiation is a requisite part of any competent journalist's repertoire. The same applies to the converse problem of fending off publicity or other foisted information. Journalists generally want industrial relations news from companies, companies wish to impart the good news about product or company developments. There is little trading of one for the other. Another form of manufactured news of which journalists are wary is the demonstration. Swedish journalists mentioned this problem particularly, though in Ireland the story was told of a political picket outside the studios. A police car had come and told them to stick to a patch outside the main gates. 'Oh, we'll be gone when the press has come', they said. The story is told, like many parallel tales of commercial publicity seekers, to illustrate the clumsy obviousness of such tactics and their ineffectiveness in the face of journalistic guile and experience. The general reaction is 'yes, it's a problem but that's just part of the job'. In the more localised Nigerian television newsrooms individual publicity seekers, perhaps seeking the glamour of having the splendours of a private party they have sponsored celebrated as a news event, are frequently and with much professional relish, repulsed from the newsrooms.

Making difficult contacts is similarly conceived as a skill to be exulted in rather than as a constraint. A Swedish journalist described a typical case in a story on mercury levels allowed in food. She had sought information from the food ministry and had eventually triumphed after insistently and patiently running the gauntlet of being passed from extension to extension on the telephone. Swedish journalists generally felt they worked in an unusually open society. Tales were told of ringing directly to the Prime Minister and getting immediate permission for an interview. The sense of being a special case is reproduced in each country. Nigerian journalists, with considerable justification, point to the unusual liberties they enjoy considering they work under a military regime and an official 'state of emergency'. In Ireland journalists remarked on 'the smallness of Irish society', 'reporters have a good idea of what's going on and who the personalities are. Everybody's somebody else's cousin'.

Two further minor constraints concern journalists – technological limitations and the various personal or departmental quirks which impinge on their work. Technology is important to the broadcast journalist; he perceives it as a constraint largely because it is cumbersome and inflexible, preventing the fast-moving slickness of the best news-gathering newspaper tradition. On the other hand it can be greeted with great acclaim when providing the visual immediacy and drama which are broadcasting's gift to journalism. At SR the inclusion in a bulletin of a 'live' goal from an evening football match provided just such a moment. Technical problems tend to be organisational problems in two senses. They often arise in the contention for facilities, such as editing, video-recording, or dubbing, which arises between departments. In addition, the suspicion with which many broadcasters view the technological competence of new staff is echoed by the concern about their own lack of training and expertise in this area which many journalists themselves expressed. The gaps created by these problems are in geographical spread (provincial news missed because too late for film processing, too few videotape machines to cope with European news and needs of other departments) and in presentation. Technical problems can appear enormously important as there are a large number of detailed ways in which they affect coverage. For example, a political reporter pointed out that there was at that time only one camera in the Irish parliamentary studio so that interviewing was difficult. The complexity, number and immediacy of technical constraints (if the telecine breaks down all the bulletin's films are jeopardised) pushes technology very firmly into the catalogue of constraints that journalists describe. The consequent concern however is to get the technology to work as it might, or to master its potential rather than to question its fundamental impact on the basic choice and definition of broadcast news.

Individual news executives and their whims and policies clearly play some part in shaping news output. That their influence takes place within the rigidly set limits of available material does not lessen the fact that they can assert some news values and dismiss others. The head and deputy head of news at RTE during our research period were seen as having introduced rigour and a sense of purpose to RTE news, an approach applauded for its seriousness and intelligence by supporters, but castigated as over-intellectual and lacking traditional news sense by detractors. As elsewhere this tends to become a personalisation of the debate between traditional 'hard' news men who know a good story when they see one, and journalists ambitious to explore 'new' approaches, expand background and analysis, and play down the entertainment or human interest emphasis in news. Some versions of this lay behind nearly all the debates about the personal influence of significant individuals. At RTE the then Head of News' known antipathy to crime news kept many such stories out of bulletins. The visibility of such authority brings other areas of discontent to focus on senior personalities. For example, several reporters blamed the Head of News for the limited news gathering done by the department. An experienced journalist working as a sub-editor remarked that there was 'too much talk and debate, no real drive, no policy, no real professional journalists at the top. Not enough money or resources but too much spent on administration instead of on getting the job done. In news there is too much comment and analysis, not the hard stuff that I had to produce on a commercial paper. All these bloody conferences and meetings but no-one really cares about the end product – news'. Swedish journalists talked in similar terms of the endless production of lists and running orders.

Some journalists pictured themselves as straining at a leash composed of interminable editorial conferences and executive hesitancy and 'reluctance to cover stories on the ground'. The straining however was not much in evidence, and the constraints seem more to do with the nature and necessities of broadcast journalism than the whims of the two executives at whom these remarks were aimed. Many of the complaints were restated in a memorandum prepared by the Irish journalists' union for submission to the Broadcasting Review Committee. The memorandum called for more opportunities for journalists to specialise, but warned against 'putting the cart before the horse – a concentration on analysis and "in depth" treatment of certain items – perhaps beyond the public's capacity or interest – while ignoring or inadequately handling other large areas of news'. The memorandum noted with concern that crime went practically unreported. The memorandum was anxious to make explicit the union's resentment at the suggestion that the blame for major deficiencies in broadcast news lay elsewhere than with management.

Departmental personalities in Sweden have already been touched on in outlining the conflict which developed over the way news should be organised under the new two-channel system. This provided us with a useful case through which to assess the relative importance of organisational constraints, journalistic imperatives and personal policies. Ostensibly the conflict over the organisation of news was a conflict over the interpretation of the guidelines laid down by Parliament for the production of news. In practice however it could be interpreted in at least four other ways. First there were personal feuds between some of the participants. This was one of the interpretations given wide prominence in the press as the new head of the Central News Department (CND) and his ex-boss in the old single-channel television organisation took the opportunity to settle some old scores. The conflict between other participants was also personalised but with much less justification.

A second interpretation given currency in the press, especially in the social democratic, Stockholm afternoon paper *Aftonbladet*, was that political motives lay behind the centralised style of organisation. Those associated with CND were known to have sympathy with the right in Swedish politics whereas those associated with the second channel and its news programme were associated with the left.

A third interpretation however was that the political coup, as *Aftonbladet* called it, related to internal rather than national politics. The new style of organisation reduced the power of the central directorate relative to the channels. In name and in practice these were to be largely autonomous. By channelling staff and resources into the central news organisation the central directorate retained control over an area of programming and moreover over a type of programming, news, which was particularly significant in maintaining the corporation's relationships with important external constituents, parliament and the government.

Fourth, there were differences of journalistic philosophy between the innovative team which gathered in TV 2 to produce Rapport and the journalists and executives associated with CND and the rival commentary programme on TV 1, Nu. The Nu team was recruited much later than the Rapport team and never developed the *esprit de corps* of their rivals. Nu had a larger audience than Rapport because it appeared on TV 1 which held most of the old single channel audience. But it was judged a failure inside and outside the corporation as it developed no distinct profile of its own. The Rapport staff were much more concerned about the competitive threat of the CND than Nu. CND was in a position to pre-empt resources and material to produce the news, resources and material which might have gone to Rapport to give them more scope with their distinctive news style. Thus there were disputes over access to the team of SR foreign correspondents, EVN and agency material and provincial stories.

Faced with internal dispute and publicised controversy SR adopted the common organisational tactic of appointing a committee to resolve the problem. From the start, it was fairly clear that the committee itself was sharply divided between a majority of centralists and a minority of pluralists. In the event it produced two recommendations, the majority advocating a single news organisation, the minority, two, one for each channel. Those who had connections with TV 1 or the central directorate of SR signed the majority recommendation; those with connections with or sympathy for TV 2, the minority. The device of appointing a committee had provided a breathing space for the corporation during which the personal feuding died down or at least disappeared from the press. However, the report left SR with the same impasse. Moreover, neither the majority nor minority advocated a solution which would fit with the restricted form of competition set out in the parliamentary proposition.

The compromise which was eventually adopted was largely based on the proposals submitted to the committee by the heads of SR's various district organisations. Their interest was mainly to get more time for provincial news, both in its own right and as part of the national news output. They advocated a strict interpretation of the parliamentary proposition so that there would be short 'fact news' bulletins produced by the CND and then two complementary commentary programmes, one for each channel, dealing with the most important items in depth. They hoped that these would have more time for provincial inserts. This proposal was particularly attractive to SR's directorate. It came from an interested source but one uninvolved in the immediate feuds. It squared with the parliamentary proposition and so did not need any further governmental sanction. It could be accommodated with only a slight rearrangement of men and resources.

This reorganisation is an interesting example of the way organis-ational constraints are liable to triumph over journalistic imperatives, and individual personalities and policies. The organisational constraint was to find a convenient method of internal organisation to take account of the existing distribution of men and resources, the interests of various sections and departments and of the corporation's external constituents who defined the situation in which it operated. In this case, having got itself into a controversial position in which press commentators had been able to accuse SR of contravening the parliamentary proposition, the opportunity to adopt a form of organisation which was almost a literal interpretation of it was particularly attractive. This in spite of the fact that few could find a good word for the short bulletins without moving pictures which were to be produced by the CND. Those working on these bulletins were deprived of most journalistic and technical satisfactions associated with the production of television news. They took some consolation from developing their skills in caption design in an attempt to make still diagrams look like moving pictures.

Individual quirks of policy in Nigeria tended to be station rather than person-specific. In RTK for example there were at this time considerable sympathies with stories that might imply criticism of federal govern-ment, and particularly its lack of attention to problems in the north. In Nigeria the personalities and news tastes of news executives were less disparaged than elsewhere, partly because the authority structure tended to be highly vertical – with considerable gaps in seniority and experience between heads of news and most news staff – and partly because the necessarily passive and limited news production process left so little room from the imposition of idiosyncracy.

Manipulation and intervention

Last, though not least, among perceived constraints on news production was the active intervention of politicians or government either insidiously or through legislation. One would expect this to be at its most obvious in a military regime. Even in Nigeria, however, the most general effect of government pressure was to reinforce the concentration of news attention on the uncontentious activities of leading political figures. Direct intervention, of course, occurs – and not infrequently. We have given some examples in Chapter 4. This is achieved either by prior definition of policies or by retrospective comment or interference. Policies tend to be for the promotion of domestic social programmes (right-hand driving, decimal currency) or in foreign affairs. In 1973 several junior reporters in NBC radio were concerned that they could never mention Bangladesh in bulletins, since the Nigerian government had not recognised its existence. This becomes a generalised feeling. 'It's difficult to maintain one's professional integrity when you have to get clearance all the time.' (Assistant Editor, WNBC)

Intervention after the event tends to be much more the work of individual aggrieved officials. Often they are treated with cynicism or contempt, though not necessarily ignored. At WNBC a Western State governor with a penchant for self-publicity happened to be on the Board of Governors of the corporation. Her frequent tirades at the failure of news cameras to follow her every public act were often mocked, but occasionally acted upon. Official complaints were often about news events, publicity of which would have been 'embarrassing' to the government or individual politicians. Strikes are a common example.

> The printing workers at the mint went on strike: they [i.e. government PR] telephoned us to say we musn't use it. (Local News Editor, NBC r)

> The other day teachers were demonstrating because they had not had their bonuses for two years. We covered it, but then we got a 'phone call from the ministry; we were told not to cover it and we dropped it. (Chief Sub-editor, RTK)

The fiction that roads are well tended and safe is maintained by constant urging not to report accidents, to keep victim numbers low or unreported. Other minor incidents go unreported; the presence of a well-known spirit healer in Ibadan prompted the local ministry of health to ask that his activities should not be given publicity.

NBC was perceived as being different in these matters, though the difference can be seen from different perspectives. For NBC people attention was seen as an indication of their importance: 'The Head of

State was going to Mali. He was delayed and WNBS announced he had already gone. Gowon phoned us. We told him he had been listening to WNBS. He said "that's OK as long as it wasn't you".' (Editor, NBC r)

To others it demonstrated NBC's slavish proximity to government: 'At NBC if Gowon goes to the toilet it's news.' (Chief Sub-editor, WNBC)

Intervention in Nigeria leads to two responses, first a reassertion of the occupational ideology in defiance of external control, second an accommodation to unavoidable interference both in practice and in ideology. Defiance is regular and takes the conventional 'publish and be damned' approach, though usually not without a careful look both ways before the road of caution is crossed.

> A former Governor once got rid of two of his cabinet. We covered it
> when the sacked Minister of Agriculture announced it at a meeting. I
> spoke to the Secretary of the Military Government. He said 'wait for the
> Gazette'. I checked with the General Manager. He said 'wait'. I put it out
> anyway and there was no reaction. (Head of News, WNBC)

Defiance is based on a reassertion of the journalists' independent judgement of news value, and brings them into conflict with organisational as much as governmental authorities. In the view of journalists, the latter can't be expected to understand – 'if they gave us our professional heads it would be to their benefit'. Broadcasting authorities, however, are if anything even more resented for their bowing to authority and inadequate defence of news staff. Their inadequacy comes from ignorance – 'what do they know about news?' Among the best liked stories were those which fended off either of these problems by the aggressive display of news values. 'The middle-east war was a good story. The editors tried to keep a balance despite official policy.' (Reporter, NBC r)

Accommodation to pressure takes a variety of forms. The most obvious is anticipatory self-censorship, which focusses the normal journalistic regard for audience response on those elite groups whose response may be swift, direct and vital.

> News is WNBS. The present government is very sensitive to news.
> Gowon always listens to our 6 o'clock and watches our 9.30. So people
> here watch us, news can decide the future of WNBS. (Chief Sub-editor,
> WNBS)

> There's no pressure, but we are self-censored. In the past three or four
> years there have been no clashes. We know what to do; we have a stake
> in the country as much as anyone. (Assistant Director News, NBC)

Anticipatory self-censorship is a diffuse awareness of a special audience occasionally sharpened by a phone call from Dodan Barracks or the military governor's office. It is spoken of as a 'presence'; 'we all understand the rules of the game'. Of course many regard this as a fair and reasonable situation; 'the government provide the money; why should they give us money to attack them?' Others give this argument a more subtle line. 'NBC is not a government mouthpiece, we just try to serve the nation. What we have is self-censorship fashioned by patriotism.' (Editor, NBC r)

Accommodation also takes the form of raising the threshold between acceptable and unacceptable pressure. A stoic shrug of the shoulders replaces the indignant rejoinder, and what might once have been an affront to the code of journalistic independence drawn from the liberal 'fourth estate' theory of the press, is accepted as yet another hazard of professional life. 'We're as free as anything compared to other radio stations. We can criticise any state government. Of course people have been taken by the police, but we still do it.' (Reporter, RTK)

Far from extinguishing the fourth estate theory such practices prompt its frequent acclamation. There is, too, an important sense in which government direction is seen not to be an invalid pressure on journalism, and that is in the notion of purposive 'journalism for development' which we shall examine in Chapter 6.

Swedish journalists felt themselves protected from government interference by their own autonomy within broadcasting and by the publicity which any government action would inevitably attract. Internal autonomy had proved important in two cases where the directorate at SR had tried to restrict news coverage, apparently at the insistence of government ministers. The first case came to be known as the 'Malta crisis' as the new Director-General was on holiday there at the time. TV Nytt had carried an advance report on the coming Swedish Budget. Despite the regularity with which such leaks occur, the Finance Minister protested to the Director-General who attempted to put an embargo on any further discussion of budget news prior to publication. Having advanced the decentralisation of SR's organisation the government found itself hoist by its own petard, unable to transmit pressure effectively via SR executives to news programmes. This was seen again during coverage of a major story involving a dramatic seige of a bank vault in which an escaped criminal was holding several people hostage. In the face of protests from the authorities the Director-General attempted to outlaw direct interviews with the criminals, but his demands were ignored by news staff who had not previously conducted such interviews. Both these cases suggest the raising of issues merely to prevent the journalists winning by default.

As in Nigeria, journalists were quick to point to their own autonomy relative to the subservience of others. Rapport staff pointed at the leadership of the CND in this way. Also, as in Nigeria, the problem was conceived mostly in terms of organisational politics. There had been some fears that, as a former trade union official, the new Director-General would bind SR more closely into the Social Democratic establishment. Most news staff felt this didn't matter. As one senior executive put it, 'some people in SR may be responsive, but they do not make the programmes'.

Ireland is a particularly interesting case in that, during our research period, journalists were operating under the unusual circumstances of a specific directive, Section 31 of the Broadcasting Act, as described in Chapter 4. As a very obvious, much discussed intervention by government in the production of news, this contentious directive had enormous impact on the extent to which journalists thought about governmental constraint, whatever its actual result in terms of changed news emphases or restricted output.

Journalists were divided on Section 31, and by and large those opposed to its activation saw it as having much impact on news coverage, while those who accepted or supported the directive felt it had had little impact anyway. Even those opposed to the directive saw its effect as indirect, in that its lack of clarity promoted indecision, caution and timorousness, at least at executive level. In turn, this became self-censorship as journalists fought shy of continually arguing the case for ignoring or infringing the directive, a fruitless and often wearying cause. Of those who supported the directive, many felt it a sensible and necessary limitation, which merely codified actions any responsible journalism would have sanctioned anyway.

> There is subversion of a serious order afoot in the country. RTE is not an evil hovering above the country just watching – it is part of the community. With due regard for journalistic standards RTE cannot ignore the position where activities of this sort are involved. Section 31 might be a bit crude, but I don't think any person of goodwill will have any trouble obeying it. (Political correspondent, RTE)

The logic has, of course, an honourable pedigree, back to Lord Reith's famous dictum at the time of the 1926 General Strike in England, that 'since the BBC was a national institution and since the Government in this crisis were acting for the people ... the BBC was for the Government' (see Tracey, 1977, Ch. 8). Whether in being 'for the Government', or in representing 'people of goodwill' against subversive elements in the community the broadcasting institution is promoting values and interests more sectional than they at first appear, is a problem we will return to in the concluding chapter. As a theory invoked for support of Section 31, this argument was widely canvassed at RTE in the months after the directive was introduced.

> I always believed that we were going to run into trouble because of what I believed was over-exposure of subversive elements. I don't feel constrained by Section 31. I would not go out of my way to cover the IRA. Anybody whose stated policy is to overthrow the government by violence and who won't put up candidates and present them to the people, etc., cuts himself off from the democratic press. (News Editor, RTE)

> I agreed with Section 31 in the national interest – a fair directive. I would cease to agree with it if the people against whom it was directed showed

an interest in local or national elections to get over their point of view ...
I think RTE has had every opportunity under the Broadcasting Act to
pursue the objectives of a civilised broadcasting organisation in a
modern democracy ... (Sub-Editor, RTE)

The main impact of Section 31 was probably to energise a debate
about RTE's constitutional obligations, a debate which, for many
journalists, led fairly steadily to the conclusion that the BBC model was
a more enticing ideal than ever before. In part, this was born of a desire to
reach what appeared an idyllic state of mature trust and mutual co-
operation between broadcasters and politicians in Britain, compared to
what many perceived as either degrading subservience or hot-tempered
feuding in the Republic. This was tempered, however, by a growing
scepticism about the BBC's coverage of Ulster at this time. More
significant was the comparatively minor impact of Section 31 on actual
daily practice in the newsroom. Of far greater importance was the
remoulding of news practices and routines enforced by the general
demands of covering the situation in Ulster.

Big news stories often stimulate quantum leaps in resources available
to newsrooms. The All-Africa Games in Lagos, for example, were used
as a lever by NBC to extract money for facilities. Many Irish journalists
were grateful to the growth of 'the North' story for expanding Ulster
news gathering facilities. An RTE office was opened in Belfast in late
1969 to ease the pressure on rather ad hoc studio facilities there and in
Derry. As one sub-editor put it, 'when this thing is over we will have
extended our organisation'. Many saw this as a boost for sadly neglected
provincial news generally, that when trouble subsided in the North RTE
would be left with a heightened awareness of provincial news. Others,
however, felt it had killed provincial news. 'The north has made bulletins
more interesting. A lot of the material that would normally have gone
into the bulletins before – a lot of provincial cameramen have bitten the
dust.' (Sub-editor, RTE)

More elevating was the sense of having discovered a world story.
Suddenly RTE had news to offer EVN; it was at the centre of world
journalistic attention. This provided more genuine satisfaction than
simply the rewards available to Irish journalists 'stringing' for American
networks, newspapers or for agencies. For many it was a journalistic
promotion to the big league. 'For $2\frac{1}{2}$ years news became something it
hadn't been for 10 years – a worldwide situation on the doorstep within
easy reach.'

The most obvious result was the firm establishment of the radio 'News
at 1.30'. Also it convinced reporters of their ability to beat the world,
'until BBC and ITV brought their big guns in'. The North became *the*
story and: 'we were almost able to salve our conscience about the way we
covered affairs in the south by our good performance in the North'.
(Reporter, RTE)

For some, at least until the novelty wore off and strains began to develop in 1972–3, the effect was euphoric:

In a way I have got to like the place – it's new, it's exciting – there is a shortage of news down here – there is little worthwhile to report in Ireland generally – but this has now put us in the centre of things – after all it is the only thing that really matters in our history. (News cameraman, RTE)

Rarely is the journalist so aware of being a primary witness of history in the making. The same heightened awareness is created at elections when the full, splendid gladiatorial spectacle of party politics is whipped up by the media ringmasters to convey the excitement of instant political history.

Coverage of the North gradually took its toll and the strains on technology, personnel and organisation intensified, while audiences, it was felt, were less and less attracted and held by events to which they had become hardened and indifferent. The strain on reporters covering the north was partly one of numbers, there just weren't enough to cover the story. 'It's a month now [November 1973] since we had a staff crew in Derry for more than a day or so.' 'We're too few people and we daren't leave Belfast empty.'

The strain also derived from the sheer physical and mental pressures of working in the North. A cameraman's car was blown up and many staff were individually threatened. The news staff fought for extra leave, special allowances and the like, but the strain still existed. Duty periods were evolved which were more like military rotas than anything else, and new insurance facilities can have been of little comfort. Within RTE the expansion of news and the high earnings news staff sometimes made from northern assignments occasionally earned resentment. Some felt that 'all they do is make a few phone calls from the office or the nearest hotel'. 'Coverage of the North for reporters means ringing up the British Army every hour for the casualty list and the shot list'. Many journalists felt the strains were not only in gathering the news. Sub-editors talked of the enormous responsibilities, knowing that news selection may provoke social responses of alarming kinds.

Some pointed to the irony that there was now a vision link between Dublin and Belfast but none between Dublin and the Republic's second city, Cork. The North threw up the conflict between the 'hard news' men and those who saw the situation as an exemplary case demanding interpretative journalism and explanation. The 'hard news' men were very suspicious of the Northern correspondent, 'not a real journalist', who specialised in speculative summaries of northern political developments. The others saw the endless catalogue of minor skirmishes as a sad trivialisation of news.

Far from distorting news values, it could be argued that the form and content of coverage of the six counties were a natural result of their application. News gathering was conducted in difficult circumstances and the consequent emphases on the immediate, accessible and dramatic stories were inevitable. So too is the emphasis on the visible, if mundane, activities of a few political leaders.

> The news is there in the North, under-reported if anything. It is under-reported because reporters find it difficult to cover for reasons of personal safety. You can report the politics – the activities of big political figures. Access to both sides is a problem for all organisations. (Sub-editor, RTE)

Similarly emphasised, as this last quote indicates, is the traditional concern to get 'both sides of the story' – IRA/British Army: Protestant/Catholic. This was a very immediate reporting problem and a major preoccupation. In general, it seems, both from our observation and in the view of the journalists involved, that the major impact of the north on Irish journalists was not through the imposition of legislative inhibitions, but the steady erosion of normal practice by the pressures of routine news gathering in Ulster. The net effect was to reassert some traditional news values and to provoke discussion of others.

In all three countries government intervention and control either seem less important, as determinants of broadcast journalism, than the values by which the job is conducted, and exert their effect through the distortion or amplification of news values.

Summary

In this chapter we have described the process by which news is produced. Our description suggests broadcast journalism is by no means random reaction to random events. On the contrary, it is a highly regulated and routine process of manufacturing a cultural product on an electronic production line. In stages of planning, gathering, selection and production broadcast news is moulded by the demands of composing order and organisation within a daily cycle. The news is made, and like any other product it carries the marks of the technical and organisational structure from which it emerges. In the following chapter we examine the results of this moulding on the product itself.

Chapter 6

The contents of broadcast news

We have seen how decisions are made, explicitly or by default, about what should be included in news bulletins. Equally we have seen how the inevitable limits of news gathering and processing impose restraints on what is available for inclusion, and also on what is likely to be chosen. In this chapter we describe the findings of our research into the resulting product; a content analysis of the output of each of the news departments during our first two periods of observation.[1] The analysis includes both radio and television news at NBC and SR, and in addition the television news of RTK. At the end of the chapter we also summarise the findings of our analysis of Eurovision news exchange material, and of Visnews.

The structure of broadcast news

Broadcast news is brief and highly structured. Like any other part of broadcasting it is a programme; a cultural construct reflecting the organisation of its manufacture and the presumed demands of its expected audience. The first limit in the construction of news programmes is that of time. The transcript of an average news bulletin, as is frequently observed, would rarely cover more than a half a page even in a moderately prose-laden newspaper. In order to include a reasonable number of stories in a bulletin brevity is essential. The length of news stories in our sample was on average 49.6 seconds on RTK and 16.1 seconds on NBC radio. Both NBC TV and RTE averaged just over 67 seconds, while TV Nytt maintained a much higher average of 114 seconds. Dagens Echo sustained an average of 80 seconds. (See Table 6.1.)

Naturally these averages conceal considerable variations. There is some tendency, though by no means a uniform one, for domestic politics to consume larger periods of time than other stories. By and large, however, the amount of air time given to a story seems to depend far less on its subject matter than on its mode of presentation. Particularly where film is available, stories become longer and the presence of a reporter on the spot, the availability of an interview, or other elaborations of presentation all contribute directly to the length of a story, regardless of its subject matter. Table 6.1 illustrates this point.

With the exception of Rapport these figures reflect the universal belief that 'talking heads are death' on television. Where no technical props are available stories are kept very much shorter, whereas film, or the less common coup of a studio interview, stretch the length of the story and in turn its implied importance. Most stories are kept technically simple. We calculated the number of discrete technical elements (i.e. a unit of film, an interview, voice-link, etc.) in each story as a measure of complexity and only Rapport achieved an average of well over two elements per story (3.6 in fact).

Table 6.1 Length of stories presented with differing technical resources (averages in seconds)

	NBC TV	RTK	RTE	TV Nytt	Rapport
Headlined	n.a.	n.a.	139.2	300.1	291.5
Newscaster only	30.5	30.4	21.3	135.2	254.1
Reporter on film/tape	n.a.	n.a.	142.3	253.7	291.3
Reporter in Studio	83.4	103.7	236.7	349.8	274.7
Studio interview	n.a.	n.a.	311.0	373.5	290.0
Film interview	73.1	0	112.5	241.3	281.7
Actuality film	99.1	93.9	128.4	226.4	290.1
Average length all stories	67.4	49.6	67.1	114.2	261.3

In order to create interest and to increase comprehensibility two types of narrative structure are often employed in news bulletins. The first comes from the journalistic textbooks and is usually referred to as the 'inverted pyramid'. This is a written style in which the major, attention-grasping fact is placed at the head of the story, the secondary facts next, and finally background elaboration to form the base of the pyramid. Though essentially derived from newspaper practice this was still felt in most newsrooms to be correct usage. News stories are, as the phrase implies, stories. They have narrative structures borrowed from other television forms. Epstein has suggested a range of such structures in common newsroom use. These story models, as he terms them, include the dialectical model, presenting positions pro and con, and the ironic; that is, the adoption of a tone of distanced scepticism to avoid polemic involvement (Epstein, 1973, Ch. 5). Green (1969) has made the general observation that 'the news broadcast is a show because it must be structured in accordance with the same psychological principles which determine the structure of a stage play, a motion picture, or perhaps more precisely, a variety entertainment show ... it must be a calculated blend of news and personality, presented as a pattern designed to hold the attention and interest of the audience'.

Narrative structures are also employed in a second way by thematically linking disparate stories to one another in an attempt to shape the miscellany of a bulletin into a news programme. Because of the technical and logistic difficulties faced by Nigerian media this sometimes produced rather odd conjunctions: 'The Japanese Prime

Minister is to visit the United States following a period of strained relations between the two countries, and in Thailand a smooth takeover of power by the army-backed revolutionary party.'

Thus quite distinct issues with similar labels are reduced to comparable aspects of the same problem. In Sweden the importation of pigs from China and Ethiopia, butter smuggling, and drink and driving in France, were grouped together as problems connected with the regulation of trade in the EEC. This same clustering technique can use geography as the thematic link, relating separate stories about the United States, for example, in sequence. The United Nations also serves this function, as for example in a sequence on Swedish radio dealing with the crisis in the Middle East and Rhodesia in terms of forthcoming UN debates. These linkages have a clear stylistic purpose, smoothing the joins in the essentially scissors and paste construction of a bulletin. In addition they supply implicit context and form by hinting incidentally at relationships between events.

An implicit context is also supplied by the varying prominence and display given to different types of story. News programmes provide for their audiences a series of cues about the importance of the news they are presenting. A longer item seems more serious than a brief one; the occasional event of extraordinary importance may explode normal boundaries, occupying half or even all of a bulletin, signalling that it is an occasion of unusual portent. A second cue is item order, the linear packaging of a bulletin providing a temporal metaphor for newspaper conventions. What comes first is what matters most, later on come the 'inside pages', at the end is light relief. Further high-lighting is provided in some news organisations by the use of aural headlines, brief capsule announcements of the main stories of the day given at the start of the bulletin. An additional cue that a story is significant is provided by the evident commitment of resources; the use of film or other visual aids, expansion on the story by a reporter in the studio, or the use of a reporter on the spot. All these indicate to the audience stories of particular note whose importance merits the use of such resources or is signalled by it. Table 6.2, which shows the ways in which different types of story are treated, and Table 6.3, which shows what kinds of story receive which types of treatment, suggest the pattern these implicit contexts follow.

Most readily apparent is the centrality of politics, both domestic and international. In Nigeria lack of local political coverage shifts the focus to visible diplomacy and its related trappings. On NBC radio 31 per cent of headlined stories were of this kind. Film stories (the ubiquitous Visnews) shared this emphasis. On NBC-TV 20 per cent of film stories were in this category and on RTK 29 per cent. Table 6.2 shows that on Dagens Echo 63 per cent of political stories merited a headline, while on RTE political stories were nearly three times as likely to get the detailed attention of a reporter in the studio or on the spot (usually the Dail) as any other type of story. Most of this attentiveness to politics concerns

Table 6.2 Presentation of different types of story

Percentage* of each type of story which: column (a) are headlined.
column (b) had actuality film.
column (c) had a reporter on film (or tape) or in the studio

	NBC TV†	NBC R‡	RTK†		RTE			TV Nytt			Rapport			Dagens Echo‡	
	(b)	(a)	(b)	(c)	(a)	(b)	(c)	(a)	(b)	(c)	(a)	(b)	(c)	(a)	(c)
Political – domestic	44	23	15	4	37	21	30	38	62	60	67	58	75	63	49
Political – internat.	47	37	26	6	21	21	5	14	38	32	86	50	88	45	27
Economic	28	32	10	0	23	54	27	46	33	46	67	67	33	43	30
Industrial	100	32	12	0	27	46	24	16	28	26	50	58	92	28	23
Agriculture	11	17	18	0	38	63	38	20	60	40	63	88	75	67	67
Technology	73	50	56	0	0	50	0	31	77	62	100	100	100	55	27
Military	59	50	29	11	12	23	11	50	65	40	100	33	100	39	23
Education	37	5	28	0	10	70	10	25	34	38	100	50	100	0	0
Culture	89	29	29	0	0	50	13	20	0	40	100	100	100	30	20
Religion	78	30	22	0	67	0	33	100	0	100	100	100	100	0	0
Crime/legal	36	17	9	0	15	27	6	19	38	14	67	50	83	39	24
Sport	45	7	47	0	0	60	0	9	37	5	100	50	50	7	2
Welfare	67	18	33	0	14	57	29	63	0	88	91	91	100	21	29
Tragedy/disaster	45	17	44	0	18	36	9	8	38	15	100	100	100	30	30
Human interest	36	0	50	0	0	100	0	0	50	100	0	0	0	0	0

Notes: † No headlining system used.
‡ Radio programmes, no film.
*Percentage rounded to nearest whole figure.

Table 6.3 Presentation of different story types

Percentage* of all (a) headline stories
(b) film stories
(c) stories using reporter on film or tape or in studio in each story category.

	NBC TV	NBC R	RTK		RTE			TV Nytt			Rapport			Dagens	Echo
	(b)	(a)	(b)	(c)	(a)	(b)	(c)	(a)	(b)	(c)	(a)	(b)	(c)	(a)	(c)
	8	10	10	15	35	13	39	23	19	27	23	24	22	24	27
Political – domestic															
Political – internat.	20	31	29	38	11	7	3	8	11	14	20	13	17	19	17
Economic	3	13	7	8	7	10	11	13	5	10	3	3	1	10	10
Industrial	6	9	2	8	11	13	13	8	7	10	9	12	13	9	11
Agriculture	1	2	2	8	3	4	5	2	2	2	7	12	7	2	2
Technology	7	5	6	0	0	1	0	5	6	7	1	2	1	5	5
Military	9	5	8	15	8	10	8	12	8	7	8	3	7	10	9
Education	4	2	6	8	1	5	2	2	8	7	3	2	4	0	0
Culture	5	4	2	0	0	3	2	2	4	3	3	3	4	2	2
Religion	5	5	2	0	2	0	1	1	0	2	1	2	1	0	0
Crime/legal	7	6	2	0	16	19	7	6	5	3	5	4	7	12	11
Sport	9	2	9	0	0	2	0	9	17	4	3	2	1	2	1
Welfare	8	5	4	0	2	5	6	7	10	6	13	16	14	2	4
Tragedy disaster	4	1	7	0	4	6	3	2	3	2	1	2	1	3	3
Human interest	4	0	4	0	0	2	0	0	1	2	0	0	0	0	0

*Percentages rounded to nearest whole figure. Column totals = 100%.

the affairs of the medium's own country; the internal political affairs of foreign countries receive only cursory treatment. Occasionally, however, the stops are pulled out for major events.

The Swedish news departments were particularly sensitive to the criticism that television news skated along the surface of events, providing no background and explanation. In general there was an aim to give the foreign staff time to comment on new developments overseas on which the audience would lack contextual information, as for example when the 1971 coup occurred in Thailand, or when Brandt's *Ostpolitik* became an important issue in the West German Elections. Beyond that TV Nytt introduced a series of longer, avowedly educational pieces designed to bring the viewer up to date on some subject which was or would be news. For example, when China joined the UN they carried a series of lengthy pieces on recent Chinese history to compensate for the lack of regular news coverage in the past. In view of the discussion about Sweden's possible entry into the EEC, they carried similar pieces on the structure and function of the Common Market. These pieces were usually hung on some news peg in the day's bulletin but were quite clearly intended to be background education rather than news, and so were a matter of some controversy in the department. RTE similarly carried an item on Vietnam introduced as 'an historical background to the Vietnam conflict'. This was compiled by a freelance attached to the newsroom and lasted just over three minutes. It exemplified two currents of thought in the Irish newsroom, the belief of the Head of News in serious discursive news, and the general but seldom satisfied yearning to cover foreign items other than from London or Belfast. Such background pieces were normally reserved for dutiful summaries from the Belfast desk of recent events in Ulster. Rapport was unusual in devoting film and reportorial resources to a wider range of stories, and in dealing with stories in depth.

A third element of structure is that provided by news-pegs and news angles. News-pegs are solid newsworthy events on which to hang whatever material is being considered for inclusion. This may lead to items being included simply to provide such a peg, as the 'softer' elaboration is not of sufficient news value to merit inclusion by itself. The longer stories were often of this kind, arising from the preparation of a background piece or its accidental availability (e.g. from Visnews in Nigeria), and the subsequent search for a story to which it could be appended. What the news could not be was an analytical piece with no news-peg. The admission of China to the UN was such a news-peg in our period, and prompted long (i.e. several minutes) items on the background to the event, its significance as an example of the changing configuration of international relations and the state of China in general.

The news angle is a journalistic device for converting raw material into a story. Where the news-peg device is the use of a news event to justify lengthier explication, the news angle is used to inject news-worthiness into an event which has failed to live up to its news potential.

Many predictable events which are routinely defined as news require shaping round a focal point of interest whose detection and elevation to prominence are rated key skills of journalism. Common examples come from speeches by major political figures. The fact that they have spoken is not in itself news and the speech has to be searched for a novel or startling pronouncement, a 'revelation', or key dictum to provide the story. Aware of this, political figures themselves highlight such elements in their speeches with an eye to journalistic requirements. A simple example was a story on NBC radio coming from a Federal Information Service release about the visit of the Commissioner for Mines and Power to the Red Cross Annual National First Aid and Home Nursing Competition. The story was buttressed by the appearance in it of a Federal Commissioner and the authority of the FIS. His formal and conventional words at the gathering were, by normal journalistic standards, totally unnewsworthy. But a headline and angle were eventually created from his incidental remarks on the need for more training for voluntary services. Thus a story was created, and, in both senses, news was made.

A further important aspect of story structure is the use of vocabulary. For example, a story which described Fidel Castro's tour of Chile was at one level being purely descriptive when it told that 'President Castro meets students and joins them in chanting slogans . . .'; but at another level it is evaluating the situation: chanting slogans is the senseless act of fanatics or manipulated mobs; chanting connotes mindless repetition, slogans are vacuous war-cries used in lieu of serious political thought. An RTE story about street fighting began, 'In Belfast, there was a gun battle this afternoon between British troops and civilians.' It is unlikely that a British medium would have used the word 'civilians' there with its heavy connotation of innocent victims, rather than 'gunmen' or some other label implying legitimate target of military aggression (see Elliott, 1977). In Sweden the NDP in Germany were characterised, by way of explanation, as the New Nazis. Newsmen in SR reported that as the government had taken a more anti US line on South Vietnam so they had been allowed to use less favourable terms to describe their actions in the war, e.g. 'terror bombing' of the north instead of just 'bombing'.

Labels and phrases readily express the assumptions and understandings behind the journalistic view of the world. Stereotyping is a further aspect of this, a categorisation by fiat which draws on an unarticulated set of concepts and beliefs about people and processes. The cold-war vision of East–West relations, for example, persists in news agency coverage of kremlinology which continues to influence coverage of East European affairs. Typical was an NBC story, one of very few indeed on Russia or East Europe, on the seizure of an underground journal by the KGB. The 'just what you'd expect in such a country' selection and tone of, particularly the American agencies, stereotypes what little coverage there is of these regions. In European media, stereotypes of life and customs in foreign parts play a large part in the treatment of stories from the third world. Excitable mobs of Latin Americans, exotic primitives in Africa, incomprehensible mystics in the East continue to populate news bulletins, not because of any malicious intent to perpetuate pernicious myths, but in an innocent attempt to render usable and comprehensible the range of data which is the raw materials of news.

Many journalistic assumptions and understandings are shared with the audience, and linguistic usage is a good example of this. Connotations and implicit explanations lie embedded in a syntax and vocabulary which is redolent of a rich set of conventional usages. In Ireland, for example, the appended phrase 'the accused refused to recognise the court' at the end of a brief court story identifies the defendant as a member of the IRA. Similar understandings are shown in such stories as a civil rights march in Ballyhaunis which ended: 'The organisers of today's rally – called the New Ireland Peace Rally – say it could be one of the most significant events in the West since 1879 ... (Pause and Out).' The deep folk memory of the Irish audience is often tapped in this way as in another film story on a march in the North whose commentary began 'And as the Orangemen went on parade the familiar tunes were heard again. ...' Tone and language can, in this indirect way, provide unintended, or at least implicit contexts for baldly narrative material.

The contexts given to stories may be either explicit or implicit. Implicit contexts place a story institutionally by association, or explain its importance by allusion. For example, RTE coverage of rent strikes in Ballyhaunis always linked the story to industrial strike news by placing it next in the bulletin, or by a linking phrase 'and in Ballyhaunis'. The rent strike was thus given context by implication and displayed as an event of the same order, and therefore having the same aura of undesirable militancy as the industrial strike. Explicit contexts, other than actual explanation by a correspondent or reporter, can derive from many of the processes already discussed. A headline, for example, may capture tersely the context of the story it heralds, such as the Swedish story which started with the question 'Are we all equal before the law?' before reporting a decision of the ombudsman in a case involving public transport in Stockholm.

A final aspect of broadcast news structure is that of the visual elements in bulletins. We have shown how the availability and quality of film significantly influenced the choice, priority and length of items. There have been few significant attempts to analyse the visual symbolism of television news and our own analysis is almost entirely concerned with texts, although shot lists, and in Sweden and Ireland videotapes, were used for the analysis. Gaye Tuchman has attempted to analyse what she calls the 'technology of objectivity' (Tuchman, 1973a). She argues that newsmen draw on cinematic conventions to reinforce visually role definitions, while at the same time drawing on sets of rules and technical procedures which guarantee objectivity. Most important of these rules is the use of a fixed, head-on camera position for interviews, statements, press conferences and the like. She suggests also that a certain discrete distance between camera and object suggests detachment. That is, physical distance suggests social distance. Comment of this kind has focussed on the interview. Gelles (1971) has written of the construction of television interviews, and emphasises the technological constraints which shape the presentation of interviewees. Much of such writing tends to impute too self-conscious a motivation to newsmen in the planning of interviews. For example, the status of an interviewee is implicit in his or her presentation. High status interviewees will be seen in the respectable surrounds of their office, and in the quiet formality of the interview can establish their status. Low status interviewees will often be presented in busier locales – they have no command over territory to use for interviewing; they are being interviewed, not granting an interview. Yet this has more to do with the pragmatics of production than any intent to present status differentially. Some confirmation of Tuchman's observations come from a study by Frank which used coders' observations of different presentation of political figures to measure the way in which different shots give a more or less favourable impression; tight shots seemed warmer, more favourable, and so on (Frank, 1973; see also Baggaley and Duck, 1976).

A variety of visual techniques contribute to the presentation of prominence or contexts. For example, a strike by workers at the Waterford gas plant was illustrated by a still of a housewife at a cooker. The visual definition was of the strike as a cause of domestic hardship for tens of thousands of families waiting for a hot meal. This common emphasis in strike stories on the harmful effects of the strike and its status as a social problem frequently receives comment (Glasgow, 1976; Hartmann, 1976). Visual back-ups of this kind serve as expressive cues as to what a story is 'really' about.

Table 6.4 Modes of presentation – all stories (%)

	NBC TV	RTK	RTE	TV Nytt	Rapport
Headlined	*	*	21.3	18.7	76.0
Newscaster only	34.3	71.3	32.2	78.7	61.5
Reporter on film	*	0	5.1	15.9	53.1
Reporter in studio	1.4	4.1	10.2	9.8	32.3
Studio interview	0	0	8.2	2.3	2.1
Film interview	2.0	0	25.6	17.9	62.5
Actuality film	45.5	24.6	22.2	33.1	71.9
Stills – people	12.6	†	15.1	22.8	29.2
Other stills	3.1	†	7.1	14.4	43.8
Map	1.1	†	2.4	12.7	28.1
Voice link	*	*	0	2.9	2.1

Notes: Totals will exceed 100 per cent since more than one form of presentation may be used per story.
*Technique not used or not technically available.
†Information not available as analysis not based on production study.

Film, especially visually arresting film, is the most likely aid to technological lapel grabbing. Table 6.4 summarises the modes of presentation used on stories in our sample. Frequently the time devoted to stories or their inclusion at all, will be directly determined by film quality. In Sweden a demonstration by artists, and another involving a kite display, were of this type, while stories about the Indo-Pakistan war dramatically lengthened when graphic film of the fighting filtered through. At the other extreme, lack of presentational back-up often shortens a story to near incomprehensibility, as for example an announcement in Sweden that Japan had decided to upvalue the Yen by some undisclosed amount on a date yet to be decided, according to Reuters Bureau in Tokyo. Similarly, in Nigeria just 18 seconds were devoted to the announcement that Portugal had promised new autonomous power to its colonial territories. Lack of film and research facilities rather than ignorance of the potential significance of this story for an African audience kept it brief to the point of obscurity.

The Nigerian media are particularly prey to the tyranny of film in this way because of their complete reliance on Visnews for foreign news film. A desire to emphasise the importance of some foreign stories is often frustrated by the lack of related film with which to do so. Consequently relationships between story and film become uncomfortably tenuous. A story about the meeting of the East African Economic Community in Nairobi for example was illustrated by the only East African film around at the time, a story about a Salvation Army rally in Kenya. In the long term the use of the more visually exciting aspects of news may have a cumulative impact on the way particular social relationships and institutions are perceived. A content analysis of industrial relations news on British television has suggested that an emphasis on 'photogenic discord' creates an impression of industrial relations which suggests irrational, violent, and discordant elements in trade-union behaviour (Glasgow, 1976, p. 127).

Social process in broadcast news

To understand the picture of social process provided by broadcast news we need to examine the events which are chosen for inclusion. The first point to note is that news is indeed about events rather than process. The Spanish philosopher Ortega y Gassett had a healthy contempt for journalists, 'one of the least cultured types in contemporary society', a view based in part on what he saw as the journalist's inability to deal with process.

> . . . the journalist's profession leads him to understand by the reality of the
> times that which creates a passing sensation, regardless of what it is,
> without any heed for perspective or architecture. Real life, is, certainly,
> purely of the present; but the journalist deforms this truism when he

reduces the present to the momentary and the momentary to the sensational (Ortega y Gassett, 1944, p. 98).

Table 6.5 Anticipatory and follow-up stories (as percentage of all stories)

	Anticipatory	Follow-up
NBC TV	8.7	14.4
NBC R	5.8	8.7
RTK	10.1	9.8
RTE	3.6	16.2
Dagens Echo	5.7	19.9
TV Nytt	7.8	15.3
Rapport	12.5	23.9

News is essentially a topping-up mechanism, a means of adding to areas of defined interest and importance the latest incremental happenings within them which become apparent. The very periodicity of news demands a daily supply of discrete times with which to construct a news bulletin. Some temporal continuity is achieved by including stories about the build up to forthcoming events, or alternatively stories about the aftermath of events that have already taken place. Table 6.5 shows that such anticipatory or follow-up items were fairly common. Anticipatory stories tend to be notices of forthcoming meetings or formal events dug out of the diary when news is scarce. They both feed off predefinitions of newsworthiness and also guarantee it by inducting events into the news before they occur. Follow-ups tend to reflect continuity of coverage rather than continuity of the social process being observed. The commitment of resources, particularly manpower, to a story requires returns in kind – two or three days worth of stories. Nearly a quarter of stories produced by Rapport were of this kind. The Rapport policy of providing more background to make events intelligible tended to show itself in providing more run-up stories to elections and other predictable events overseas, and follow-up stories to domestic events in greater detail than the other programmes. 'Background' in this context tends to mean a summary of recent related stories, compilation rather than analysis. A background story on the Anglo-Rhodesian talks, for example, was a narration of previous meetings rather than a discussion of the social sources of tension and dissension within Rhodesia. Particularly is this true where lack of staff or other resources prevent the luxury of library research or time to prepare. But the important point to note is that it is this definition of what kind of material serves to provide 'depth' or 'background' rather than the unavailability of resources to provide such perspectives that it is the prime limitation to explanation.

What kinds of events, then, appear in the news?

Table 6.6 shows the main categories of story which appear in the news. Most immediately striking is the prominence of political stories, both national and international. But what kind of political actions are being conveyed to news audiences? International relations appear

Table 6.6 Main story types by subject categories (%)

	NBC TV	NBC radio	RTK	RTE	TV Nytt	Dagens Echo	Rapport
Political – domestic	9.7	11.3	14.3	18.9	14.4	14.2	24.2
Politics – internat.	20.7	21.4	25.1	9.4	14.4	16.2	17.2
Economic	5.5	10.2	8.8	5.8	6.9	8.7	4.0
Industrial	2.7	6.9	4.7	8.3	12.6	12.5	13.1
Agricultural	2.7	2.2	3.0	1.8	1.4	0.9	9.1
Technological	4.6	2.2	2.5	0.4	3.7	3.2	1.0
Military	6.7	2.2	5.8	12.8	5.7	9.0	6.1
Education	5.8	7.6	5.0	2.2	2.3	1.4	2.0
Cultural	2.7	2.5	1.9	1.8	1.4	2.9	2.0
Religion	2.7	3.6	2.2	0.7	0.3	0	1.0
Crime/legal	9.4	8.4	6.3	20.7	6.1	11.0	6.1
Sport	8.8	5.1	4.4	1.4	22.9	12.5	2.0
Welfare	5.5	6.2	2.5	3.1	2.3	4.1	11.1
Tragedy/disaster	3.3	2.2	4.1	4.9	3.7	2.9	1.0
Human interest	3.8	0	1.7	0.2	0.6	0	0
Other	5.8	8.0	7.7	7.6	1.3	0.5	0
Total	100	100	100	100	100	100	100
N	329	275	363	445	348	345	99

largely as the meeting at top level of major political actors, a personalised encapsulation of diplomacy concentrating on the public and symbolic trappings of multi-national politics. The Swedish media appear less prone to this, giving more attention to other aspects. Many Swedish journalists wanted to replace conventional 'visits and meetings' news with stories which would be more informative about life in other countries. They were limited, however, both by the supply of stories through Eurovision which tended to be of the conventional type and by a feeling that they could not ignore the activities of heads of states, even if they ended up with conventional, uninformative news stories. The Nigerian picture is to some extent an artefact of presentation. Frequently a story which in the Nigerian bulletin is left baldly as a statement that A is visiting B might be embellished in better endowed newsrooms by extracting a statement or event on which to peg the film of the visit, thus forcing out a story from the unpromising material to hand.

Given the common criticism that news is unduly concerned with entertainment it is worth noting the infrequent inclusion of human interest items, those quirky stories about children, animals or simply the odd and the bizarre. Broadcast journalism differs markedly from press journalism on this point, particularly the style of the popular press, or what in Sweden was known as evening paper journalism. Broadcast journalism tends to be preoccupied with the type of news which William Randolph Hearst denigrated as 'merely important' as compared to the 'interesting', 'gee whizz' news which would attract the attention of a mass public. For various reasons broadcasting organisations, almost universally, have taken a serious view of their responsibilities in providing news. Some lighter, human interest items have been inserted with an eye to closing the news show and returning the audience smoothly to the remainder of the programme schedule. While the British media still seem to rely on this device it was far rarer in the three countries in this study, especially in the radio bulletins (Dagens Echo, NBC radio) as one would expect, and on RTE where the general sobriety of the news from Ulster could make such items tastelessly frivolous. The essentially visual character of television news has led to the adoption of sports items to perform this curtain-dropping function, in place of the more traditional journalistic rubric of 'human interest'. Sports items accounted for up to 23 per cent of all stories, with RTE again registering the low point, a result of deliberate policy.

A great deal of news is about what the American historian, Daniel Boorstin, calls the 'pseudo-event' (Boorstin, 1963, pp. 19–54), happenings he castigates for their 'synthetic novelty'. Boorstin argues that they signify a transference of responsibility from news gathering to newsmaking. But in an important sense news gathering is about the collection and processing of material made available by newsmakers. There's no need to wear a deaf-aid when some people are shouting: the pressurised newsroom is glad to receive material from the more vociferous and productive newsmakers.

Table 6.7 Type of action or event in story (%)

	NBC TV	NBC radio	RTK	RTE	Dagens Echo	TV Nytt	Rapport
Formal statement	6.8	6.8	5.5	7.8	10.4	6.2	1.8
Speech	14.7	15.8	22.4	15.7	11.6	9.9	9.7
Travel	9.9	10.0	10.3	3.7	4.6	4.5	4.4
Meeting/conference	9.2	14.0	8.9	9.0	11.6	10.4	6.2
Personnel change	3.0	1.8	3.7	1.0	2.8	3.0	2.7
Organisational change	3.3	8.6	7.2	1.4	3.8	5.7	10.6
Official report	3.3	2.5	1.4	3.9	3.3	4.3	11.5
Formal event	12.6	5.7	4.9	7.6	1.8	1.1	4.4
Other event	29.0	31.2	30.7	37.8	29.9	42.8	28.3
Violent mass action	3.3	0.4	2.3	5.5	8.1	6.2	5.3
Non-violent mass action	1.9	2.2	2.9	5.3	5.1	3.0	10.6
Other	3.0	1.1	0	1.2	7.1	2.9	4.4

These characteristics of news are summarised in Table 6.7. A very large proportion of news stories concern the prepackaged statements, press conferences and public meetings of publicity-seeking bodies. Statements are included because of the authority of their authors, particularly where they are able to expect or insist on such courteous coverage as in Nigeria. Thus the content or substance of the statement may have very little news value even in conventional terms.

The North-Eastern State Commissioner for Health and Social Welfare has urged nurses to exercise great patience and tolerance in dealing with the sick.

General Gowon has said that Nigeria will stand by any decision she arrives at on the Rhodesian issue.

This last example, quite meaningless in substance, nonetheless is obligatorily included because of its source. In general, this table illustrates the extent to which news is about the predictable and manageable, and also the extent to which it derives from material made available by authoritative sources in those arenas under observation. Commonly, 30 per cent or so of the stories were of this kind.

To a very large extent broadcast news is a fragmentation of reality, selecting those snippets of action which are drawn to its attention by groups and institutions with privileged access to the public ear. Social process becomes a missing dimension, quite impossible to reconstruct from the limited range of information elements daily provided in bulletins. A further important dimension of social description is that of power, and we can turn next to the way power appears in broadcast news.

Power in broadcast news

In looking at the events in broadcast news we have been seeing how news tells us what happens in the world. But it also tells us how and to whom. To examine the picture of power and influence provided by news we have taken three key issues. First, what kind of institutions are portrayed in broadcast news? Second, where do news events occur? Third, who are the characters portrayed in broadcast news?

Institutional definition

News creates an agenda of significant social events and issues, as can be seen in the analysis. This is achieved by a process of institutional definition, in which certain arenas of social life are selected as consistently worthy of journalistic attention, and certain among them are given priority. As we have seen, the agenda is headed by activities in the central political institutions of parties and governments. Often stories from other institutional spheres are referred back to these arenas for context and significance, as in the following item.

In London, the three-day sale of books from the Dublin library of King's Inns started at Sotheby's today, after thirty-eight lots out of more than eight hundred had been withdrawn. The books were withdrawn following objections to their sale outside this country ... The matter had been raised in the Dail last week. ...

The same tendency is repeated at international level by the prominence given to the conflict-resolving processes of the major powers and inter-governmental news-creating bodies like the UN. Stories about, for example, the anti-colonial fighting in Mozambique were consistently placed in the context of the more easily describable and accessible meetings of the UN decolonisation committee. Stories about conflict in the Middle-East or Africa become readily translated to ramifications of great power diplomacy.

Table 6.8 Domestic political stories
Giving a breakdown of the subjects of all stories dealing with politics within one country, whether that of the medium concerned or not. Totals may exceed 100 per cent because individual stories might deal with more than one subject area.

	NBC TV	NBC radio	RTK	RTE	Dagens Echo	TV Nytt	Rapport
Comment/statement	30.4	24.7	35.7	33.9	31.8	19.5	16.1
Legislation	2.4	4.9	1.0	4.9	3.5	3.2	3.6
Policy forming	3.8	5.5	5.6	9.3	14.9	22.3	21.4
Executive action	12.8	20.8	17.0	6.0	17.7	11.8	3.6
Opposition within legislative bodies	1.9	4.0	0.6	14.2	16.2	9.1	14.2
Other opposition	5.7	4.0	9.5	20.6	14.9	10.5	17.8
Power conflict	2.8	2.4	4.6	2.0	21.1	12.5	16.1
Elections	1.4	0.9	3.9	2.4	4.2	3.9	5.3
Change of government	0.9	2.4	2.9	0	3.5	2.7	0
Local/regional	5.7	19.9	6.8	20 2	4.2	3.2	5.3
Other	9.5	18.3	19.7	11.3	5.7	11.8	19.7

Executive action and comments or statements by political actors far outweigh other facets of politics, as Table 6.8 illustrates. Political process is very much less likely to register than the actions or pronouncements which periodically surface to signal particular developments. Focussing on personalities draws attention to the executive rather than the gradual formation of policy or legislation. This is particularly true of foreign news. In addition the politics of foreign countries is rarely covered unless there are international connotations to the event. Thus politics is essentially about the actions of domestic political elites and seems considerably less complex in other countries. Very little reporting deals with the political process in other countries in its own terms, in a way which would elucidate the balance of forces, and the course of political debate in that particular country. Reporting election campaigns and results provides one possibility for such coverage however. This emphasis on the visible activities of the executive has been noted by other content analysts. Frank's research on American network television news led him to conclude that 'overwhelming emphasis across all three networks was in covering "executive action" to the exclusion of judicial and legislative action' (Frank, 1973). Rositi, in an analysis of television news in four European countries, has also drawn attention to the focus on formal politics and the activities of executive elites. (Rositi, 1975, pp. 25–30).

All this is to define politics in a fairly conventional and confined way. Looking more broadly at politics as contention for power and influence in any institutional sphere there is a marked lack of news coverage of politics away from the central institutions of government and legislation. As we shall show further on, there is a surprising lack of financial and industrial elites in the lists of actors in news stories. This is paralleled by the emphasis in economic news on those aspects of the economy managed by the state. With the exception of Dagens Echo none of the media conveyed many news stories about financial affairs, while industrial news is primarily about industrial disputes. In Nigeria, where strikes, though present, are officially proscribed, this gap was filled by concern with the structure and state of industry, mostly in the form of official releases about production figures or the siting of new factories. In Sweden the ban on advertising in SR programmes also has the effect of making journalists suspicious of company announcements of new industrial developments as simply an attempt to publicise the company or its products.

Institutional prominence on the news agenda is directly the product of news production procedures. Because of its reliance on an emulation of Western news sources, Nigerian media replicate the agenda defined by those sources. The relative prominence of industry and agriculture is a case in point. News in Nigeria about the production of goods is almost entirely confined to the small industrial sector, while the productive activities and problems of 80 per cent of the population go unrecorded. The economy, to the extent that it appears on the agenda at all, is a relatively remote and unfamiliar one to most of the population.

The geography of news

By concentrating on some areas of the world and ignoring others the news creates a mental geography for its audience. This is particularly important given the frequent research finding that media material is particularly influential in topic areas about which the audience is comparatively ill-informed. Despite the increase in travel, most people spend most of their lives, and a large number all their lives, in their own country, and knowledge of foreign parts and peoples is derived almost entirely from the mass media. Of course impressions, stereotypes and understandings are created during the cursory exposure to geographic wisdom most people receive at school. But these are substantially nourished by media material, and perhaps most of all by the news.

News geography is a product of news history. News comes from places which are centres of news production, collection and distribution because historically they have been important for news audiences. Thus commercial centres, major trade posts in the colonial territories, and the major capitals of Western Europe and North America have always housed the majority of media and agency correspondents. It is the regular production of routine news from such 'news capitals', rather than the occasional production of news from 'news provinces', which draws the boundaries and shapes the contours of the news atlas.

Table 6.9 Location of news events
Percentage of all foreign news stories located in the following areas

	NBC TV	NBC radio	RTK	RTE	TV Nytt	Dagens Echo	Rapport
Supranational	5.7	10.1	3.7	2.4	4.7	3.3	0
W. Europe	13.6	12.7	10.3	75.3	40.2	42.8	70.8
USSR/E. Europe	6.0	5.5	2.7	2.6	8.1	8.9	3.1
Middle East	9.5	6.6	7.7	2.4	5.2	7.4	2.0
Africa	29.7	38.0	44.5	3.0	4.9	4.2	3.1
Asia	17.2	9.9	17.3	8.0	19.9	20.7	12.4
Cen./South America	2.8	2.1	4.2	0.6	2.8	1.7	4.2
USA	7.7	4.6	3.9	3.2	7.1	7.9	3.1
Other	2.8	0.1	2.4	0.8	1.2	1.4	1.3
Space	4.0	6.4	1.4	1.4	1.2	0.6	0
Multi	0	3.1	1.4	0	0	0	0
Unidentifiable	1.0	0.9	0.6	0.3	4.7	1.1	0

Table 6.9 gives a simple picture of this pattern. Latin America and Asia almost disappear off the map, but for the continuing interest in Vietnam (the two study periods included the US blockade of North Vietnamese ports, and the fall of Quang Tri) and the fighting between India and Pakistan in 1971. A good war is always news, and a continuing war, drawing the permanent commitment of resources, is a steady source of film material. Africa too is an invisible part of the globe for the European media, whose massive concentration on Western Europe reflects both the distribution of their own correspondents and the convenience and prominence of Eurovision material in the processing of foreign news. By contrast, roughly a third of the foreign stories in the Nigerian media were located in Africa, although of necessity they are forced to ignore most other areas of the developing world that might be of interest to their audiences. Because of the determined efforts in the Nigerian newsrooms to include as much African material as possible, the agency wires are scoured for suitable stories. The proportion of African stories is thus pushed up to a respectable proportion but at the expense of other news values – relevance, importance and so on. Thus comparatively trivial or meaningless items are included because they are African. The audience learnt simply, for example, that 'The President of Mali has sent messages of solidarity to President Nyerere of Tanzania and President Siaka Stevens of Sierra Leone.' A large proportion of the African stories in our period dealt with the visit to Rhodesia of the then British Foreign Secretary, Sir Alex Douglas-Home, and the announcement of the Anglo-Rhodesian settlement proposals. Without one or two major items like this, involving the interests of the agencies' major

customers in the developed world, African news is hard to come by, even in Nigeria.

When stories from these hidden areas do surface, it is because they satisfy criteria of news value other than their geographical or cultural proximity to the news medium. A major military clash, the death of a political leader or his overthrow in a dramatic coup will meet the bill. One of the few times South America appeared in our four weeks of Swedish news was in pictures of a bus crash in which 40 people died. The corollary of this is that such events will submerge as quickly as they surfaced. The death of Nkrumah, a giant on the African political scene, was just important enough to register in the bulletins of RTE but very quickly disappeared, while Nigerian newsrooms worked overtime to keep the story alive, in a desperate attempt to make the limited material at hand stretch to match the importance journalists there accorded the event.

Newsmen often have other explanations for the absence of news from particular areas, usually in terms of the problem of news collection. The foreign editor of the London *Times* has suggested that 'it is extremely difficult to cover Africa. Apart from the fact that there are so many countries, few of them have the political and social infrastructure necessary for the production of news'. This is a very clear statement of the rigid definitions attached to news; if a country fails to meet these criteria it can be assumed to, and indeed quite literally does produce no news. A broadcaster has written that among the problems he faced was 'an absolute dearth of news in the Gulf region where the excessive heat of the summer does not permit any important events to happen' (Kandil, 1975, p. 61). By axiomatically declaring in this way when and where news does not get made, such senior practitioners are indeed erecting the barriers which guarantee a lack of news, and ensuring the fulfilment of their own prophesies.

While foreign news is geographically distorted in this systematic way, it is still only a part of news bulletins. The more obvious geographical imbalance is the heavy concentration on domestic affairs and events. Home news represented from 30 per cent of the stories on RTE (this excludes Northern Ireland stories which accounted for another 36 per cent) to over 50 per cent on Rapport in Sweden. The Irish concern with Ulster of course influences the figures there, while in Nigeria the relative simplicity of dealing with foreign news contrasts with the difficulties of local news gathering, particularly in television, where foreign news is two-thirds of the total. But generally the world news is first and foremost a domestic affair.

One frequently offered explanation for the rationing of foreign news is the low interest in it displayed by audiences. 'They don't want it, they don't like it, they don't understand it', as one news executive explained. However, journalists feel duty bound to provide a full account of world events; expensive and technically complex resources are devoted to their observation and processing and they are regarded as important.

Therefore they must be tailored to the audience's capabilities and interests by linking them to domestic concerns or by focussing on their entertaining aspects. Two ways of doing the former are noted in Table 6.10

Table 6.10 Foreign and domestic stories (%)

	NBC TV	NBC radio	RTK	RTE	TV Nytt	Dagens Echo	Rapport
Home news abroad*	7.8	5.1	3.9	5.8	6.6	6.2	2.1
Foreign news at home*	9.6	4.4	5.6	8.7	3.6	1.8	2.1
Other 'real' foreign news	46.4	38.3	52.4	55.0	41.0	46.6	41.7
Uncertain status	0	0	0	0.2	1.0	2.3	1.0
Domestic	36.1	52.2	38.1	30.2	47.9	42.8	53.1
N	332	274	357	447	332	341	96

*See text for explanation of these terms

The first, '*home news abroad*', concerns stories which, while the events they describe occur abroad, are of concern at least indirectly to the domestic audience. The foreign travels of a home political leader or the successes of a native sports star overseas are examples. Alternatively, domestic interest in a foreign story can be actively injected: Irish viewers were informed of Senator McGovern's political position after he won the Massachusetts Primary in April 1971 by the observation that the Senator, 'who supports a withdrawal of troops from Northern Ireland', secured 51 per cent of the votes. McGovern's Irish connections were affirmed by a short clip of his victory speech in which he quoted from W. B. Yeats. Similarly in Sweden an interviewer doggedly chased after 'the Swedish concern' in a story about the legal status of the moon. An alternative and common strategy is the 'translocation' of news events. That is covering not the remote and inaccessible event itself, but the reaction to it in a news capital. The most common form of this is the use of the United Nations as a news source. Up to 5 per cent of all stories in some media were located at the UN or other similar supra-national bodies. In many cases this was because of debates about or statements on events in less journalistically accessible or newsworthy locations. The other side of this coin is '*foreign news at home*', the attempt to make international affairs appetising because they occur in the audience's own country. Visits by foreign dignitaries, international conferences in the capital and domestic reaction to international events are common examples. These two categories contained a large proportion of foreign news stories, as Table 6.10 shows.

Because foreign news has to justify its inclusion by having enhanced news values, stories from abroad tend to be longer and more visual than others. They also tend to retail events of greater news significance; bigger crashes, more famous or elite personalities and so on. The exceptions to this rule in our study were RTE (average domestic story

83 seconds, average foreign 57 seconds) and TV Nytt (average domestic 132 seconds, average foreign 111 seconds). The RTE figure is explained by the very large number of short Northern Ireland stories (foreign in our classification) which distort the average for foreign stories. In Sweden there was a continuing legacy from the days when news bulletins had simply relayed wire service telegrams. More typical is NBC where foreign stories, because they are far more likely to include film, average 75 seconds against 59 seconds for domestic stories.

As we have argued consistently in this study, news is largely an artefact of the supply of information made available to the newsroom. This is particularly true of foreign news since the cost of foreign news gathering on any significant scale is prohibitive. Table 6.11 shows the source of foreign news (it includes only those news programmes in which observation was conducted to verify this data for the content analysis period). Immediately apparent is the direct relationship between the availability of foreign news from the organisation's own staff and the resources available. In Nigeria funds did not extend to the posting of permanent correspondents, and with the exception of foreign tours by the head of state or very occasional major events like an OAU summit conference, foreign news was obtained entirely from agency sources, most importantly, in television, Visnews. RTE had a few correspondents but still only obtained a third of its foreign news from them. Rapport, with far greater resources available, got nearly two-thirds of its foreign news from its own correspondents, though this is more often from freelancers and from home-based journalists travelling to the event than from permanent offices abroad.

Table 6.11 Sources of foreign news stories (%)

	RTE	NBC TV	NBC Radio	Rapport
Own correspondent	32.8	0	0	61.9
Reuters	n.a.	20.7	47.8	n.a.
Associated Press	n.a.	28.3	33.6	n.a.
Agence France Presse	n.a.	0	2.3	2.4
Visnews	1.2	37.1	0	0
Eurovision	11.1	0	0	42.9
BBC	8.8	11.8	11.1	4.8
Other	12.9	0	3.2	2.4
Unidentifiable	33.2	2.1	1.6	9.5

Notes: n.a.: figures not available
N.B. More than one source may be used on a single story, thus column totals may exceed 100 per cent.

Because of its dependence on external sources, not merely the extent but the type and content of foreign news stories are dictated to a smaller, less well endowed, newsroom. Perspectives are inevitably second-hand, not only in the sense of imported bias, but in the structure of assumptions and in the very language in which news coverage is embedded. First, the selection of stories reflects the interests of their primary producers and their major audiences. NBC radio in our period included brief stories on an epidemic of Asian flu spreading through Hungary, and the suspicion that Queen Elizabeth was developing chicken pox, both given prominence in the BBC bulletins from which they were borrowed, both surely of dubious medical significance to the Nigerian population. Second, although a story may recommend itself in outline, its treatment may be more alive to the views of its European producers or audience than its Nigerian customers. Anxious to use a story about the financial problems of neighbouring Ghana, one of the Nigerian newsrooms was obliged to transmit the agency's brief explanation that it was all due to 'absenteeism among civil servants'.

A final aspect of the geography of news is the distribution of reported events within each home country. All the organisations were committed to the idea of more regional news and less concentration on the capital, or, in the case of WNBC and RTK, their home city. Table 6.12 shows the

Table 6.12 Location of domestic news stories

Sweden	**Dagens Echo**	**TV Nytt**	**Rapport**
Stockholm	54.6	45.5	30.8
North	5.7	3.2	0
Central	11.3	15.4	5.8
South	11.3	6.4	13.5
West	4.9	11.5	3.8
General/multi or unidentifiable	12.1	17.9	46.2
N	141	156	52

Ireland	**RTE TV**		
Dublin	52.2		
E. urban	9.7		
E. rural	7.5		
W. urban	21.6		
W. rural	9.0		
General/multi/unid	0		
N	134		

Nigeria	**NBC TV**	**NBC radio**	**RTK**
Lagos	78.4	30.5	15.4
West	11.5	22.7	11.5
North	4.7	14.3	45.5
East	5.4	20.1	8.3
General/multi/unid	0	12.3	19.2
N	148	154	156

domestic distribution of news stories. In each case between a third and a half of the domestic stories were located in the home city. In Ireland rural areas (containing roughly 48 per cent of the population) accounted for only 16.5 per cent of all domestic stories. In Sweden the north and west were particularly poorly represented, while in Nigeria each station was heavily committed to its own area in a very localised sense – even the west produced only 11.5 per cent of domestic stories on NBC TV. There is clear conflict here between policy and the pragmatics of news production. The triumph of the latter can be explained by the concentration in the capital of the people and events most highly valued as newsworthy regardless of their location. National legislatures, for example, command permanent attention from newsrooms. But, exemplified by the relative attention given to Lagos and to Northern Nigeria on RTK, ease of access and production play a part, amplified by the concern in this case to satisfy the needs of a local audience.

Dramatis personae

Quite obviously very few people in the world merit the daily attention of journalists, and very many escape their attentions eternally. The resulting cast list in news bulletins amounts, in aggregate, to an implicit account of who are the significant individuals in public affairs. As a first approximation to this account Table 6.13 shows the occupational roles or institutional background of all the main actors in the news stories in our sample. By actor here is meant any individual, group or organisation portrayed as the subject of whatever events or activities the story describes.

The most obvious generalisation indicated by these figures is the heavy concentration on formal political leaders, both the major party figures in domestic politics and foreign heads of state. Political figures dominate news bulletins almost independently of the significance of their actions; indeed their actions are given significance by the elite status of the actor. This routine coverage of political elites inevitably produces a good number of stories which might seem trivial measured by other criteria of news value. Thus when a routine visit to Derry by the British Minister for Northern Ireland turned out to be an uneventful and uninformative affair, a note was despatched by the RTE correspondent pointing this out to sub-editors in Dublin. Nonetheless an interview had been booked and a lengthy, though futile, film of the visit and the interview was included in the bulletin. SR tended to give less attention to the Swedish Prime Minister than the other media devoted to their own respective national leaders. In Ireland the Prime Minister featured in 12.6 per cent of domestic news stories, in Nigeria the then Head of State, General Gowon, was the focus of between 7 and 11 per cent of domestic news stories. On NBC TV and radio his activities, of course, received pride of place at the start of the bulletin.

In contrast to the spotlight thrown on the political elite other political actors are comparatively shrouded. Non-legitimate political groups are unable to register their dissidence because of their absence from the locales of legitimate political gamesmanship. Thus their illegitimacy is

Table 6.13 Main actor in news stories

	RTE	NBC TV	NBC radio	RTK	Dagens Echo	TV Nytt	Rapport
Sweden							
Prime Minister					0.3	0.3	1.0
Government					9.5	4.0	6.3
Other ruling party					0.3	0.9	1.0
Bourgeois parties					3.4	2.0	3.1
Communists					0	0.3	1.0
Ireland							
Prime Minister	4.9						
Government	2.1						
Other ruling party	1.7						
Other parties	3.2						
Church	1.0						
IRA/Sinn Fein	1.2						
Nigeria							
Gowon		5.1	4.0	3.2			
Service chief		0.3	0	0.7			
State government		3.9	11.5	8.9			
Federal commissioner		3.6	3.6	1.3			
State commissioner		1.8	3.6	2.5			
Other state government		0.3	2.9	1.6			
Trad. ruler		0.9	0.7	1.0			
Expat.		1.2	0.4	0			
All nationalities							
Pol. leader	4.8	12.9	10.4	16.8	9.5	9.5	14.6
Symbolic/nominal head	0.3	0.6	0.7	1.3	0	0.3	0
Civil service	1.7	3.0	6.1	4.3	3.7	3.2	3.1
Ambassador	0.5	0.6	0.7	2.1	0.9	3.2	2.1
Other diplomat	1.7	3.6	4.7	2.4	1.8	0.6	1.0
Ruling group	6.6	5.4	2.9	5.1	8.9	6.3	3.1
Executive/legislature	1.4	0.6	1.8	1.6	1.2	2.0	2.1
Legit. pol. opposition	6.3	0.9	1.1	1.4	2.1	1.7	4.2
Non legit. opposition	0.3	0.3	0.7	0.8	0.9	2.0	4.2
Military	12.2	5.1	1.4	5.4	5.8	3.5	17.7
Industry	4.1	2.4	2.2	2.9	4.6	8.9	5.2
Labour/unions	5.2	0.3	0	0	8.6	9.2	1.0
Religion	2.9	2.4	3.6	2.2	0.3	0.3	2.1
Local/community	2.5	2.1	1.1	0.8	0.9	0.3	0
Pressure group	3.4	1.5	0.4	1.1	0.6	0.3	0
Celebrity/sports	1.8	10.5	4.0	3.8	12.0	23.6	2.1
Media	0.8	1.2	0.4	1.8	1.8	1.4	0
Academic/educ.	1.4	3.6	6.1	5.6	3.7	4.3	9.4
Police	2.6	1.8	2.5	0.8	2.5	1.2	3.1
Lawyers/judiciary	0.8	2.7	2.2	1.8	0.3	0.6	0
Criminals/prisoners	3.2	2.4	2.5	1.6	5.5	1.2	1.0
Nation(s)	1.4	6.0	7.6	7.9	2.8	1.2	2.1
Other	19.1	10.3	9.7	9.0	8.0	7.6	5.2

enhanced and their credibility diminished. International diplomacy is portrayed as an endless succession of air flights by national leaders, perenially waving greetings of arrival or departure on the steps up to the plane. Industry is manned by the conciliatory leaders of employers federations, large industries or major unions. The analysis compared the number of actors who were leader figures in their field with ordinary members of whichever institutional or organisational spheres were mentioned in the story. In nearly all cases the former were much more frequently portrayed.

Table 6.14 Nationality of main actor in news stories (geographical areas simplified) (%)

	NBC TV	NBC radio	RTK	RTE	TV Nytt	Dagens Echo	Rapport
UN/OAU Etc.	1.5	7.3	5.1	0.6	0	0.9	1.0
W. Europe	7.4	5.2	7.2	84.0	70.4	67.2	68.7
USSR/E. Europe	1.5	1.1	0	0.9	4.5	4.1	3.1
Middle East	6.3	3.3	4.3	0.9	1.5	6.2	2.0
Africa	58.3	69.6	60.3	0.9	1.9	2.1	3.1
Asia	11.0	3.6	9.5	4.6	10.5	12.8	14.6
USA	8.8	3.7	3.7	3.0	6.5	6.2	7.3
S. America and all other countries incl. multi-national	5.2	6.2	8.9	4.7	0.5	0.2	0.2
Total	100	100	100	100	100	100	100
N	327	272	350	436	336	341	96

The concentration on elite figures increases the further away, both culturally and geographically, a story is located from its intended audience. Thus while the population of domestic stories is a varied, if limited one, more distant areas are portrayed almost solely by the deeds of one or two major figures. The affairs of more distant parts are thus reduced and simplified to their barest political bones. Table 6.14 shows the nationality of the main actors, Table 6.15 shows in summary form this tendency to focus on elite figures at a distance. The figures in Table 6.14 are simplified from a more detailed analysis.[1] This computation shows the heavy concentration on actors from the medium's own

Table 6.15 Elite figures by nationality
Figures show the ratio of political leaders and members of the ruling group to all other actors in three areas of the world. The highest figure thus indicates the heaviest concentration on elite figures.

	RTE	NBC TV	NBC radio	RTK	Dagens Echo	TV Nytt
Domestic	0.010	0.035	0.049	0.039	0.009	0
W. Europe	0.181	0.167	0.400	0.786	0.513	0.304
Third World	1.11	0.596	1.00	1.335	0.575	0.795

country. On RTE for example 36.9 per cent of actors were from Ireland, on NBC TV 42.9 per cent were Nigerian and on Rapport 55.2 per cent were Swedish. Beyond this each culture has a secondary sphere of interest; Scandinavia for the Swedes, Britain for the Irish, and Africa for the Nigerians. Table 6.15 shows how this three-fold division of the world is in fact common to all countries, being dictated by the news provision of the wire agencies. Thus even in Nigeria news of Third World countries is simplified to the acts of symbolic rulers. For them any increase in Third World news is only achieved by using a greater proportion of the news made available to them, allowing greater quantity but not greater depth. It is news *of* Africa but *for* non-African audiences.

Table 6.16 Dimension of main actor in story (%)

	NBC TV	NBC radio	RTK	RTE	Dagens Echo	TV Nytt	Rapport
Individual	50.5	41.8	49.3	40.0	35.2	37.5	39.1
Small group	20.8	25.8	17.5	24.0	17.6	20.5	5.4
Large corporate group	10.7	5.8	6.6	12.7	8.4	4.6	7.6
Large informal group	3.4	4.7	7.2	6.0	5.2	6.6	7.6
Organisation – national	6.4	9.1	3.9	8.7	24.5	28.2	38.0
Organisation – supra-national	1.2	2.9	2.8	1.1	1.2	0	0
Nation – state	5.8	8.4	8.0	3.3	2.9	1.2	2.2
No main human actor	1.2	1.5	4.7	4.2	5.2	1.4	0

News is about people, and Table 6.16 shows the extent to which events are portrayed by the activities of individual actors. Organisations and groupings appear less often than isolated individuals as the prime movers in the historical process captured by news stories. Roughly half the stories were concerned with the activities of an individual, not with the kinds of process which would require narration in terms of more corporate entities. This focus on personalities rather than groups inevitably shapes the portrayal of events themselves, suggesting the powerful and sudden influence of personalities as the potent drive in affairs rather than any less tangible, or less objectifiable subjects. The spokesman, the leader and the chairman are more likely elements in a story than the groups or sectional interests behind them. This is just one aspect of the difficulty faced by news broadcasters in the presentation of abstractions. The very rhetoric, technology and language required for journalism demands the concrete rather than the abstract, the person rather than the social group.

One indirect means by which a context is given to events is to refer them for comment to people involved in the event or to related experts. This provides a richer background for the story while giving the desired personalisation to it. As well as calculating the distribution of main actors in the stories the analysis looked at the use of secondary actors and commentators. The most common source of commentary were the media's own correspondents, though this practice was virtually unused in Nigeria. Rapport in Sweden made the most prolific use of film and studio explanations by its reporters and also used the filmed interview a great deal (on nearly two-thirds of its stories). Of the commentators used in Rapport stories 34 per cent were media personnel, but less typically nearly 14 per cent were academics of various kinds. This is because of the tendency to use comments and explanatory interviews most often in politically non-controversial stories, technological advances and the like. TV Nytt and Dagens Echo, committed to a more traditional 'just the facts' style of news, used commentators far less. Interviews and commentaries are generally most common in those institutional areas where public pronouncements are in plentiful supply by participants – formal politics, major industrial disputes and stories about celebrities. In these areas the pronouncements of major participants are not merely commentaries, they are themselves news. The stage army of what one analyst has termed 'accredited witnesses', is composed largely of subjects of events not their objects, those who act, not those acted upon (Hall, 1975). More significantly it is composed of those willing and able to become sources of commentary and observation, able to play the role of news source and benefit from it.

Of course there is an area of discretion in which the news media are casting directors. The choice of interviewees is often governed by a set of understandings about which are the pertinent interests affected by an event and who are their legitimate spokesman. A Swedish story about government tax plans included interviews with leaders of all the opposition parties except that of the Communist Party. In the continuing struggle to show evident impartiality, claim and counter claim must be displayed. But where this necessitates the active seeking of counter claims it activates deep-rooted understandings about the relevance of different voices. To a surprisingly large extent however this power of definition was unavailable to the news media in our study. Very few stories included interviews and of these only a handful included second or third interviews with contrary viewpoints. This practice is a luxury available only to the best endowed newsrooms able to commit considerable resources to a single story, and among those we studied only the Rapport team in SR was able to attempt it regularly. Of course comments and reactions can be indirect rather than interviews. Here, much more clearly, the news was dependent on what could be termed the information-producing strata of society, leaving unheard those with no access to publicity or no desire for it. The stage army of news performers tends not to include owners of big business, bureaucrats, financiers or ordinary people with no special or bizarre circumstances to thrust them into prominence.

News agencies

Since we are emphasising the important influence of material available to newsrooms in determining the selection and presentation of news, it was necessary to analyse the most regularly used and voluminous inputs, those from the news agencies and from Eurovision. We therefore conducted a content analysis of all news stories circulated by Eurovision and Visnews for the four weeks of our main analysis.

Eurovision[2]

For this analysis we included all stories in the midday offers ('EVN-1') for the two 14-day periods of our content study, a total of 345 cases. Of these, 19 per cent were accepted by RTE and 35.5 per cent by Sveriges Radio. Of course acceptance does not necessarily lead to inclusion in the bulletin; Table 6.11 shows that RTE used considerably less Eurovision material than Rapport in Sweden. However, European costings are based on, among other things, acceptances rather than use, so these initial choices are the result of some consideration.

The main characteristics of these Eurovision offers are shown in Tables 6.17, 6.18 and 6.19. Three subject areas dominate; international politics, military encounters and sport. All three have the general marketability required of a commodity which has to satisfy a variety of national organisations. All three subject areas are international and have visual appeal. The military figure is boosted by Vietnam and India from where film material was supplied by the agencies (Visnews, UPITN and the American CBS).

Geographically, the focus is on the same news capitals as in news media generally. Almost a third of the stories were in Western Europe, and a further 9 per cent in the USA. Obviously the main function of the Eurovision network is to distribute material produced within Europe. But increasing participation by the film agencies has made the Eurovision news circuit a general source of foreign news, particularly of course for smaller stations with few foreign news gathering resources of their own. Thus the very limited coverage of South America and Africa is not compensated for by other sources.

A similar unequal exchange operates between East and West Europe. In our period 13.5 per cent of stories came from behind the iron curtain, but they included such items as a new breed of speaking parrots, an art exhibition and the discovery of a mammoth fossil. Varis and Jokelin (1976) in a study for the EBU on this exchange, have noted the apparently different emphases in news values between EVN and Intervision members. Eurovision offers to IVN in their study period were almost entirely international politics (53%), sport (18%) or catastrophies (15%), whereas the offers from IVN included 16 per cent on economic affairs and 31 per cent on cultural, social and scientific affairs. The political content of stories from IVN was muted; Varis and Jokelin point out that 'of the IVN political items, almost 90 per cent dealt with visits of heads of state or other high government or party officials to other countries'. One third of the newsfilm received from

Table 6.17 Eurovision: stories by subject matter (%)

Domestic politics	2.5
International politics	27.8
Economics	2.5
Industrial	2.1
Agricultural	0
Technological	1.4
Military	21.5
Education	0.7
Cultural	1.4
Religion	0.7
Crime/legal	4.6
Sport	19.4
Welfare	1.4
Tragedy/disaster	4.6
Human interest	4.2
Other	5.3

Table 6.18 Eurovision: Geographical location of stories (%)

United Nations	1.7
Other supra-national bodies	1.2
Britain	7.8
Scandinavia	0.3
Other W. Europe	32.9
USSR	4.9
E. Europe	8.6
Middle East	4.0
N. Africa	1.4
W. Africa – Anglophone	0
W. Africa – Francophone	0
E./Cen. Africa	0
S. Africa/Rhodesia	2.9
China	0.3
Japan	1.7
Other Asia	19.0
Cen./Latin America	2.3
USA	9.2
Australia/Canada	0
Other	1.7

Table 6.19 Eurovision: event in story (%)

Press conference	2.1
Other speech	10.8
Travel	13.3
Meeting/conference	14.2
Formal Event	3.9
Mass behaviour – violent	1.8
Mass behaviour – non-violent	7.2
Other violence – military	9.0
Other violence – criminal	1.8
Other	35.8

IVN by Eurovision members dealt with sport. Even given the limited flow from East to West, most EVN members took less than 5 per cent of stories offered by IVN, and this in a period including Dr Kissinger's visit to Moscow.

Eurovision stories are about the formal, prepackaged events which are as much addressed to news media as discovered by them. Statements, speeches, airport arrivals and departures, meetings, conferences; in other words the visual accessories of international protocol. To a large extent use of Eurovision material requires pre-planning; producing countries have to make their offers and receiving countries need to plan their requirements. Programming considerations plus a certain sensitivity to likely demand evolved over the years determine the type of story distributed through the network. A large proportion of stories came from a very few sources. The film agencies supply about half the EVN items and, of the remainder, the larger organisations supply all but about 20 per cent. Smaller organisations, like SR and RTE, play a relatively insignificant part in the provision of news to EVN.

Visnews

Visnews, 'the world's leading supplier of international news actuality material for television', supplies a considerable proportion of film stories to Eurovision. It also distributes air freighted film packages throughout the world. Indeed, many television newsrooms in poorer countries are entirely dependent for foreign news film on either Visnews or its major competitor, UPITN.

We analysed all air-freighted stories circulated by Visnews in this way for 4 weeks, a total of 371 items. The most obvious feature of these stories is their 'soft' nature, that is their lack of spot news, hard up-to-the-minute events. Because of the comparatively slow means of distribution, Visnews stories are mostly designed to be of use for several days or even longer. In our sample period only 4.1 per cent of the stories were 'hard' news, though 78.5 per cent dealt with events in the very recent past, while the remaining 17.4 per cent were of no specially topical significance. It is for this reason that air-freighted film news is of such limited use to newsrooms in Europe (see Chapter 5).

Table 6.20 shows the types of news story distributed by Visnews. Again, the predominance of formal politics is marked, though with perhaps a surprisingly high proportion of internal domestic politics (16.6% of such stories recorded election results). Because of the loss of immediacy, sports, crime, and tragedies and disasters are less prevalent than elsewhere since their impact and utility depend so much on just that immediate presentation which Visnews cannot provide.

To counter this loss of serviceability, the agency includes among its packages a large number of 'featurettes' or general interest items. In our period examples included the annual festival of Children's Fortnight in

Table 6.20 Visnews: types of news story by subject (%)

Domestic politics	19.4
International politics	16.8
Economics	4.0
Industrial	2.4
Agricultural	0.3
Technological	7.4
Military	20.7
Education	1.9
Cultural	2.4
Religion	2.4
Crime/legal	2.7
Sport	8.0
Welfare	1.6
Tragedy/disaster	1.9
Human interest	5.1
Other	3.0

Zaire, a facelift received by the British liner, Queen Elizabeth, in Hong Kong, and the presentation of an elephant called 'Prosperity' to Los Angeles Zoo by the Cambodian Premier. The significance of these stories is not their triviality and whimsicality, but that they represent the only film news from these areas available to newsrooms like those in Nigeria. As professionally produced film items, they rank highly for inclusion in bulletins, especially because of the 'any news from X is better than no news' syndrome.

Table 6.21 Visnews: geographical distribution of stories, and of main actors in stories (%)

	Story location	Main actor
UN/Other supra-national bodies	2.8	0.6
Britain	9.7	10.6
Other W. Europe	17.1	13.7
USSR/E. Europe	2.5	2.4
Middle East	10.5	8.7
N. Africa	1.9	1.6
W. Africa	6.6	5.7
E./Cen. Africa	4.9	4.9
S. Africa/Rhodesia	3.0	1.6
S.E. Asia	10.3	10.4
Indian sub-continent	6.8	6.8
Other Asia	6.0	6.0
Cent./S. America	4.3	4.9
USA	9.2	13.6
Australia/Canada	0.5	0.3
Space	1.1	0
More than one area	2.8	8.2

Table 6.21 shows the geography of Visnews stories. Over a third of the stories are situated in western Europe and North America, and a similar proportion of European and American personnel populate the stories. The familiar gaps recur in Latin America and Africa, though some

attempt is made to cater for the large number of customers in the latter continent. The people in Visnews films tend to come from the same limited strata as in news generally, with a heavy concentration on political leaders (who were the main actors in 21.1% of stories). Only military figures (14.6%) approach this level and this largely because of their guaranteed appearance in news production from Vietnam.

Because of its 'soft' function, Visnews tends to carry even more than other agencies of the formal, predictable meeting and conference stories, comprising routine set-piece film of similar people sitting at similar conference microphones. But perhaps the most interesting aspects of Visnews stories are features no quantitative content analysis can illuminate. The language of commentaries is one such facet. Visnews stories are written largely by European, especially British, journalists for audiences all over the world. The assumptions and standpoint of the writers may be very different from those of the audiences. Vietnam stories invariably were filmed from the American side of the battle-front. The advance of 'Communist troops' or even 'Communist tanks' was always a threat, the fall to them of a hill or a town a further tragedy to be mourned over. Further, the viewpoint is clearly seen in such phrases as 'military sources fear twelve US advisers have been left behind on the retreat from Quang Tri, as well as hundreds of Vietnamese'. This is not the place to go into media coverage of the Vietnam war, but such perspectives were typical of much western agency coverage. For African newsrooms the implicit and often explicit treatment of Africa is a constant source of annoyance, though much is accepted and unquestioned because of the absorption of western news values. A story about the visit of the Foreign Minister of the Ivory Coast to Brazil was set in the context of international relationships between African countries and Brazil. But the relationship was set at the level of diplomacy and culture, not a common interest in anti-colonialism. After film of a visit to a museum in which the cultural legacy of African slaves in Brazil was stressed, the film ended as follows:

> Many of the exhibits display styles and techniques that can be found throughout Brazil's modern culture. [Shots of wooden carvings of women, and a wooden Hippo with headdress.] The Brazilian government recognises the natural affinity between their country and the African nations, and it sees Africa as an important market for its booming export trade. The Africans consider that the obstacle to improved trade is Brazil's friendly relationship with Portugal – a country that in African eyes continues to refuse independence to its African colonies.

Only after some discussion (Visnews items were rarely altered) was this changed in one newsroom from 'Africans consider' to 'People here in Africa', and 'perpetuate atrocities in' substituted for 'refuse independence to'. But the continual third person treatment of Africans spills over into the selection and treatment of stories, not just the odd phrase.

This is seen in the persistence of stereotyped featurettes. So we have the 'colourful Africans' angle, as in a story on the fiftieth anniversary of the King of Swaziland; the 'primitives still abound' angle, as in a film report about a visit by a team of anthropologists to a 'stone age tribe', in the Philippines, and the 'strange and fascinating customs' angle as in a story about 'drugged villagers' celebrating the end of the dry season with 'weird dancing' in scanty 'tribal' costumes. Such film stories are clearly tailored for European audiences, but in fact are more often used by newsrooms in Africa. Lacking alternative African news film sources they are grateful for whatever they can get. How cynically such items are received by the audiences is impossible for us to judge, but at the very least they displaced more serious attempts at continuous television journalism on African affairs for African audiences.

Summary

It is possible to disappear beneath a deluge of statistics and lose sight of the overall anatomy of broadcast news this analysis reveals. Broadcast news is a passive reflection of the information provided for it by the information-producing strata in society and by its own gathering mechanisms. Both these sources are severely restricted. The news is packaged like any other programme, and supplies implicit explanation and context by default. In being restricted to the passive transmission of observed events it satisfies explicit demands for neutral, objective reporting while necessarily providing a limited, and persistent view of social reality. This view is a construction based on the built-in production procedures and values of broadcast journalism. Social process is fragmented and ultimately lost, while social power is masked by a concentration on formal political institutions, a geography created by the cartography of the long-established contours of cultural colonialism, and a personalised cast-list of news performers in line with the limited institutional structures described.

We have stressed that the cultural artefact we call broadcast news is shaped not by the personal whims or professional inadequacies of individual journalists, but by the systematic routines and occupational traditions within which they work. In the next chapter we examine these routines and traditions through the eyes of the journalists themselves.

Notes

1. For reasons of space we have not included the coding schedule in this book, nor full tabulation of the results.
2. For a fuller analysis of Eurovision news see Varis and Jokelin (1976). For a detailed study of the wire agencies see Harris (1977).

Chapter 7

Journalists in broadcasting

Popular attitudes to most occupations tend to be highly ambiguous. Alongside the image which reflects credit on the practitioners as true servants of a noble calling, there is another which contemptuously and irreverently cuts them down to size. In journalism the main contrast has been between the journalist as a man of letters and a man of influence, the consort of the great and famous in politics, literature and society, and the journalist as commercial hack, titillating the baser appetites of a gullible public. There is a narrower contrast, however, within the specific field of broadcast journalism between the glamour of the new technology and the contact it allows with important people and events and the subservience of the broadcast media to state power. In the case of broadcast journalism, for commercial hacks read government hacks.

The relevance of such images to the journalists in the three countries we studied is a point to which we shall return at the end of this chapter when we discuss the social role of the journalist, his status as an intellectual and creator of ideas and his concern for the social obligations and implications of his work. The data in this chapter comes from a survey carried out in the news departments towards the end of our research.[1] Both the design of the survey and the use we make of it in this chapter were informed by our experience of observing these and other journalists at work during the whole of the study.

In this chapter our concern is to examine the broadcast journalists themselves, who they are, how they work, their careers and aspirations, relationships and views. We shall deal with four aspects of broadcast journalism as an occupation. First, the educational and demographic backgrounds of our broadcast journalists. Second, their role as employees with particular interest in how they divide their commitments between broadcasting and journalism and how being a journalist in broadcasting compares with newspaper work. Third, we shall consider the professional values and characteristics of journalism, reformulating the usual questions about the professionalisation of journalism in a broadcasting context. Finally, we shall return to broader questions about the journalists' role in society.

Origins and education

Broadcast journalism is a middle class occupation in the sense that few journalists in any of the countries had fathers who were manual workers (Table 7.1). Interestingly, the proportion was highest in Ireland even though industry is only a small part of the Irish economy. In all countries a large proportion came from what might be termed the educated, literate or professional elite. This was spectacularly true of Sweden, where 45 per cent had professional fathers. But there is little evidence of journalism becoming a self-recruiting profession. There were no more than one or two second generation journalists in any country. A smaller proportion of journalists came from business and industrial homes. In Ireland, reflecting the still rural character of the

Table 7.1 Journalists' fathers' occupations (%)

	Nigeria	Ireland	Sweden
Journalist/other Media	1.2	3.5	4.8
Teacher/academic	6.0	7.1	4.8
Civil servant	16.9	10.7	1.6
Politician	1.2	3.5	1.6
Other professional	4.8	3.5	32.3
Sub-total	(30.1)	(28.3)	(45.1)
Farmer	24.1	25.0	3.2
Trader or small business	12.0	14.3	0
Other non-manual	25.3	14.3	38.7
Other manual	8.4	17.8	12.9
(N)	83	28	62

country, a quarter of the journalists were farmers' sons. Nigerian journalists were very frequently from the 'new bourgeoisie' or 'modernising elite' groups who form the urban middle class of Third World countries. Many had fathers who had risen to lesser ranks in the colonial civil service. Of course, these bald figures disguise the complexity of the Nigerian occupational structure. In addition to the 24 per cent whose fathers were farmers a good proportion felt their roots to be in rural village life, though they themselves were the successful products of educationally facilitated mobility and were seldom able to visit their home areas due to new commitments and associations.

Educationally the journalists tended to be above average, though not spectacularly so (Table 7.2). In Ireland three-quarters of the journalists had acquired the school leaving certificate. All but one had left school after their sixteenth birthday, which is exceptional for the age range represented. In Sweden three-quarters had their 'student examen' (equivalent to matriculation or university entrance standard). The majority (four-fifths) had stayed at school until 18. In Nigeria a quarter had gone as far as the Advanced Level General Certificate. This had often involved many years of post-primary education into the late teens and early twenties, after delayed or interrupted primary education. Although education has expanded rapidly in Nigeria, the goal of a

Table 7.2 Education(%)

	Nigeria	Ireland	Sweden
(a) Age on leaving school			
12–15	6.0	3.6	1.6
16–17	19.3	28.6	16.1
18+	28.9	67.9	82.2
Late entry 18+	45.8	—	—
(b) School qualifications			
Nigeria: Leaving or West African School Cert.			48.2
'O' Levels			18.1
'A' Levels			24.1
None			9.6
Ireland: Inter			10.7
Leaving			75.0
None/Other			14.3
Sweden: Real Examen			9.7
Student Examen			74.2
None			16.1
	Nigeria	Ireland	Sweden
(c) Further education			
Journalism	1.2	—	4.8
Other technical/prof.	16.9	—	3.2
University – 1st degree	6.0	21.4	21.0
higher degree	1.2	3.6	6.5
uncompleted	3.6	10.7	30.6
General educational	9.6	—	6.5
None	61.4	64.3	25.8

national minimum of 50 per cent in primary education by the mid-1970s was not achieved. The figure was far below this level in the north. As we shall see, most younger Nigerian journalists see their education as unfinished and hope for further qualifications. A job with a government-backed corporation is the best base from which to realise such aspirations.

In all three countries the recent or contemporary experience of the social changes associated with industrial and urban development meant that education was generally highly valued. Irish journalists were exceptionally committed to higher education: 21 per cent had a university degree and a further 11 per cent had gone to university without graduating. In Sweden, where 22 per cent of the male population go to university, again 21 per cent had a degree and the proportion who had gone to university abortively was as high as 30 per cent. Swedish universities developed on the continental, particularly the German, model, in which it is not unusual for students to attend for a few lecture courses and then drop out.

The career of the broadcast journalist

A major contrast between Nigeria and the two European countries was that in the latter employment in television news represented a career peak, while in Nigeria it was more often a stepping stone. Most Swedish and Irish journalists expected to continue their careers with their present employer. This expectation reflected partly the specialisation involved in broadcast journalism, partly the lack of alternative venues in which to practise this specialism and partly, at least in the Swedish case, the growing prestige of broadcast journalism in relation to other types of journalism in the country. Nigerian journalists were younger (average age 31) than Irish and Swedish journalists (average age 38 in both cases) and so had more of their career ahead of them. They were also less likely to think of themselves as restricted simply to a career in journalism.

Nigerian journalists were predominantly spiralists, in the sense that they were not tied to a single employer or type of employment. They often expected to change their jobs to seek advancement. Prior to taking up their present employment, journalists in Nigeria had had mixed careers, and less than a third had spent all their working lives in journalism. In Sweden and Ireland by contrast two-thirds had pursued careers entirely within journalism. Prior to entering journalism many Nigerians had worked in junior civil service jobs and a large number had taught, reflecting the usual structure of salaried employment opportunities in a developing country. Very few had worked outside the public sector.

The Nigerians also differed from their contemporaries in the other two countries in terms of their career intentions. Less than a quarter of Nigerian journalists saw their future in their present jobs, whereas nearly three-quarters of Swedish journalists felt they had arrived to stay. Irish journalists were less entirely satisfied and a quarter suggested they would like to move back to print media. Nigerian journalists were younger, and therefore less set on an undeviating career path. In addition, their skills were saleable in a far wider range of emerging occupations than the more differentiated and rigid occupational division of labour in industrialised countries. For similar reasons entry into broadcast journalism in Nigeria was frequently less deliberate than elsewhere. For many it was just one of a variety of possible ways of exchanging their general educational qualifications for entry into the elite occupations in government or industrial administration. Swedish or Irish journalists were advancing their careers as journalists; Nigerians were advancing their careers.

Swedish and Irish journalists were more likely to give both negative and positive reasons for moving out of other types of journalism into broadcasting (Table 7.4). They were also more likely to have been positively recruited to work for the organisation, reflecting the expansion of broadcast journalism and its growing importance alongside the print media. In Sweden the traditional career route led from a period as a 'volunteer' on a local paper, to employment by a local

Table 7.3 Previous journalistic employment (%)

	Nigeria	Ireland	Sweden
Other domestic broadcasting organisation	10	—	—
Local or provincial newspaper	28	61	85
Metropolitan paper	30	96	77
Weekly magazine	6	11	18
English media	5	18	0
Other foreign media	2	4	2
Other	7	7	13

Note: Totals may exceed 100 per cent as more than one type of prior employment may have been mentioned.

paper, then on to a large regional centre, to a metropolitan paper and then to SR (Table 7.3). Several of those whose careers followed this sequence referred to it as the 'old route' or 'the long way round'. They contrasted it with a more modern tendency for SR journalists to be direct entrants from higher education, especially the Stockholm Journalism High School (see below). The Irish career route was similar though a smaller proportion had worked on a paper in the provinces and almost all the journalists had had experience on one of the Dublin papers. Their commitment to their present employer was less however. Broadcast journalism had yet to achieve the prestige in Ireland that it had achieved in Sweden.

The length of time working in their present job averaged just under 5

Table 7.4 Reasons for joining present employing organisation(%)

	Nigeria	Ireland	Sweden
Conditions of employment including salary and security	15	57	18
Contact reasons including invitations to posts and previous freelance experience	13	40	53
Negative reasons – dissatisfaction with previous journalism job or job folded	13	18	23
Positive reasons connected with media, e.g. the challenge of a new medium with new techniques, broadcasting a better form of journalism, wider audience, glamour of broadcasting	27	47	51
Other	0	0	15
No special reason/Don't Know	8	0	5

Note: Totals may exceed 100 per cent when more than one reason given.

years in Nigeria and between 7 and 8 years in the other two countries. This masked what appears to be a sequence of generations. Three recruitment periods were important in Sweden; pre 1968 when television news was only slowly growing; a period from 1968 to 1970 when expansion and the second channel induced additional recruitment and mobility within the corporation; and the subsequent period with recruitment continuing slowly but subject to severe restraint as budgets became tighter. The middle period of expansion saw the greatest influx of journalistic talent into the corporation. Many of those involved in television news in the early days were more professional broadcasters than professional journalists. In the final period the pattern of entry had shifted towards direct recruitment from the Journalism High School (JHS) of students who had managed to arrange to serve their practical training period at the corporation. This development suggested the possibility that broadcast journalism might become more of a specialism in the future.

In Nigeria the main generational split was between the older journalists with long experience in newspaper journalism and broadcasting in the days of politics (to 1966), and the younger recruits, mostly products of expanding educational opportunities whose aspirations lay beyond their present job. This provided a clear split in commitment between the older men with traditional journalistic ideas and the younger men, many of whom saw their future outside journalism, or at least in the private sector. Among the older men many dreamed of retiring to set up public relations firms of their own or of moving back to a senior post in newspaper journalism. As the various Nigerian states began to set up their own broadcasting organisations the opportunities for younger men with limited experience to gain rapid promotion, particularly if they were from the state in question, began to attract younger men away from the more usual escape route into government or commercial public relations.

The most obvious comparable employment for broadcasting journalists is in newspapers and the most apparent index of difference, their income. In Sweden most felt themselves to be better off in broadcasting and generally regarded SR as a good employer. There was some recognition that a comparison of real income might not be that simple. 'We have the salary and they have the perks' was how one Swedish newsman put it. But overall only a tenth felt they would be financially better off in newspapers. By contrast, Irish journalists, almost to a man, felt themselves worse off. This reflected a recent settlement with journalists on the *Irish Independent* whose basic pay had been raised above that of RTE journalists. Similar settlements for journalists on other papers were in the pipeline. It will be remembered that half the Irish journalists gave salary as their original reason for joining RTE. Journalism in Dublin is a relatively small world in which such comparisons are easily made and important. In Nigeria opinions were divided; a third described themselves as worse off and a third as better paid than if they worked on newspapers. This largely depended on their reference point. The highly successful Lagos *Daily Times* was much envied. High salaries were the main reason it had attracted and held a trained, proficient and skilled corps of journalists. Journalists, in particular those at WNBC or RTK, who chose a regional newspaper as the most realistic reference point felt less deprived. In fact, reaching the point on salary scales where one can attract loans and perks is often more desirable than salary increments for many in Nigeria, and this may be more likely in a small expanding government corporation like broadcasting.

Salaries in Nigeria were not, of course, on the scale of those in Europe. At the period of our research annual household income for rural families was estimated at about £125 p.a. A junior reporter at RTK was getting about £310. A survey in the Kaduna textile industry (reported in the Nigerian *Daily Express*, 16 October 1973) found average annual earnings of about £185 though they were rather higher in the 26–30 age group. At the other end of the scale, however, the editor of the *Daily Times* was believed to be on a salary of about £6,000. Salaries were generally higher at NBC at this time (1973) though WNBC has made up much of the ground recently. For example, a chief sub-editor at WNBC was getting £876 while his equivalent at NBC was on £1,020. However, even editors at NBC were on a scale whose maximum was £2,380. In fact few Nigerian journalists mentioned salary as their reason for joining their present employer though many mentioned it as a reason for wishing to leave.

The Swedes were most content with their present jobs. Over three-quarters intended to stay even when invited to hypothesise on possible moves they might advantageously make. Of course this partly reflected a period of settling in after some considerable organisational shuffling. Many had moved within SR, particularly with the introduction of Rapport and the second channel. As emphasised before in this chapter, this also reflected the growth of broadcast journalism and of its prestige in the country. In Ireland there was less certainty. Less than half the Irish journalists were definitely committed to staying and an equal proportion were unsure. Of those who had thought of leaving over half had in mind the press, perhaps with the recent wage settlements in mind. In Nigeria only a quarter were committed to their present position. The two-thirds who expressed uncertainty were voicing the obvious indeterminacy of careers which had either just started, or were based on skills which were in increasing demand from a proliferation of employers and occupations. Despite the known financial rewards of commercial public relations, the favourite choice of those who named one was once again in newspapers.

The broadcast journalist as professional

The literature on journalism, particularly in the United States where there is a vast academic industry training journalists, is much taken with the question of whether or not journalism is being 'professionalised'. As has been the case in similar occupations, much of the discussion turns on the relationship between education and values, with the occupation concerned to claim professional status and the educators concerned to emphasise their role in allowing the claim to be made (Elliott, 1972b, Ch. 3). Articles on this subject recur frequently in *Journalism Quarterly*, published by the (American) Association for Education in Journalism. In one sense, of course, this is nonsense. Those traits normally isolated as peculiar to the professions – personalised client relationships, skill based on theoretical knowledge, an ethic of altruistic service, organisation, control over entry to the occupation – are very largely absent from media occupations, and indeed the notion of direct individual client service is quite contrary to the defining nature of mass communications. Some professional characteristics are present, however, and it is their diffusion which is taken to signify 'professionalisation', notably increased training and professional education, association into professional organisations, and an ethos of service to the public and disinterested vocation. The growth of broadcasting has stimulated a global expansion of education in mass media skills and techniques, and more generally in mass communications, frequently misunderstood as a discipline in itself.

The approach to the study of professions which depends on identifying traits and totting up a score for or against, ultimately has more to do with debate than analysis. Johnson has neatly released us from the fruitless task of deciding whether broadcast journalism is or is not a profession by pointing to the importance of professionalism 'redefined as a peculiar type of occupational control rather than an expression of the inherent nature of particular occupations. A profession is not, then, an occupation, but a means of controlling an occupation' (Johnson, 1972, p. 45). Not that the control is necessarily exercised by the occupation itself through its own association. This was the pattern in the nineteenth century when authority was delegated to the occupational associations of the classic professions. Broadcasting at least when organised on the British broadcasting authority model which, as we have seen, was particularly influential in all three of these countries, is a good example of authority being delegated to a corporate body which includes various occupations rather than to the occupations themselves. In such cases the distinction between professionalism and bureaucracy, another central tenet in accounts of the professions, becomes blurred (Elliott, 1972b).

To justify its independent exercise of that authority the corporation develops its own notions of professionalism. It may come to stand for the occupation in the sense that the interests of broadcasters are represented as those of the broadcasting organisation. Broadcast journalism as the occupational title makes clear however has both an internal and an external referent. In press journalism two notions of professional independence have commonly been mixed in the ideology of the free press. One is the claim to independence from commercialism particularly associated with the great nineteenth-century writing editors, and the other the claim to political independence from government (Elliott, 1978). In recent years this has led to rudimentary forms of self-regulation such as press councils in some countries as a response to continued pressure to raise standards. Broadcast journalism is more exposed on the second count than the first in countries such as those considered here in which the authority is established by the state with little or no commercial involvement.

Table 7.5 Journalism training (%)

	Nigeria	**Ireland**	**Sweden**
Any type of 'professional' or journalism training	38.6	3.6	33.9
In-house technical courses	8.4	14.3	14.5
None	53.0	82.1	51.6

Table 7.6 Professional qualifications (%)

(a) Ireland and Sweden	*Ireland*	*Sweden*
Any	10.7	11.3
None	89.3	88.7
(b) Nigeria		
Nigerian degree		4.8
Nigerian diploma		16.9
Foreign degree		2.4
Foreign diploma		22.9
Other		3.6
None		49.4

Among these three countries, Ireland most clearly reflected British influence in the lack of professional training and antipathy to it. The strain of anti-intellectualism or anti-academicism in British journalism is associated with the commercialism of the British press and the recruitment traditions of both countries. Untrained entrants are likely to be more amenable to the practices of the organisation they join and to cause less resentment among those already in post. Only 11 per cent of journalists at RTE had any professional qualifications and none intended to seek one (Tables 7.5 and 7.6). There are two kinds of suspicion, one of graduate entrants who would mistake education for capability and assume unwarranted and unworked-for success. The other comes from the view that journalism is an innate art, impossible to teach and requiring inborn talent and experience rather than training and much despised 'paper qualifications'. This view is fostered, of course, by the experience of 'learning by doing' in low status jobs on regional newspapers.

I like to see graduates coming in but would be afraid of having graduates per se – you need a capacity to boil down stuff to lay terms – it's akin to a natural flair for teaching. Some people have it naturally, it's difficult to impart. There must be something more than academic ability. (Correspondent, RTE)

Some feared the move towards employing graduates. 'They are going for intellectual types rather than hard-bitten reporters – a mistake from the news point of view' (Reporter, RTE).

Many were willing to concede the need for technical training, and indeed expressed a desire for its expansion. This amounted to insisting that journalistic skills remained unteachable, but that their implementation was frustrated by the technology of broadcasting, the mysteries of which should be revealed to allow the journalist the fullest opportunity to perform.

Training should remove fear of machines, particulary among people from the newsroom going down to other areas. This fear will otherwise inhibit the use of the machines. Television training is needed to get over an inferiority complex, for example with graphic artists, directors, film editors, VTR operators who want to be stroppy. (Chief Sub-editor, RTE)

A similar distinction was drawn by Swedish and Nigerian journalists. One Swede pointed to other incapacities which might frustrate the journalist in the exercise of his function.

You need a feeling for journalism. It is a great advantage then to be qualified in a language, for example for interviewing. It's often necessary to have specialised knowledge in a field and it's also necessary to have the technical knowledge to be able to recognise the potential of a piece and tell the technicians what to do. (Executive, SR)

Basic professional training is essential for television journalism, especially in production techniques. Journalism, though, is learnt on the job. (Senior Sub-editor, NBC TV)

In Nigeria, however, some older journalists spoke sceptically of the newer entrants, whose commitments to journalism they thought limited, and whose training in production skills they thought valueless without a solid core of journalistic instinct and 'feel'. By and large, however, most expressed satisfaction with the change in the occupation since entry qualifications had appeared. This was seen to have raised the status of journalism in Nigeria and offered hitherto unexpected opportunities. Nigerians see themselves, and are seen by others, as obsessively eager for paper qualifications, a not unusual characteristic in a developing country where service occupations, and particuarly the civil service, are expanding very rapidly and competition for favoured employment is intense as educational opportunities expand. As Lloyd (1966) and others have argued this usually works to the benefit of already favoured groups. Regardless of age, many Nigerian journalists were keen to acquire further professional qualifications (only 8% were not planning to do so), with a fairly even split in intentions between Nigerian and foreign degrees or diplomas.

For many of the younger Nigerians qualification per se was the attraction. As educated members of the 'modernising elite', their reference groups were neither other journalists nor other broadcasters. 'I've always believed in academic excellence. I don't believe in on-the-job training. Most of my friends are professional people. I don't want to be left out of the race' (21-year-old reporter, WNBC).

Of course the industrial context has changed. Instead of working for small entrepreneur proprietors or shoe-string political party papers, journalists in Nigeria now work for large, mostly government corporations, with intricate career and salary structures and well defined, if contentious, grading schemes and entry and seniority requirements. In theory, criteria for selection and promotion have changed in sociological terms, from the particularistic to the universalistic. In practice, of course, as in any bureaucratic structure run by human beings, friction is created by the frequent collision of these two norms.

Nigerian journalists tend to enter professional training programmes after initial experience. For one thing, this means employers will second them and foot the bill. It also means they are most likely to enter specifically vocational courses even though they intend to use the qualification as a general entry to elite occupations. Thus the courses tended to be praised for 'broadening horizons' or providing a general educational veneer. Of Nigerian journalists who had been on a course the commonest was the one-year scheme at the Lagos University Institute of Mass Communications. The institute was, at this time, in the process of moving to new large, UNESCO-financed, quarters, and had introduced a three-year degree scheme in 1969. Courses tend to follow the pattern of American journalism schools with a smattering of 'mass communications theory'. Also popular were the courses run by the Nigerian Institute of Journalism, originally founded by the International Press Institute and resurrected by them after the Civil War with the support of Nigerian editors' and newspaper proprietors' associations. Funds for the IPI Africa Programme came largely from the Ford Foundation. The courses were primarily press orientated and solidly rooted in occupational skills and practice ('use of the library', 'shorthand and typing', 'law and the journalist').

Europe and America influenced Nigerian journalism education in two ways. First, the schemes set up in Nigeria were initially run by expatriates and revolved round European and American notions of the functions, skills and values of a professional communicator. Second, many journalists, unable to find a place in Nigeria, sought training abroad, either by going to a foreign college or university, or by correspondence course. No less than 64 per cent of Nigerian journalists had done, or were doing, part-time or correspondence courses, the majority in general education fields rather than specifically in journalism, indicating again the commitment to career rather than profession. Younger journalists were often to be seen in their breaks huddled over an antiquated teach-yourself text on 'British Constitution' or 'advanced level accountancy', as they painfully sought approbation from remote supervisors and the eventual, dearly bought but vital certificate.

This need has been much exploited by British and American 'schools of journalism'. The scale of their operations is phenomenal. To take one example, the School of Television and Journalism based in one of the English Home Counties claims to accept no less than about 350 pupils annually from Nigeria. Students are given a choice of free books on enrolment including 'Make Yourself a Master of Magic Phrases' and are promised the gift of 'Word Power', and instant elevation to the pinnacles of their chosen profession. Needless to say, the cost is heavy and a constant worry to many younger journalists, desperate for a quali-fication from Europe and unable to acquire one any other way. Even a local course can be expensive. One journalist estimated that two years at the Jackson College of Journalism at Nsukka would cost him £300 a year, while fees alone at the Nigerian Institute of Journalism were £150 p.a. in 1973–4. Overseas training and attachments provide an ever more costly and more direct exposure to news values and practices abroad, which we have discussed above in the context of the general influence of foreign media. (For an extended discussion of media professionalisation in Africa see Golding, 1977.)

In Sweden only 11 per cent of the journalists had any professional qualification (Table 7.6) and very few thought of seeking any. Seven had attended a Journalism High School (of which there were then two, one in Stockholm and one in Gothenberg) and another 14 had attended either the Journalists Institute or Poppius' Journalists School, which preceded the JHSs. Many of the older journalists expressed distrust of the JHS and as elsewhere contrasted the over-intellectualised and probably left-wing attitudes they encouraged with the more solid journalistic virtues acquired by a sound grounding in newspaper journalism. 'I don't like the JHS. There used to be good fellowship in the press in the old days based on hard work, lengthy experience, and conscientious attitudes. We didn't sit around and talk as they do now' (Reporter, SR).

Such resentment was by no means universal however. There was a general sense that education was a good thing however sceptical journalists might be of it as a specific training for journalism. Moreover different levels of education tended to be used as markers for different generations of recruitment. In the early years the only place for journalists to come from was the press but now entrants tended to be better qualified and there were more opportunities for direct entry. One reporter who was very sceptical of the educational value of the Stockholm JHS pointed out that taking the course there was useful as a way of making contact with the corporation in the hope of gaining regular employment after graduation. Level of education and recruitment generation also served as markers for the different styles of journalism which had been the source of much controversy within the organisation. Where the traditionalists, such as the reporter quoted above rejected education for producing too much talk, their opponents tended to value it for producing a wider sense of commitment.

> It's very good that there is more education and training for journalists. Those without tend to be negative and uninspired. It would be dangerous if they were all to be educated the same way. We want journalists from different backgrounds, with different experiences. But it's good they are younger, better educated, critical towards society and authority and committed towards getting things done. This is happening everywhere but maybe it's more common among young journalists and discussion at the high school and such places has strengthened these commitments. It's certainly caused problems for the high school and the newspapers, especially the conservative papers who attack the 'red high school' and threaten not to employ its graduates. But it's not as bad as they make out. When they get a job on a conservative paper they do it. We've taken some from the high school and we've had no trouble. (Executive, SR)

In broadcasting, part of the good fellowship of earlier years had arisen from common problems with an unfamiliar technology. A recording of the first Swedish news bulletin on television was a treasured momento of those years complete within its technical mistakes and presentational *faux pas*. In common with journalists elsewhere, Swedish journalists often made wistful reference to the need for technical training. In theory,

Table 7.7 Membership of unions and other associations (%)

(a) Unions	
Sweden SIF	8.1
SJF	6.5
Both	80.6
Non-members	4.8
Ireland NUJ	96.4
Non-members	3.6
Nigeria NUJ	62.7
Non-members	37.3
(b) Other associations	
Sweden PK	33.9
Parliamentary group	4.8
Other	4.8
Ireland	0
Nigeria ARJON	41.0
Other	4.8

new recruits to SR went through a short technical course to acclimatise them to the medium, but there seemed to be many who had either missed such a course or only gone on an abbreviated one. Initial recruits to Rapport had had a particular advantage in this because of the long planning period they had had prior to going on the air. Part of the Rapport philosophy was to make news with the television medium rather than to make news which could then be transmitted through it. The commonest attitude of Swedish journalists to training was caught by one who thought that 'journalists are born and not made, but once born an education certainly helps'.

Membership of unions in Sweden and Ireland was virtually total. Swedish journalists were generally rather puzzled to be asked why. Their answer was simply 'its natural' and so it was. Unions have played a prominent part in the life and government of the country. Union membership was not just uncontroversial but an expected feature of citizenship. In Sweden one union, Svenska Journalists Forbundet (SJF) organises journalists while another, white-collar union (SIF) organises SR staff. Most were highly dissatisfied with the SIF on the grounds that it was not a journalists' union and paid little attention to their special problems such as odd working hours and shift systems. In Ireland the primary commitment was to the Irish National Union of Journalists. There is no house union at RTE and most other broadcasters are in one of the larger multi-industry unions. Oddly the newsreaders were in Equity, the actors' union, which occasionally led to problems. Here even more clearly than elsewhere the prime commitment was to journalistic association rather then organisation as broadcasters, though more particularly commitment was to the RTE branch of the NUJ, and the formation of this 'chapel' was generally welcomed. Nearly half said they were 'not very satisfied' with the work of the union, though more had some kind words to say for it.

In Nigeria broadcast journalists were less unionised, only three-fifths were in the Nigerian Union of Journalists, though many of the younger journalists intended to join as and when invited to do so. Membership was largely nominal outside a few highly committed stalwarts. Although there were no staff associations, there was an Association of Radio and Television Journalists of Nigeria (ARJON) to which 41 per cent belonged. Both the NUJ and ARJON were primarily concerned with issues of work conditions; salaries, hours, appointments, fringe benefits and the like, rather than 'professional' issues such as training, ethics or qualifications. However, both occasionally arranged courses abroad, particularly in eastern Europe, though it would be more correct to say that east European sponsors, often journalist unions themselves, channelled their scholarships through the unions. This naturally led to charges of corruption and nepotism, and these were prominent amongst a barrage of accusations many members threw at the unions. Other charges included the view that the unions were weak and ineffective and very poorly organised.

It is interesting to compare these findings with those of Johnstone *et al.* in the United States, where a national survey found only 28.8 per cent of American journalists to be members of guilds or unions. In a country where it is claimed the professionalisation of journalism is highly developed, still only 45 per cent were in professional organisations of any kind, most of them local. Journalists have a conventional dilemma between professional association and occupational unionism. Broadcast journalists occasionally try to have it both ways though the solution, as H. L. Mencken pointed out long ago, is thrust upon them. The journalist, he wrote in 1927, 'is probably somewhat in error about his professional status. He remains, for all his dreams, a hired man, and a hired man is not a professional man' (Mencken, 1955, p. 216). Nevertheless in Sweden, where unionism was strongest, there was also a journalists' club which formed the basis of a professional association. About a third of the journalists belong to the Publicists Klubben (PK), the most prominent and longest established journalists' club in Sweden. The leadership of PK had become involved in pursuing a professional policy for journalists in matters of controversy. Many of the internal regulations on liability, for example, which were drawn up prior to the passage of the Broadcasting Liability Act were taken from PK recommendations and codes.

Journalists point out that their odd working hours destroy normal social life, so that they are thrust for conviviality into the company of their colleagues. We asked how many of their friends were journalists. In Sweden over a third (35.4%) said most or all of their friends were journalists, though another third (33.8%) said not many or none of their friends were journalists. There were several husband and wife pairs among those who had journalists in the family. In Ireland only 21.5 per cent said not many or none of their friends were journalists, while nearly 40 per cent said all or most. In both Sweden and Ireland many of the journalists were totally uninvolved in an occupational culture based in leisure shared with colleagues. Either because of involvement in other activities or family commitments, they avoided the conviviality of regular drinking with colleagues. In Sweden this was sometimes a matter of regret. Some journalists pointed out that as there was no bar in the building there was little opportunity for getting together socially after the programme. In Ireland social groups revolved round three or four distinct common interests; Irish speaking, horse-racing, politics and a group of more stereotypical regular drinkers from which the occasional permanent casualty emerged.

The pattern was very similar in Nigeria with as many very involved in a spill-over leisure pattern as avoided it altogether. Generally, the younger journalists retain social links with school or college friends while older journalists are enmeshed in a network of acquaintances acquired through years of working in different newsrooms. At the time of our interviewing there were no well-established journalists' clubs, though it was ubiquitously seen to be desirable. In RTK, to an even greater extent than at the other two stations, short staffing meant heavy overtime commitment and minimal opportunities for a full social life. Many journalists worked anything up to a fourteen-hour day (with some hours break during the afternoon), often with only three or four days off in a month. Nonetheless, there were hopes of a press club and the local police club served informally as such for the time being.

We have been emphasising the extent to which many of the journalists saw themselves as journalists first and broadcasters second. But of course there are very many ways in which broadcast and newspaper journalism differ, and many were acutely aware of these. We have touched earlier on the differences in the two fields as forms of employment. Here we turn to substantive differences in ideas and practice. Some of the perceived differences in status emerge from these. In Sweden many referred to the status which attached, or which they believed others attached, to SR in particular and television in general. 'We have to work with the more important things in this job. We don't have to deal with non-news. That makes it more satisfying. Everyone else thinks television has status too' (Editor, SR).

Several referred to the glamour of television as an '*open sesame*' when enticing sources. Some, however, thought this was wearing off, partly through public beliefs that SR had shifted politically leftward and partly as people became more used to television. For the individual journalist the visibility he obtained by a newspaper by-line had been exchanged for more direct exposure to the television camera or microphone. This meant exposure to the general public which in the Swedish case had been amplified by newspapers' fascination with television and those working for it. The publicity given to Swedish broadcasters in the early days was felt by them to have been rather like the publicity treatment given to film stars. Most were ambivalent as to whether this was flattering or intrusive but were generally agreed it was inappropriate to news and no help to good journalism.

> When television news started there were few broadcasters and they were glamorous stars but now the glamour is gone and it's a tough job. News journalism has developed much with many people involved. At the start there were few and you did not need to know so much but to have the right face. (Editor, SR)

There were mixed feelings about this in the other countries too.

> The prestige position of Dublin journalists on papers has been raised by the scope given by the *Irish Times* – by-lines, features. I think the prestige between television and newspaper journalists is roughly equal. I would have less prestige than a specialist on a newspaper, but no more no less than a general reporter. As far as prestige is concerned, the general public is not very important. Journalists are keen on how their fellow journalists rate them. (Reporter, RTE)

> Personally television suits me. This business helps me because I'm a performer. (Reporter, RTE)

On the other hand a Nigerian journalist was less enthusiastic.

> Writing on a paper gives you freedom, independence and a by-line.
> People know you exist. You come here and you're forgotten. (Reporter,
> NBC TV)

In Nigeria, as in most developing countries, radio is the major medium in terms of audience size, and probably influence. Television is a minority medium, however elite and influential its small audience. Newspapers, less closely controlled by government, are seen by many journalists to offer greater licence for the exercise of professional skill and discretion. 'Newspapers are more exciting because there aren't such limitations. There's self-censorship here, much more than on a paper. You find there are certain things they won't like' (Editor, NBC r).

The audience figure prominently in journalists' assessment of their relative status and in comparison of work in different media. Irish and Swedish broadcast journalists were mostly convinced their work had greater impact than that of pressmen. They valued working for a large audience through television though there was a common view that television news audiences are in some sense passive, less attentive or comprehending than when reading newspapers.

The most immediately obvious differences are in the style and practice of work. The rhythm and pressures of day-to-day routines are perceived as very different, and many journalists expressed nostalgia for the more familiar news production cycle they remembered in their newspaper days.

> If I'm out on a story with other newspapermen, they are working hard
> over a longer period. For the comparatively short time I'm working, I'm
> working harder. (Reporter, RTE)

> Television and radio are much more demanding for shorter periods.
> There are long hours of boredom and minutes of extreme pressure. TV is
> damned by the technicalities and the things that can go wrong.
> (Reporter, RTE)

The sentiment that newspaper work was real journalism, broadcast journalism a truncated and compromised form of the art, was frequently expressed, and explained by the exigencies of electronic news production. Short bulletins meant there was little time to go into any subject in depth. Many journalists missed the opportunity to exercise their original skill of writing.

> If you are writing, you read and learn more. Maybe my knowledge of
> economics, politics and the labour market is what I learnt 10 years ago.
> In this kind of job you are not forced to keep up. The best way to learn is
> to write. (Executive, SR)

> ... I miss the hustle and bustle of newspaper newsrooms. I miss a lot of
> the feature work that I would be doing on a newspaper. There's a

tremendous difference in language. I've learnt to write simply ... I don't know how to use big words any more. (Reporter, RTE)

It's boring here, newspapers are more enterprising, more challenging. You're regimented here to certain forms. In a newspaper you could spend two months on a story. (Reporter, MNBS)

However there were many journalists particularly in Sweden who valued the technical challenge and the opportunities it gave them.

There is a good chance of being first with the news here and what's more we have the technology to bring it straight to the people. (Reporter, SR)

You don't have to arrange an interview and then write it up like a newspaper journalist. You can actually show people the interview so they can see what he said and how he said it. (Editor, SR)

Many Nigerian journalists saw newspaper journalism as more active, more exciting. Similarly, many Irish journalists thought newspapermen had this more creative and positive job. This was often expressed, however, as the probable viewpoint of others, suggesting it was tinged with just a little doubt and perhaps a hint of romantic exaggeration of the lack of routine determination in a newspaper newsroom. 'Within the profession newspaper journalists think of themselves as doing a more worthwhile job' (Reporter, RTE).

The major technical differences are thus the amount of copy that has to be produced, the pressure under which it is produced, and its technical form. The newspaper journalist is seen to have more time, more leisure to produce more material about fewer stories. He is more active, more a news gatherer, less hampered by technology. The general job satisfaction most journalists expressed voiced a satisfaction with career and occupational opportunity rather than with professional practice. This was less true in Sweden where a period of expansion and change had resulted in television journalism 'coming of age'. Rapport was admired by newspaper journalists and readily attracted staff. The reorganisation however which produced news bulletins without moving pictures was seen as a throw-back to a more controlled, bureaucratic type of journalism.

The limitations of television did prompt serious concern. There was the problem of making room for background and explanation and other ways in which they intruded into root elements of the occupational ideology.

From an analytical point of view newspapers are better because you can present a longer and more balanced picture. You're not so much at the mercy of time and facilities as you are in television. Journalists have more scope to present a fairer, truer picture on a newspaper largely because in a visual medium you've got to be prepared to sacrifice some of the balance of newspaper reporting for the sake of visual impact. That's your limitation. (Sub-editor, RTE)

It is interesting to see how journalists assess the work of colleagues. Most broadcast journalists are voracious consumers of news from their own and other media. They are selective in this, in that their general consumption of broadcasting is not particularly high, and very much curtailed by the demands of evening and weekend working. In Nigeria many of the journalists had no television set, though evening newsroom routines were leisurely enough for them to take in more or less as many programmes as they wanted to. But for them, as for the majority of their audience, radio was the prime medium. Predictably, broadcast news was of major interest to journalists in all three countries, including radio news, which was listened to 'more than once a day' by 69.4 per cent of Swedish journalists, 85.7 per cent of Irish journalists and 80.7 per cent of Nigerian journalists.

Consumption of news media other than their own products is important for broadcast journalists in two ways. First, it provides a reinforcing mechanism by which items introduced onto the news agenda in one medium are likely to be picked up by other media, assuring a general, across the board, rough agreement about news selection. Second, it is a source of models and approaches to news production which generally promotes the tendency to homogeneity in news output. As a very rough generalisation, it seems that radio is often the main source for agenda-setting, while newspapers are the main source for news values and models for television journalists. Radio or agency reports provide the initial cue that something has happened, press attention the confirmation that it is 'big'.

Table 7.8 'As a journalist, which of the (country) papers do you regard most highly?' (%)

(a) Nigeria	
Daily Times	48.2
New Nigerian	43.4
Nigerian Observer	4.8
No particular one	3.6
(b) Ireland	
Irish Times	78.6
Irish Press	10.7
Irish Independent	7.1
No particular one	3.6
(c) Sweden	
Dagens Nyheter	75.8
Svenska Dagbladet	8.1
Aftonbladet	1.6
Expressen	3.2
Arbetet	3.2
No particular one	8.0

Journalists were asked to assess newspapers produced in their own countries, with the results shown in Table 7.8. In Ireland and Sweden there were clear favourites. All Swedish journalists read the two Stockholm morning papers. *Dagens Nyheter* was the clear leader because of its more comprehensive coverage based on a large staff and resources, but *Svenska Dagbladet* was often applauded for its foreign coverage. Journalists who chose papers other than *Dagens Nyheter* did so almost as a gesture of defiance to show they knew other papers were published and wished there was more variety in the Swedish press. In Ireland the *Irish Times* was conceded to be the best paper by three-quarters of the journalists who felt it clearly stood alone in comprehensiveness and style as a quality paper. Other virtues were discovered in other papers, the 'Indo' (*Irish Independent*) for its 'well-subbed' clarity, the *Irish Press* for journalistic resourcefulness. Occasional loyalty to an old stamping ground biased assessment in all three countries. There was often a split between a public assessment – 'Well, of course everybody acknowledges that X is the best paper' – and a private professional view – 'but you've got to admire Y for its subbing, layout, speed, editorial vigour, etc'. Generally newspapers are evaluated as professional products rather than as purveyors of a favoured political line or editorial stance. A Swede who cited the popular afternoon paper *Expressen* on which he had worked, was relatively unique in praising the techniques of popular journalism. Generally the broadcast journalists were up-market consumers of newspapers.

In Nigeria the poll was split between the Lagos *Daily Times*, a commercially successful independent paper originating in the heavily supported chain of International Publishing Corporation papers in West Africa, and the *New Nigerian*, published in Kaduna in the north and jointly owned at this time by the six northern state governments. The *Daily Times* attracted support for its professional approach, its comprehensiveness and objective, reliable coverage. The *New Nigerian* was appreciated, often almost in awe, for its fearless and outspoken editorial audacity.

Home-produced news magazines were only moderately supported and there was little feeling that they were required reading for the up-to-date, well-informed journalist. Apart from *Hibernia*, a Dublin-based political fortnightly which was read by over 70 per cent of the Irish journalists, most were only read by a minority of journalists, and often only casually because they were left lying around the newsroom.

Far more important were the international news magazines,

Table 7.9 Readership of foreign news magazines (%)

	Nigeria	Ireland	Sweden
Newsweek	75.9	17.9	45.1
Time	71.0	35.7	33.8
Any UK weekly	20.4	39.3	9.6
Other European	3.6	0	41.9
West Africa	18.0	—	—
Africa	14.4	—	—
Drum	38.5	—	—
Other	18.0	10.7	4.8

particularly the giant American weeklies, *Time* and *Newsweek* (Table 7.9). The impact of these magazines on general news awareness and in supplementing the news available from the initial agenda-setters is enormous, particularly in countries like Nigeria, where alternative sources of foreign news are so scarce. It would be too much to argue that a monolithic 'Newsweek culture' is spun around the journalistic globe, at least in advance of research, but it was clear both from these readership figures and from observation that the major American news weeklies carry great authority internationally in the choice of stories and the perspectives with which they are viewed.

Table 7.10 Readership of foreign newspapers (%)

	Nigeria	Ireland	Sweden
British 'popular' daily	19.2	17.8	0
British 'quality' daily	48.1	64.2	20.6
British Sunday 'popular'	8.4	10.7	0
British Sunday 'quality'	10.8	89.2	11.1
American	13.2	10.7	22.2
Scandinavian (not Sw.)	—	—	19.0
Other European	2.4	—	28.6

Foreign newspapers received less attention, though British 'qualities' (mainly *The Times* and *Sunday Times*) were widely read (Table 7.10). These circulate widely in Ireland, of course. These figures reflect 'exposure to' rather than readership since journalists would often claim to be regular readers of a newspaper (and indeed magazine) to which they in fact gave an occasional cursory glance in its travels around the newsroom. This was particularly true of the prestigious 'heavies'. In Nigeria for example a claim to readership very often expressed an aspiration or self-deluding exaggeration. The important point is that they were seen to have value and prestige. Expense alone would have prevented many younger Nigerian journalists regularly obtaining the London *Sunday Times*. Though newsrooms generally subscribed to most of these publications, they were often much delayed or mislaid before they could filter through to the newsroom. It was noteworthy that in Nigeria African newspapers, with the rare exception of one of the main Ghanaian papers, were never to be seen in newsrooms. Although the London-based *West Africa* and the Paris-based *Africa* are seen, apart from *Drum*, a general feature magazine published in London, hardly any Africa-based publications find their way into Nigerian newsrooms. Once again their source of Africa news and views comes from outside the continent.

The influence of foreign media did not only derive from direct regular exposure. Foreign news programmes were known from travel or by repute. In some cases they could be received directly. Swedes were well aware of British, German and American productions, and there was a long tradition of interchange with overseas stations, particularly the

BBC. The innovative executive responsible for Rapport was modest about his achievements saying he had done no more than bring to Sweden a style of broadcast journalism common in Britain and America. Latterly in Sweden, the thirty-minute ITN (London commercial television) News at Ten had displaced BBC news as the most admired overseas news programme. Nevertheless, there were Swedes, and not only those connected with Rapport, who rejected the term admiration and felt that Sweden could now hold its own in any international comparison. In Ireland ITN secured a firm majority (57.1% to BBC's 21.4%) based on admiration for its slick unadorned presentation. For many Irish journalists this was the model towards which they were working. At this time a thirty-minute news programme for RTE was under active consideration. Foreign news programmes were generally admired for doing well what others did inadequately rather than for doing different things. That is, they were praised for their 'professionalism', for being attractively packaged, slick, clear, rather than for being innovative or attempting to redefine or expand conventional notions of news.

There are three further ways by which foreign news media exert an influence. First, journalists are often sent on attachments to work or train with major overseas news media or educational establishments. For Nigerians this was a perk which was much sought after, both for its intrinsic satisfactions and for the boost to career prospects it would provide. Not surprisingly, young Nigerian journalists would eagerly seize the opportunity to travel and study and acquire foreign experience and qualifications, and with them a sense of news values. The BBC, to whom nine had been for training and to whom several more were sent or attached during the research period, is particularly admired. The Thomson Foundation, which ran a Television Centre in Glasgow and concentrated on short technical training courses, was also a much sought-after goal. Eastern European broadcasting organisations and schools of journalism are increasingly providing places and scholarships for African journalists, and competition for these places is intense. Many older Nigerian journalists complained that people came back from all these places full of unusable ideas, technically far in advance of anything practicable with the resources available. European or American experience was also valued by journalists in the other two countries, though it was less likely than in Nigeria to involve them in a formally organised training course. In both cases the key role which the BBC had played as a source of advice and overseas experience was still evident but younger journalists tended to have had a wider range of contacts.

Relatively few journalists were involved in the second source of influence, that of actually working for foreign news media on a freelance basis. The exception was Ireland, where a quarter of the journalists provided material for foreign, mainly British and American media, mostly arising from their knowledge and coverage of events in the north. None in Ireland or Sweden acted as 'stringers' for the agencies. In

Nigeria over 10 per cent claimed to do this, though this was quite certainly another exaggeration born of a sense of where status lay in the news-gathering ranks. It was in fact expressly forbidden by work contracts in some newsrooms. Finally, a few were members of international journalists' associations, or of the journalists' associations of countries in which they had trained or formerly worked. Foreign specialists were particularly enthusiastic about these as providing an opportunity to socialise with their international colleagues.

By and large foreign media exert their greatest influence where they are a source of actual material, as for example in the case of the BBC in Nigeria, or, in Europe, the different types of material available through the Eurovision news exchange. The variety carried by EVN was particularly important in allowing standards of comparison and evaluation to develop. Training programmes, international circulations, foreign visits and postings serve merely to reinforce the international conventions and standards of news content and presentation which are in any case rooted in the routines and limitations of television news production anywhere.

Whether the broadcast journalist is a 'professional' or not, his occupational values and ambitions are far from autonomous. The bureaucratic and work routines and exigencies that surround him severely compromise the free exercise of ideals or professional intent, and in turn such values come to incorporate and reflect such limitations. Sigelman has written, perhaps underestimating journalists' self-awareness, that 'the reporter's perception of his role is sufficiently narrow and technical that he does not feel that his functional autonomy is jeopardised.' (Sigelman, 1973.) In some ways the broadcast journalist resembles the form of professional described by C. Wright Mills (1956, p. 112), to whom 'much professional work has become divided and standardised and fitted into new hierarchical organisations of educated skill and service, intense narrow specialisation has replaced self-cultivation and wide knowledge; assistants and sub-professionals perform routine, although often intricate tasks. ...' The triumph of routine over professional ideology results from the technical complexities and scale of broadcast journalism, which make it a segmented and passive craft, often removed from the newspaper practices in which its ideology was formed. In many ways the broadcast journalist remains a journalist by design, a broadcaster by necessity.

The social role of the broadcast journalist

Broadcast journalists are aware of the power of their product as a force in the world. They reflect on their social role and changes in the image and nature of journalism. Many see a fundamental change in attitudes as younger men, not imbued with traditional newspaper practices or ideas, take up the reins, and as audiences become more sophisticated and demanding. Rapport in Sweden was deliberately making an attempt to foster these changes and further the cause they heralded. Much of our research has suggested that ambitions of this kind are necessarily frustrated by the nature of the task. We now turn to the journalists' views of this situation, and their general notions of their own social role and purpose.

Much recent analysis has drawn a distinction between two types of journalist, the one interventionist, socially committed and motivated, the other detached and uninvolved, concerned to preserve the objectivity and impartiality of journalism. These distinctions involve both a sociological and a social theory. Sociologically it is possible to argue that by the nature of the work he does the journalist is unavoidably the producer of an ideology, however implicit or incoherent. As a social theory it would be possible to argue that journalism *ought* or *ought not* to be committed to the dissemination of certain ideas rather than others. In debate these two strands of argument are often confused, though clearly if the sociological position is correct the choices made by a theory of what journalism ought to be are only one element among many shaping the occupation and the news it produces.

In a major study of American newsmen, Johnstone *et al.* have looked at the social correlates of what, borrowing from Cohen (1963), they term 'participant' and 'neutral' journalists. For the former 'that which is most worthwhile journalistically is believed to emerge from the active involvement of the journalist in the news-gathering process'. For 'neutrals' 'the news media constitute an impartial transmission link dispensing information to the public'. In sum, 'the neutral journalist allows the control of content to be vested in the events observed, while the participant sees control as vested in the journalist himself'. Johnstone's research consisted largely of identifying journalists who adhere to either of these positions and comparing them. The researchers found that 'participants' tend to be better educated, more likely to work in big organisations in the main cities. Interestingly they suggest that the relationship with education arises because 'neutral values are a product of apprentice-type experiences, of career lines in which one learns to be a journalist in the context of practical skills and concrete routines rather than abstract principles and theories'. However, commitment is one thing, practice another, and the researchers conclude that 'participants' are 'inspired by an image of professional practice which in large part is incompatible with organisational realities'. The conclusion is echoed almost inadvertently in a Scandinavian survey of different orientations among Nordic journalists which failed to find any correlation between demographic variables and orientation. 'This was read as a sign of *widespread consensus on professional values*, either as strongly positive, as neutral or as strongly irrelevant' (Høyer and Lorentzen, 1977, p. 113, emphasis added).

The general distinction has been reviewed by Janowitz in a paper contrasting the gatekeeper with the advocate as alternative professional models for journalists. A rather overdrawn version of the same distinction has been provided by Merrill, who writes of journalists with an 'Apollonian' orientation, inclined to be scientific, detached, aloof, and of the 'Dionysian' journalists, who are committed and involved. Merrill argues for a synthesis of these two, into an orientation bearing the ugly neologism of Apollonysian! A similar, if less pretentious, account appears in Argyris, who finds three job conceptions, that of the traditional reporter, concerned only with objective facts, the reporter-researcher, who wishes to provide interpretation, and the reporter-activist, who sees journalism as a means to an end (Argyris, 1974).

Other writers have looked at this distinction historically and we shall return to their approach in Chapter 8. The argument is that there has been a general shift from journalism requiring the exercise of an intellectually creative and politically critical skill, into journalism demanding technical proficiency and mastery of technique. This has resulted, first, in the elevation of these techniques and skills to defining characteristics of the special nature of the occupation and second in a residual nostalgia or ambition for socially creative and involved journalism. This latter strain lies behind much of the debate about 'the new journalism' in the United States, and its equivalents elsewhere. To argue for a general shift however is to risk succumbing to a tyranny of the present in which current trends are extrapolated as evidence of major change. Rather one can point to a continuing oscillation which has gone on throughout the history of journalism accompanying changes in market, technical factors and systems of control (Elliott, 1978). In terms of technique and control broadcasting is particularly characteristic as a restricted type of journalism.

Table 7.11 Journalists' opinions of organisation as 'mouthpiece of government'. (%)

	Sweden	Ireland	Nigeria
Agree	0	7.1	37.3
Not Sure	14.5	14.3	26.5
Disagree	85.5	78.6	36.1

One of the main tenets of the ideology of a free press as disseminated throughout the western world is its independence from government and political control. For journalists working in corporations established and financed, however indirectly, by government this is liable to be specially problematic. In Nigeria more than a third of journalists were prepared to accept that their organisation was a government mouthpiece and to justify this on the grounds that it was necessary if the people were to be properly informed in a developing country (Table 7.11). Only a few felt this reduced their own role. Most felt theirs was an important job which contributed to development. Nevertheless almost as many Nigerian journalists completely rejected the suggestion that they were a government agency. Journalists in the other two countries rejected this view even more vehemently. In Ireland this was in spite of the recent experience of the invocation of Section 31 of the Broadcasting Act, as described in Chapter 4. This led to a certain amount of sophistry as journalists tried to be realistic about their avowed ideology of freedom.

> Generally I don't know. Certainly in the newsroom every executive would deny it. As to what happens in the head of department's or the Director-General's mind in reaching judgements I don't know. I think that they are on the side of the angels – freedom/objectivity, but how they interpret it in the Irish context – how close to the bone they feel able to go I couldn't say. No television station is the mouthpiece of government, even if the government is running it. In a lot of areas you could say what you like. It is the narrow contentious areas that are a problem. (Reporter, RTE)

The Swedes however were much more confident in their denials. Those who recognised the problems associated with finance and periodic government reviews were still prepared to argue that SR was a special case. This they argued on two grounds. The news departments within the two channels in SR had a high degree of autonomy. The news structure of SR had created additional buffers between external pressures and the newsrooms. As one senior executive put it, 'Some people in SR may be responsive, but they do not make the programmes.' The second factor guaranteeing independence was the publicity which any attempt at interference would attract. Government reviews and agreements appeared to go further than might be usual in other countries in specifying details of internal organisation and programme policy. Nevertheless when it came to a controversy like the one over the organisation of a central news department the government had refused to become involved for fear of the adverse publicity this would attract. This in spite of the fact that *Aftonbladet*, the Stockholm social democratic paper, had publicised an interpretation of the controversy as an attempted right-wing coup within SR designed to frustrate the wishes of parliament.

Nearly all our broadcast journalists were confirmed in the view that as individuals they should have no political convictions, or that if they did have any they could, and should, be kept out of their work. Political allegiance was defined here as support for a party or party political position. Only two, one in Sweden, one in Ireland, were actually members of a political party. Journalists are defensive about accusations of political bias. In the early stages of this research an article appeared in one of the Stockholm popular evening papers stating that researchers from England had come to investigate left-wing tendencies in SR. Similarly, over the years RTE has been characterised as 'red Montrose' (the site of the studios). Such accusations are often advanced in evidence, along with complementary charges from the left, to support broadcasters' self-images of their own neutrality.

In Sweden one party, the Social Democratic, has dominated the political life of the country. Most journalists described themselves with words like 'I'm a social democrat, but . . .', not distancing themselves to the left or the right of the party's position but in terms of their own professional neutrality. Irish journalists avoided obvious commitment to a political party. The situation in the North had brought forward many latent, half-forgotten sympathies and attitudes. But most journalists were concerned to emphasise their responsibility by not allowing such sympathies to influence their work. For Nigerians 'politics' meant the bad old days of intrigue and corruption in the years leading up to independence and on to the military take-over in 1966. Many older journalists had been politically active, if only in the newspaper world. The Nigerian press remained a party press until very late and most journalists could still match surviving papers with the sectional interests they had once overtly supported and represented. Just as Nigerian political life more generally lies dormant, but very much alive beneath the wintry crust of military rule, so the party press and political commitments were often not far below the surface.

For the journalist political detachment is often signified by a disenchantment with the art and craft of politics. Party and governmental politics are seen as a game in which the journalist is a privileged spectator, close enough to spot the fouls and rule-bending, distant enough not to be splattered by the dirt. Epstein has perceptively described this view in his study of American broadcast journalists. In Epstein's view, journalists thought that 'neither ideology nor personal commitment to substantive goals were considered to be realistic explanations for [political actions]'. Instead, the tussle for electoral success was seen to dominate the strategy and statements of politicians whose hypocrisy was to be debunked by the journalists. The heightened cynicism he found among American journalists however was not in evidence in the newsrooms we studied.

In Sweden many journalists felt there was too much political news, that they had become too engrossed by the political football game. 'Sometimes the political game gets too much attention – very often it's not important. The problem is that journalists get more involved and interested in it than it's worth to the audience' (Reporter, SR). This judgement about the relative unimportance of political news was echoed in complaints that in general there was too much 'duty coverage'. An example commonly cited was the reporting of the Swedish king's funeral, a recent event at the time of our survey. Many felt too much attention had been given to a ceremony which would not bring about any change in Swedish society. Others, however, were pleased with the level of technical and professional accomplishment which had been shown in the coverage. 'Duty coverage' was regarded as unimportant in the sense that it involved the reporting of the unimportant acts of the powerful or the acts of those who were no longer powerful. It was supported more by tradition than a contemporary evaluation of the significance of the people and events.

Table 7.12 'In general would you say the contact you have had through your work with politics and politicians has given you more or less respect for politicians and the work they do?' (%)

	Nigeria	Ireland	Sweden
More	32.5	25.0	30.6
Not sure	43.4	39.2	40.3
Less	24.1	35.7	29.0

Table 7.12 tabulates the journalists' views about politicians. These figures disguise what were often mixed feelings about politics and politicians. For journalists, politics was not a remote process to be judged in terms of ideology and theory, but a system of administration manned by individuals. Politics was seen in close-up and thus judged as the acts of individuals were judged – in terms of integrity, efficiency, administrative skill, guile, charm and intelligence. 'There are differences between the various politicians. But if we consider the important politicians then my respect is greater. In general they are open, frank and decent' (Executive, SR).

A common journalistic critique of politics is to call for 'greater use of reason' as though this were a quality apart, a moral end in itself, a corrective to the untidy and unscrupulous interplay of individuals which is politics as it appears to the close-up observer. But another part of the journalistic view of politics was the acquisition of an informed sympathy; 'we understand their difficulties'. Involvement in the political game, in which the journalists were included, made them appreciate the difficult mechanics of political life, and to realise that they are too complex for anything much ever to be achieved.

A third, though less widely held, view was that all politics is corrupt, the political machine merely a vehicle for the ambitious and the cynical. To view politics in this way was by implication to contrast it with the integrity of journalism. The journalist was the voice of the people bearing an integrity no longer present in politics.

In general, the journalists' concept of politics equated it with government rather than with power, with office holding rather than social influence. The study of content in Chapter 6 showed that power is largely invisible in broadcast news. This has much to do with its absence from the journalistic view of politics. Nevertheless, there was some awareness, particularly among the Swedes, that this was a view broadcast journalism was constrained to take. Their ideal was to shift the focus of attention towards real centres of power and influence, though they realised that the odds were against dramatic change.

In as much as journalists felt entitled to introduce an explicit political view in news, this was largely restricted to foreign affairs. In Sweden, for example, Spain and countries like it were perceived as unarguably a target for criticism, countries whose political arrangements could safely be condemned without stepping on Swedish political toes. This licensed a more tendentious selection and treatment of news of such countries than would be considered fair in other areas. In Nigeria, South Africa was seen in the same light. In domestic politics the issues are less clear-cut and the rule of non-partisanship so central to broadcast (as distinct from newspaper) journalism is inviolable. In effect this means the underlying political ideology draws not on explicit or conscious political argument, but on unconsidered consensual values derived from more generally accepted ideologies in society. The consensus implicit in news is thus, by default, derived from the broader prevailing social consensus or ruling ideology. The exceptions, such as the cases cited above, are those which the political ideology of the country itself allows; progressive internationalism in Sweden, anti-imperialism in Nigeria and a certain pride in independence from Britain in Ireland.

The notion that broadcast journalism should serve some social purpose has a greater and a lesser implication. The lesser is that the news should provide a public service of information. A common critique of present practice on this ground is that, to do so fully, it should include information that is at present lacking and the background and analysis necessary for that information to be fully understood and useful. The greater view is that the news should explicitly serve defined social purposes, that it should be a means to well-considered and generally accepted ends. Journalists were frequently wary of more background and analysis because they saw it as leading towards this second view of news, the interventionist approach rather than the neutral, reportorial approach. Not only would more analysis soften the hard factual news which was the traditional journalists' stock-in-trade, it would allow the intrusion of unwarranted opinion which was beyond the journalists' right or duty to provide.

In Sweden, it was assumed that the trend was toward more background and commentary. This was partly because it was associated with the policy of Rapport which was accepted as the current pace-maker in journalistic style. But many were cautious about going too far in this direction, pointing out that current affairs was designed to provide such material: 'Background is very important but we have to avoid becoming an educational type of programme. This is *news* after all' (Editor, Rapport SR). Many Irish journalists were also unconvinced: 'I don't think you can successfully marry straight, objective news and current affairs comment and discussion. People should know quite clearly that it is the news they're looking at' (Reporter, RTE).

Because of their lack of specialists and resources, Nigerian news staff envied the extent to which European and American news media were able to provide such limited analysis as they do. This was seen as of paramount importance, though the same misgivings about stumbling into controversy and illicit opinion-mongering were common. Most newsrooms had plans to include short commentary sections in their bulletins. RTK had already done so and WNBC began to shortly after our research period. But in the struggle to get more film and adequate reporting staff these seemed remote objectives. To satisfy them 'background' was sometimes described in fairly limited ways. 'Yes, you have to delve a little. For example, that accident we had, we should add it's the worst since X' (Reporter, WNBC).

To some journalists background was acceptable, analysis not, though this seemed a circular way of begging the question of where contextual information ends and contentious perspective begins.

> It's important to get the background to stories. By background I mean the origins of the story. Analysis is trying to predict. (Reporter, RTK)

> Background, yes – there should be lots more of it, but analysis smacks of too many opinions. (Reporter, RTE)

Most journalists fell back on the organisational solution to this dilemma. News provided the facts, current affairs provided the analysis. News should be brief, factual, 'the biggest story of the year in $2\frac{1}{2}$ minutes, the biggest story of the night in 45 seconds – subbed down, crisp, down to the bones', as one Irish sub-editor put it.

The most common feeling was that expansion of background and analysis or the provision of context were tasks for specialists, with whom no newsroom believed itself to be sufficiently endowed. But many spoke of 'the news itself' or 'the actual news' as a separate entity, to which context, background and analysis were added or not, as considered desirable or feasible. Few considered the possibility of implicit context or analysis by default. The predominant view is that news is news, background or explanation are adornments which can be (and in the view of many should be) separated from that output labelled news.

Despite this idea many journalists felt strongly that there were some areas of news which were missing or inadequately covered. Thus they conceded that in the pursuit of improving their service to the public they should actively manipulate the content of news and that this might well be against the immediate tastes and wishes of the public. They were equally sure that some news items recurred too frequently or were given excessive prominence – Northern Ireland or religious ceremonies at RTE, 'duty' political coverage in Sweden, 'call-upons' in Nigeria. The gaps most commonly identified were geographical (either domestic, provincial or foreign) and what was often referred to as news about ordinary people. In Sweden widely publicised research of news content by PUB, the SR research department, had drawn attention to 'the blank spaces on the map'. A few journalists related this to the further need for non-crisis, non-topical coverage:

> We miss out on areas of the world in foreign coverage, for example China. But then what about the Indo-Pakistan war now, or South Vietnam now, or Bangladesh now? It's the result of news evaluation. There is no continuity. You do get it a bit in documentaries, but it's not the same. (Reporter, SR)

The problem with the other type of news identified as missing is that it is not news as conventionally understood. Swedish journalists referred to the difficulty of giving news about 'the real life of ordinary people' in two or three minutes. Both format and sources were a problem. While leaders and elites were available, the standard ways of contacting others either relied on the pot luck of their chance involvement in 'real' news, or in the occasional truncated interviews in street corner 'vox pop' sequences. The gap was explained by the difficulty of getting and packaging the information. Leaders and elites were not only available, they expected to be used and to make news. They had no doubt that their views and actions were important. Journalists were also frustrated by the way other types of news would be defined away by editors as 'not news'. This was particularly so in Sweden. Some pointed to the paradox that editors who were keen to get different types of stories at the planning stage or when discussing policy issues in the abstract might well rule out the end product when forced to decide what was to go in the programme on the night.

> We should do more on daily life, the hospitals, the courts, information on people's rights and where they can get help. The problem is in coming down from top people. It's difficult to get information and find out how it works. (Executive, SR)

> We could do more about ordinary people, more filmed reports – there is too much chat. Then too the party leaders push all the others out in parliament. Now we have to do more duty coverage. It means there is more traditional, hard leader type news than there used to be in Rapport in the past. (Rapport reporter, SR)

> We should do more on daily life. How people get along and how different decisions affect people and families. It's difficult to do in a concrete and comprehensible way. It's easier to take official statements and then all the parties and politicians are very content. (Reporter, SR)

In Ireland it was the senior news staff who were more likely to question conventional news values. Gaps were identified as arising from the undue prominence given to news from the North, especially the repetitive detail of shootings and bombings. Here news as social record was considered to have usurped news as entertainment or social service. Irish journalists were particularly concerned by the dearth of provincial stories, often mentioning local government issues. This may have been the provincial newspaper journalist view fighting through the metropolitan gloss acquired in Dublin broadcasting. Yet again the absence of this desired category was explained by difficulty of access – train times, video links – as well as by the intrusion and expansion of Ulster material. Because of this major concern with Ulster, RTE journalists spoke less of missing news of ordinary people than their colleagues in Sweden and Nigeria.

Demands for the provision of news for and about non-elites took their most focussed form in Nigeria. As well as expressing similar wistful and vague regrets about the lack of concern with ordinary people in news bulletins, a more explicit notion of 'development news' had evolved which is very different to the conventional definitions of news in the western tradition. The tensions between the idea of news as information deliberately selected and shaped to serve defined social purposes, and news as an objective and randomly selected capture of reality disinterestedly distributed, often proved difficult for Nigerian journalists, trapped between two currents of thought. It is a difficulty commonly found in African newsrooms and rooted in the very late transition from a political press to the adoption of those notions of objectivity associated with the western 'fourth estate' and the commercial press. For western experts it is a problem to be solved by education and experience until an adequate professionalism is acquired. Frank Barton, for some years director of the International Press Institute's Africa Programme, has written of 'the clash of loyalties between journalism and what might be called the African idea' which he says tormented his trainees. His book (Barton, 1969), which describes the work of the IPI training centre in Nairobi, describes very well how these torments arise and are administered.

Of course, the 'African idea', despite its local flavour and idiosyncracies, has a wider pedigree. The collision of journalistic ideologies which occurs within many newsrooms has much wider referents to styles of politics and government which are very apparent to the participants. Reuven Frank provides a good example of one side of the argument.

> Our system does not provide for working toward social good. Let us even postulate that there is a universally accepted social good which TV journalism should set itself to achieve or promote. And the decision would be made by five Albert Schweitzers sitting around a table. Whoever put them there could in time – perhaps far, far off in the future – replace them with five Joseph Goebbels or five Joseph Stalins, or five George Lincoln Rockwells. You see, it's not the five Albert Schweitzers who are important, but the table. I say the table itself is evil ... The only safeguard is free journalism, journalism without directed purpose, because whether that purpose represents good or evil depends on who you are. (Quoted in Small, 1970, p. 284)

The other side of the debate is represented by the publications of the Prague-based International Organisation of Journalists, and claims descent from the writings of Marx, and especially Lenin. The IOJ television journalism textbook, for example, suggests that:

> It is not too much to say that the journalist is the central figure in the process of social guidance – the man entrusted by society to express its interests, the bearer of the ideology of his class, the gatherer, supplier and interpreter of socially significant information. (Boretsky and Yurovsky, 1970, p. 20)

Thus in Africa the IOJ view is of the media, in Lenin's terms, acting as 'the tool of the economic education of the working masses' (see Ullrich, 1974). In Nigeria this view did not derive from considered immersion in the writings of the IOJ, Lenin or even Nkrumah. Rather it was a natural view of journalism on which the neutral, non-purposive ideology of the western 'fourth estate' had been imposed. Thus the same journalists would argue that they were neutral or 'middle of the road', yet reserve an unapologetic commitment to development news or African news. 'I've no political commitment, but I am an African, when they [the agencies] call freedom fighters guerillas, I regard them as my people . . . We have to champion their cause' (NBC newsreel reporter).

The view of the journalist that emerges is of an intellectual catalyst, prompting action and response by elites and masses alike.

> Our aim should be to try and help guide society. The journalist is in touch with people all the time, especially opinion leaders. If they are misinformed, it is our duty to guide him, to give our objective opinion on issues. You can show both sides and educate them. (Head of news, RTK)

This odd conflation of conflicting ideologies – the phrase 'objective opinion' is symptomatic of this as much as a verbal slip – is expressed by many African journalists. Their natural inclination to see journalism as socially purposive is given a guilt complex by training in the creed and practice of objective reporting as it is preached and conducted in European and American media.

The methods by which development journalism is produced are of four main types. First, there is a stress on the generally educative function of news, either about specific pieces of information or by the arousal of general awareness of events and their implications.

> It educates the mass public. People listen to different events, and learn from them. They want to know what causes things, like this middle-east business; we can learn lessons from it. (Reporter, WNBS)

> News can aid development a great deal. Farmers want to know about new brands of fertilisers, they want advice about what is happening in other parts of the world, when to plant. (Assistant editor, WNBC)

Second, whatever their reservations about the ethics or efficacy of military rule, most Nigerian journalists saw news as a channel of communication between government and governed, providing the former with clues about popular needs and demands, the latter with guidance about executive action.

> The media should show how people underneath live, so that those at the top know about living conditions. For example, this drought, we should show the scramble for water, or when the electric goes we should show the effects. (Reporter, NBC-TV)

> But for NBC people wouldn't know about government thinking. (Chief reporter, NBC-r)

The third, and favourite, method of using news to promote development was the 'spur to emulate' method. This exploited local pride and envy, by broadcasting news of developments in one place in the hope that others would rise to the bait of relative deprivation.

> If you give news about a village launching a development fund, others hear about it and it encourages them to do it too. (Editor, WNBC)

> The news is educative, it draws people nearer to government. Like the self-help projects – bridges, roads, piped water. Other people hear that and want to do the same themselves. At Ikiri, for example, the people hold meetings after hearing about such things on the radio. (Reporter, WNBC)

Of course, in many ways the political thesis behind such a view has all sorts of implications about the causes of underdevelopment and the nature of development. Specifically, it tacitly accepts the notion that 'peasant apathy' is the problem and mental stimulation the solution (Golding, 1974a). The final method of promoting development news is more populist at root, though aimed both at government and masses. 'We can stir up thinking, yes. If a Commissioner is talking about slum conditions we should go out and do a piece on it. We could give people a feeling of awareness, not just be a tube talking at them' (Reporter, NBC TV).

Such a view, of course, is quite consistent with conventional news values, relying as it does on a prior news-peg. More openly aggressive are views directed at reassessing authority. 'Not just development, revolution, especially with international news. If you report a major development in, for example, students changing the system or workers changing machinery elsewhere, or how peasants do things elsewhere, it will influence people here (Chief Sub-editor, RTK). Similarly, 'Yes, it can. For example, stories from the outside world. The Agnew resignation shows it could happen anywhere, it shows no-one is too big for the law' (Reporter, NBC r).

Both the Agnew resignation and the Watergate saga were followed with avid interest by Nigerian journalists and given great prominence. Both a gleeful, almost mischievous, delight in the embarrassment and humbling of a super-power, as well as the subtle moral parallels for their own country, where government corruption was a persistent topic of concern, made these stories unfailingly fascinating to Nigerian journalists. Watergate carried with it, of course, the additional attraction of being a running tribute to the social importance and professional power of the journalist. This made it an attractive model in all three countries. The 'Swedish Watergate' duly took place during the time of our survey though there were considerable differences of opinion on whether the affair was important and the parallel accurate. (For an account of the case see Guillou, 1974 and Stothard 1975–7.) From the point of view of our study of news making, the important point was not the incidents which occurred so much as the clear case they provided of the diffusion of frameworks throughout the international news system through which such incidents could be located and interpreted.

In Nigeria, journalists at RTK took the most developed social catalytic view of their role probably for the reasons outlined in Chapter 3. During the drought in the north, the governor of one of the northern states, conspicuously inactive himself in assistance plans, had made a rather feeble call for special taxes to aid the stricken. RTK repeated his speech two or three times 'to expose his irresponsibility. I'm sure people knew that was the idea behind it', as a senior news executive explained. One current affairs executive felt that the drought story had been the Watergate of the Nigerian media, another case of conceptual diffusion. Clearly a self-congratulatory glow of satisfaction added confidence to many of the agitational stories produced on this issue. The centre of production was in current affairs.

> The news people have a BBC view; they aim at truth, attempt to be fair to both sides. We want to take the government to task on this drought thing. Crucially we support northern interests, the north must catch up. We tell new staff they must advocate the cause of the common people. Of course we try to influence decisions. We reported on malpractices in distribution of the drought relief funds. The Governor sent five Permanent Secretaries to see what was happening. (Head of Current Affairs, RTK)

This journalist was convinced that the news should become like current affairs. It was interesting that other Nigerian journalists, when advancing the cause of development news, often slipped into the habit of labelling the desired material current affairs, unable to get away from the ingrained limited notion of non-purposive news. 'Yes, of course we must do more development news. Next year we are doing a programme, The Nation in Action, with interviews with Commissioners, or we'll do a programme asking people on a site when they will be finished' (Reporter, NBC r).

At RTK, however, development news via agitational prompting was common, despite the scepticism of the current affairs department, ever scornful of the abilities of their less educated, less qualified colleagues in news. A short comment on a donation to the drought relief fund by an army chief read: 'this is only the second donation from a military leader'. Both in choice of material and in treatment, RTK were stretching the bounds of conventionally understood objectivity and news values.

This brings us to the problem of whether such 'participant' or 'activist' notions of journalism are demographically derived. Our research suggests that it is the organisational and political context, and in turn the work situation, which can promote such approaches rather than age or education or other individual differences. RTK journalists were not notably different in such individual respects from other Nigerian journalists, but their relationship with government was. Similarly, in Sweden the significant differences in journalistic attitude were between departments. Rapport, a new programme produced by a new department, set about creating a different identity for itself within the context of broadcasting news and current affairs in Sweden. This meant less emphasis on authority and credibility as sanctified by traditional, corporate broadcast news values and a willingness to reappraise the notions of importance which they embodied. This was most effective in terms of output in the early days when the programme was less constrained to provide a comprehensive service of news as traditionally understood and was able to cover a few stories every night in more of a current affairs format. The obligation to provide 'news' limited the scope for autonomous decision over selection and presentation. By this time the 'Rapport ethos' had been diffused quite widely throughout the corporation. What was missing was the opportunity to realise its results in practice in the reorganised departments and news schedules. The work situation and organisational context allows such differences in approach to develop among journalists and these become critically important in allowing such differences to be reflected in different output styles.

We shall return to the implications of this, and earlier findings, for the notions of objectivity and impartiality in journalism, in the concluding chapter. It is no new dilemma. In 1920 Walter Lippmann was complaining that 'the work of reporters has thus become confused with the work of preachers, revivalists, prophets and agitators. The current theory of American newspaperdom is that an abstraction like the truth, and a grace like fairness, must be sacrificed whenever anyone thinks the necessities of civilisation require the sacrifice' (Lippmann, 1920, p. 8). The questions this begs must be answered, or at least considered in the conclusion to this study.

Note

1. Lillian Nowak conducted interviews in Swedish for us. We are grateful to her and to PUB, the audience research department of SR, for invaluable assistance with the research.

Chapter 8

The problem of broadcast news

We have seen in the previous chapters how news is shaped by a variety of organisational, cultural, economic and normative restraints. At the end of a tightly structured and highly organised production routine emerges a cultural package called news. This research, together with other comparable investigations, has shown how this package is more nearly a reflection of the forces that produce it than of the events and processes in social reality it claims to portray. This could hardly be otherwise, though we sometimes forget just how limited and oblique a view of the world around us is provided by news. Its limitations, especially in broadcasting, are frequently forgotten in the face of the apparent authority and credibility of both the medium and of broadcast journalism in particular.

In the last few years more and more journalists have themselves begun to question the nature and function of broadcast news. An increasing number of analyses and critiques have trickled down from broadcasters as evidence that within the profession the seeds of doubt are germinating. Especially within television, as a generation of purely broadcast journalists has come to maturity, a growing concern with the limitations of television news as conventionally organised has begun to gnaw away at old certainties and assumptions. It is no longer enough to point to criticisms from each end of the political spectrum and claim, 'You see, we must be OK, they both think we're biased.' For the first time it has become plausible that perhaps these criticisms are symptomatic of a deeper failure of news broadcasting.

In this chapter we review the responses to these new doubts. First we examine the implications of our own and similar research for the evaluation of broadcast news. Then we pursue the solutions, tried, suggested or ignored, which address the inadequacies of broadcast news.

Bias, objectivity and ideology

In Chapter 2 we rejected the claim that news is 'random reactions to random events'. But it is equally possible to see broadcast news as simply the result of the bias of individual journalists, committed either to professional notions of how news should be structured, or to social views of the ideas it should convey. For David Brinkley, the authoritative American newscaster, 'News is what I say it is. It's something worth knowing by my standards' (Brinkley, 1964). Whether this is unguarded arrogance, or hyperbole to make a point about the essential indefinability of news, it represents to many people the most likely explanation of news output. The newscaster is the visible tip of the news production plant, a visual or aural reminder that it is a process handled by people; fallible, biased and opinionated, like the rest of us. The obvious weakness of this explanation is that the news changes very little when the individuals who produce it are changed. An occasional shift in partisanship may be detected in the reporting of particular issues, but the events covered, and the nature of their coverage, remain the same. As this study has shown, even in highly varied cultural and organisational settings broadcast news emerges with surprisingly similar forms and contents. In addition the division of labour required for production limits the impact of individuals on news. This has often been observed (see Golding, 1974b, pp. 59–61). It is a central finding, for example of Tunstall's study of journalists (Tunstall, 1971, pp. 10–11) and of Epstein's study of television news production in the USA. Epstein (1973, p. 28) describes how 'News executives decide on the deployment of correspondents and camera crews; assignment editors select what stories will be covered and by whom; field producers, in constant phone contact with the producers in New York, usually supervise the preparation of filming of stories ... editors ... reconstruct the story on film ...' and so on.

Yet the notion of group, if not individual, bias persists. Whale (1972, p. 48) suggests that 'most journalists working for organs of mass communications can be said to be on the side of established order'. Smith, by contrast, argues that, in the 1960s at least, broadcast news was 'left-wing' because broadcasters 'accepted the view that this was the general drift of events' (Smith, 1973, pp. 101–2). The notion of bias is often contrasted with objectivity, and for clarity's sake two distinctions should be made. First impartiality and objectivity are distinct. Impartiality implies a disinterested approach to news, lacking in motivation to shape or select material according to a particular view or opinion. Objectivity, however defined, is clearly a broader demand than this. A journalist may well be impartial towards the material on which he works, yet fail to achieve objectivity – a complete and unrefracted capture of the world – due to the inherent limitations in news gathering and processing. Second, the bias of an individual reporter dealing with a single event may be reduced or even eliminated by, for example, the deliberate application of self-discipline and professional standards of reportorial fairness and accuracy, or by the use of several reporters of known and differing views. This form of bias must be distinguished from bias inherent in the practice of journalism per se. The former is conscious or at least detectable in individual reports, the latter is accumulative and results from news collection and production as a total process. In other words we should distinguish bias as the deliberate aim of journalism, which is rare, from bias as the inevitable but unintended consequence of organisation.

There are, then, three possible views of journalistic objectivity and impartiality. First, there is the professional view that it is possible to be both, based on the idea that objectivity and impartiality are attitudes of mind. Second is the view that objectivity may well be a nebulous and unattainable goal, but that impartiality is still desirable and possible. Thus, Brucker argues that 'objective reporting is nothing more than what good reporting has always been: the work of a disciplined professional who has tried his damnedest to get the whole story and then to present it accurately and honestly without letting his own bias creep into it'. (Brucker, 1973, cf. McDonald, 1971).

It is this claim that is challenged by the various studies of the reporting of particular events by the media (Halloran *et al.*, 1970; Lang and Lang, 1953; Benet, 1970), and indeed by the common observation of anyone who has witnessed an event, yet finds it barely recognisable from an obviously honestly intended news account. The third view, that neither objectivity or impartiality are in any serious sense possible in journalism, comes from a change of analytical perspective, from the short-term and deliberate production of news stories to the long-term and routine, unreflective practices of journalism as we have analysed them in this study. Objectivity and impartiality remain the aims of most day-to-day journalism. But we should understand these terms as labels applied by journalists to the rules which govern their working routines. Objectivity is achieved by subscribing to and observing these sets of rules, which are themselves the object of our analysis. We have seen how these rules, both the explicit regulations of organisational charters and newsroom manuals, and the implicit understandings of news values, are derived from the currents of supply and demand which eddy round the newsroom.

The assumed needs and interests of audiences on the one hand, and the truncated supply of information into the newsroom on the other, both exert pressures to which the organisation of news production responds. What are the consequences of these pressures?

When we come to assess news as a coherent view of the world, that is to step up from news values to social values, we enter an altogether more complex and tangled argument. News is ideology to the extent that it provides an integrated picture of reality. But an ideology is more than this; it is also the world view of particular social groups, and especially of social classes. The claim that news is ideology implies that it provides a world view both consistent in itself, and supportive of the interests of powerful social groupings. This can come about in two ways.

First, news is structured by the exigencies of organised production which are the main concern of this study. These allow only a partial view of the reported world which may or may not coincide with a ruling ideology. The historical process by which this coincidence occurs is more than accidental, and is rooted in the development of news as a service to elite groups, as described in Chapter 3. Thus most of the basic goals and values which surround journalism refer to the needs and interests of these groups. Second, in attempting to reach widespread, anonymous audiences news draws on the most broadly held common social values and assumptions, in other words the prevailing consensus, in establishing common ground for communication with its audiences. In the case of broadcast journalism the complex relationship with the state exaggerates this need to cling to the central and least challenged social values which provide implicit definitions of actions and events as acceptable or unacceptable, usual or unusual, legitimate or illegitimate.

To elaborate on this we can generalise from the analysis in Chapter 6. There are two key elements to the world of broadcast news; the invisibility of social process, and the invisibility of power in society. We can discuss these two lacunae separately. First, the loss of a sense of social process. News is about the present, or the immediate past. It is an account of today's events. The world of broadcast news is a display of single events, making history indeed 'one damn thing after another'. Yet in this whirl of innumerable events the lingering impression is of stasis. Events are interchangeable, a succession rather than an unfolding. What is provided is a topping up of the limited range of regularly observed events in the world with more of the same. A reassuring sameness assimilates each succession of events to ready-made patterns in a timeless mosaic.

This fragmentation of social process, evacuating history, has been described as 'a kind of consecration to collective amnesia' (Gabel, 1967, p. 113). In a real sense reason disappears as actors flit across the journalistic stage, perform and hurriedly disappear. Walter Lippmann described news as 'not a mirror of social conditions, but the report of an aspect that has obtruded itself'. Or more metaphorically he writes that 'the news does not tell you how the seed is germinating in the ground, but it may tell you when the first sprout breaks through the surface' (Lippmann, 1922). Thus industrial relations appears not as an evolving conflict of interest but as a sporadic eruption of inexplicable anger and revolt (Hartmann, 1976; Glasgow University Media Group, 1976). Similarly the political affairs of foreign lands appear as spasmodic convulsions of a more or less violent turn, while international relations appear to result from the occasional urge for travel and conversation indulged in by the diplomatic jet-set.

The second absent dimension in broadcast news is that of power. News is about the actions of individuals, not corporate entities, thus individual authority rather than the exertion of entrenched power is seen to be the mover of events. News, and broadcast news in particular, is the last refuge of the great man theory of history. Yet faces change, power holders are replaced, and such changes take pride of place in the circumspection of the news. The continuing and consistent power of the position is masked by concentration on the recurrent changes of office-holder.

In domestic news the focus is on central political elites and their daily gamesmanship in the arenas of conflict resolution. Groups which may exert power but which do not make news disappear, by definition, from view, and with them the visibility of power itself. Prominent among the absentees are the owners of property and their corporate representatives. Of all the institutions which contribute to social process none is so invisible to broadcast news as the world of the company boardroom. In international news the world revolves round the news capitals in Europe and North America. For audiences in the Third World their fellows in three continents are invisible, a communality of interest cannot emerge and problems appear particular and separate to each watching nation. Thus it is not the *effect* of the rich and powerful nations on the Third World that is seen, but their attractiveness as models, benevolence as aid-givers and convenors of conferences, or wisdom as disinterested umpires in local disputes.

Power disappears in the institutional definitions the news provides, an agenda of issues and arenas to which attention is directed. In particular politics is separated from power. Power is seen only in the public display of formality, gesture and speech by major political actors. It is defined by reference to government and the central institutions of political negotiation. Rositi has similarly drawn attention in his analysis of European television news to 'the primacy of formal politics' in the television news world (Rositi, 1975, pp. 25–30), and remarks on the absence of financial and business elites. Thus power is reduced to areas of negotiable compromise, and politics to a recurrent series of decisions, debates and personalities. It is removed from the institutions of production. Thus news bears witness to the institutional separation of economics and politics, a precondition for the evacuation of power from its account of the world. Power is absent from news by virtue of this severance of politics from economics; power is located in authority not in control, in the office-holder not the property owner. News thus provides a particular and truncated view of power, and in this sense power is a dimension that is effectively missing from news.

With these two missing dimensions – social process or history, and power – news indeed provides a world view. The question remains to what extent this is a coherent ideology. Analyses which see news as necessarily a product of powerful groups in society, designed to provide a view of the world consonant with the interests of those groups, simplify the situation too far to be helpful. The occupational routines and beliefs of journalists do not allow a simple conduit between the ruling ideas of the powerful and their distribution via the air-waves. Yet the absence of power and process clearly precludes the development of views which might question the prevailing distribution of power, or its roots in the evolution of economic distribution and control. A world which appears fundamentally unchanging, subject to the genius or caprice of myriad powerful individuals, is not a world which appears susceptible to radical change or challenge.

There are three ways, then, in which broadcast news is ideological. First it focuses our attention on those institutions and events in which social conflict is managed and resolved. It is precisely the arenas of consensus formation which provide both access and appropriate material for making the news. Second, broadcast news, in studiously following statutory demands to eschew partiality or controversy, and professional demands for objectivity and neutrality, is left to draw on the values and beliefs of the broadest social consensus. It is this process which Stuart Hall, 1970, p.1056) describes as 'the steady and unexamined play of attitudes which, via the mediating structure of professionally defined news values, inclines all the media toward the status quo'. The prevailing beliefs in any society will rarely be those which Stuart Hall, (1970, p.1056) describes as 'the steady and merely reinforce scepticism about such divergent, dissident or deviant beliefs. Third, as we have seen, broadcast news is, for historical and organisational reasons, inherently incapable of providing a portrayal of social change or of displaying the operation of power in and between societies. It thus portrays a world which is unchanging and unchangeable.

The key elements of any ruling ideology are the undesirability of change, and its impossibility; all is for the best and change would do more harm than good, even if it were possible. Broadcast news substantiates this philosophy because of the interplay of the three processes we have just described. What are the implications of such an analysis for proposals to improve or refashion broadcast news?

Reforming broadcast news: improvement or redefinition?

The many criticisms of broadcast news which have appeared in recent years have been accompanied by recommendations for reform. The twin dilemmas of broadcast news outlined in Chapter 2 have been attacked from a variety of angles, from the merely cosmetic alteration of presentation style to the wholesale reformulation of programme construction. But in essence all such recipes for reform boil down to two strategies. Either news must clarify its objectives and be more successful in achieving them, or it must change those objectives. That is, either news must be improved in its own terms, or those terms must be redefined. We can look at the suggested improvements first.

One solution recommended to the problem of brevity and incomprehensibility in news is to lengthen news bulletins. By doing this, it is argued, broadcast news would be able to relax its stringent selection procedures, and offer a more complete and explanatory service of news and background. Breakthrough in this direction began in the United States in the early 1960s, and the near half-hour news on the British commercial network (extended to this length in 1967) has been a model admired and imitated in many countries. By extending the news even further, perhaps to an hour, most of the limitations to broadcast news will disappear, it is suggested. For some this means taking broadcast news back to the true spirit of journalism as exemplified in newspaper practice. As noted in Chapter 7, for many broadcast journalists the newspaper world of printers ink and lengthy copy is the true home of their craft, and the more broadcast journalism can be moulded to this form the better it can achieve its ends. A British broadcaster, Robin Day, has argued strongly for a one hour news, significantly referring to it as 'a newspaper of the screen', having the 'depth and variety' lacking in the usual provision (Day, 1975, p. 68). But as with many who argue for this, he is really after not news at length, but news in depth, that is not more news but different news, and that brings us to a different set of arguments altogether.

A second solution would introduce more background information to flesh out the inadequate and superficial account of events at present given in bulletins. This approach tackles one of the dilemmas (comprehensiveness versus depth) and opts unapologetically for profundity. The immediate objection of course is that this ignores the dilemma rather than solves it. Finnish news broadcasting has attempted this in recent years, presenting fewer stories but providing background, analysis and comment (Nordenstreng, 1970). Apart from the obvious loss of other stories, many of the problems which arise have been seen in our discussion of the Swedish news programme Rapport, and in Finland led to an increasing dissatisfaction with the new approach. Most of all it challenges the root distinction between news and current affairs so central to broadcast journalism, and the magnetic pull away from the dividing line back to clearcut news stories is difficult to resist. It also challenges the basic values of factuality and objectivity by inviting comment in the guise of analysis, partiality in the guise of background, and for these reasons is unpopular among journalists. At least within the rubric of news it seems unlikely that this solution is possible insofar as it threatens the defining characteristics of news itself.

A third solution is seen to lie not in changing the product, but in changing the producers. If only journalists were better trained they would produce better news, this argument implies. One form of this argument suggests that the world has become a more complicated place, requiring more sophisticated observers to inform the public of what is happening. The journalist thus needs to be more an academic, probably a specialist, and certainly educated to know how and where to seek for relevant information. Victor Zorza, a well-known journalist specialising in 'kremlinology' suggests that 'the complexity of world affairs has become so great that for the journalist to acquire real understanding of the more important issues and to convey that insight to his readers he needs at least a week's work per issue' (Zorza, quoted in *UK Press Gazette*, July 30th, 1973, p. 10). Of course, in a form of knowledge production committed to daily output this would lead to the 'Tristram Shandy paradox', narration of events being unable to keep pace with their occurrence. More training has long been supported. Not for the first time we can go back to Walter Lippmann, finding it 'altogether unthinkable that a society like ours should remain forever dependent upon untrained accidental witnesses' (Lippmann, 1920, pp. 78–9). Yet many journalists still view their craft as a mixture of inborn talent and acquired skills, the latter best learnt in practice rather than in didactic abstraction. At best, as we saw in Chapter 7, the broadcast journalist acknowledges the need for training in the technical skills of broadcasting, so that he can better apply the innate talent of journalism. Even in the United States, where journalism education has long been a vast academic industry (by 1940 there were well over 500 schools of journalism), a recent national survey of American journalists found that 'most working journalists were not trained in journalism ... most of those trained in journalism ... do not enter the news media' (Johnstone *et al.*, 1976).

For many such writers the real issue is that training will protect the journalists from external influence. It will provide a barrier of knowledge and expertise with which to resist the blandishments of public relations and the other fall-out of the 'information explosion'. There are two schools of thought in the argument for more and better training. One school argues that specialist training in journalism would do more harm than good, leading as it does to over-institutionalisation and control (Merrill, 1974). To assist the development of journalistic autonomy more general education for recruits to the trade is necessary. The other school, while not disparaging general education, sees the need for specialist approaches. Training means professionalism, and professionalism means autonomy. Like many such recommendations, of course, the calls for more training and better professional education beg the important question: which skills, for what ends, using what techniques and grounded in what assumptions and axioms?

Thus a second series of demands for reform is less concerned with improvement than with the need to redefine news, and the task of reformulating long-cherished beliefs about journalism and its practice. One such demand suggests, in effect, that news should look more like sociology. If its basic deficiency is a lack of perspective a more sociologically informed approach, it is argued, would provide the answer. There are clearly two aspects to this, the problem of information gathering and of its presentation. Sociological inquiry, involving lengthy research procedures, is impossible in the daily routine of news production (Jacobs, 1970). But the more important point is conceptual. It lies in the argument that events should not be presented as isolated, accidental or superficial occurrences but as grounded in deeper social process. People act not as individuals but in roles, representing group interests and aggregate or collective characteristics. Rositi (1975, p. 9), for example, complains that in news 'the image of society offered is without structure but also without a subjective agent'. His analysis, which seeks news items containing 'explicit statements of links of causality not purely technical or institutionalised, for which a real or even generic law could be understood ...' (Rositi, 1975, p. 13) found very few such items, which he labels 'sociologically rationalised', in the broadcast news of the four European television stations he studied.

Clearly news is not sociology: the question is, could it be? This is not to ask for the usurpation of one professional ideology by another. Most critics of television news seem to share the views of a BBC chairman who 'would rather take my chances with journalists than have the news chosen by academics' (Hill, 1972, p. 16). But this view raises the issues of, first, selection: are there criteria other than conventional news values by which to select items for news? Second, the issue of conceptualisation; is it possible to portray social process, groups, power and institutions in news? The answer to both arises from the tautology that news is news. If it were based on other than conventional news values, it would be something else. Similarly the only way, ultimately, to portray abstractions, is to have someone talk about them, reducing television news to a narrator of ·vritten ideas – the much despised 'talking head'. There is no evidence that the advantages in a new 'visual grammar' available to broadcast news can cope with the better presentation of abstraction. Indeed, the thrust of much of this study is that television news is bound to deal only in the concrete, visual, immediate and individual to the exclusion of more basic explanatory forms.[2] In representing the group by the individual, and process by event, news is not merely rendering the difficult comprehensible; it is giving an account of the world based on entirely different premises to the sociological.

A second attempt to redefine news involves a candid rejection of objective journalism and the explicit identification of the journalist with his product. In the United States this movement has been labelled the 'new journalism', the latest in a line of styles bearing this emblem. It has been mainly associated with the work of magazine writers and novelists, providing news features of unashamed, even aggressive subjectivity, often spilling over into flamboyant egocentricity. As an influence on mainstream journalism the school, if such it is, has been marginal, except as instigator of a widespread secondary literature on its significance. In fact, the 'new journalism' is less a matter of philosophy than of style. One advocate (Newfield, 1974, p. 61) describes it thus:

> [The 'new journalists,] have successfully appropriated the forms and techniques of the short story to enrich and expand the more immediate genre of journalism. They have exploded the old, impersonal, objective journalism school formulas, to get closer to the human core of reality, to tell more of how it really is after the press agents and ghost-writers go home, to be more than 'clerks of fact'. . . . They set a mood, and experiment with character development, and try wild stabs of intuitive insight. They have a point of view and they are personally involved in

whatever they are writing about. And most distinctively, the new journalism challenges the central myth of objectivity.

This is to crucially misunderstand the objectivity claimed by conventional journalism, which though putatively an epistemological neutrality, is no more than a set of rules and procedures governing practice. It is revealing that 'the new journalism' has been predominantly concerned with character: the freakish, the colourful, the eccentric. Even less than 'the old journalism' is it able or willing to deal with social or historical process. Interesting, too, is the almost total restriction of new journalists to the print media. The forms and conventions of television news would entirely reject any reformulation in terms of news as 'wild stabs of intuitive insight' in the form of the short story. Yet ironically both broadcast news and the new journalism share two central traits. They focus on the individual and on character, and they have a love of the bizarre and the unusual. The revolution is less, perhaps, than it claims.

The third reformulation of news is an attempt to make journalism more active and less reportorial. This distinction has been characterised by contrasting 'investigative' with 'stenographic' journalism (Epstein, 1975, p. 4). The claim of investigative journalists is that beneath 'the facts' lie more facts. The job of the journalist is to seek out these hidden layers, advancing beyond the passive role of the reporter to the active role of investigator. As with 'new journalism', 'investigative journalism' is a case of old wine in new bottles. 'Trust no one' is a celebrated adage of journalism even if one more often honoured in the breach than in the observance. Its results appear more often as newsroom gossip than as public copy. The urge to investigate motive as well as report horror is at least as old as the broadside ballad. Helen Hughes (1940) noted that an important strand of popular journalism strove for understanding rather than sensational reaction. It has had such powerful advocates as William Randolph Hearst and Lincoln Steffens. The latter wrote in his autobiography, 'the true ideal for an artist and for a newspaper [is] to get the news so completely and to report it so humanly that the reader will see himself in the other fellow's place ...' (quoted by Hughes, 1940, p. 94). 'Muck-raking' also enjoyed a vogue in pre-war America and that is the style of journalism which is the direct antecedent of contemporary 'investigative journalism'. Political scandals in a variety of western countries have brought the new brand to the fore. Though Epstein and others have disputed how for it was journalism which revealed the scandals, it is significant for our argument in this chapter that it was the evidence of political rather than economic corruption which was taken as truly scandalous.

Before we turn finally to the implications of these reformulations, two characteristics should be noted. All these developments have taken place away from broadcasting. The central assumptions of broadcast news, its reportorial, truncated style and commitment to an impartial service for heterogeneous audiences, militate against any of these more discursive, print-oriented innovations. Second, the very rigid distinction between news and current affairs, legitimising in organisational form the deep-rooted separation of reportage from comment and analysis, prevents any stretching of the defining boundaries of broadcast news *per se*. One consequence is that most changes introduced into broadcasting news and current affairs are changes in form rather than content; to do with the style of presentation, the length of programmes and their positions in the schedules. Schlesinger (1978) has made this point on the basis of his study of the British experience. But it is also apparent that there has been some change over the long term in news values.

Such change has lacked dramatic markers, sudden turning points or even the extensive historic research necessary to show that it is real. Nevertheless some long-term changes in priority have taken place, and many of the journalists we talked to in the course of this research were anxious to keep the momentum going. An example was the decline in the importance of ceremonial news in Sweden. Another type of change in content, much emphasised by 'whig' historians of broadcasting like Grace Wyndham Goldie (1977), is the gradual extension of the number and range of subjects which are considered fit for broadcasting. This extension has its most dramatic impact outside news in the production of 'fly on the wall' documentaries in which microphones and cameras have been allowed into various sanctums, hitherto closed to public view. So far as news itself is concerned the gain has mainly been in topicality and style. The right to broadcast leaks and matters of controversy while still based on speculation; to treat authority figures in an inquiring rather than a deferential manner; to abandon self-imposed or official embargoes related to the nature of the medium rather than the content of the news. Such rights were the ones which many of the most self consciously innovative journalists in Sweden were seeking to establish and secure. In many ways they can be seen as attempts to put broadcast journalism on the same footing as newspaper journalism.

They are changes which bring us back to questions of presentation and style but also to reliability, impartiality and objectivity. The broadcasting of speculation and controversy for example lacks the clear marker of an event to justify its inclusion. Reporting events is both the foundation of production routines and the fundamental defence for broadcasters in their relationship with government and the state. If speculation is to be reported prior to an event then an alternative marker is needed, that the speculation is well-founded, current elsewhere, reported in the press. This means that while broadcasting *makes the news* that most people see and hear, it rarely *makes news* in the sense of introducing new items or interpretations. Broadcasting news is more about processing than gathering, and even such gathering as does go on, as discussed in Chapter 5, might better be termed receiving. Fundamentally it is a passive rather than an active agent in the general media culture (Elliott, 1972a, Ch. 8). To shift the balance would require new procedures and criteria of impartiality to be developed and accepted which would allow broadcasters to make more independent judgements.

The implication of this study is that the gods of objectivity and impartiality are not false idols, to be smashed in a revolutionary regeneration of news. They are merely labels for sets of rules and routines which are unavoidable in the organisation and established practice of broadcast journalism. These practices and routines produce a body of knowledge which, lacking the dimensions which could cope with a critical account of society, is manifestly conservative, and in the broadest sense consensual. James Carey (1969, p. 35) has summed up some of the implications of this:

> What are lamely called the conventions of objective reporting were developed to report another century and another society. They were designed to report a secure world of politics, culture, social relations, and international alignments about which there was a rather broad consensus concerning values, purposes, and loyalties. The conventions of reporting reflected and enhanced a settled mode of life and fleshed out with incidental information an intelligible social structure ... one can be content with 'giving the facts' where there are generally accepted rules for interpreting the facts and an agreed set of political values and purposes. Today no accepted system of interpretation exists and political values and purposes are very much in contention'.

But not, it should be added, in the world portrayed by news, which does indeed have its own 'system of interpretation' in which dissenting perceptions and values are made to appear peripheral or ephemeral.

The more contentious the subject, the more manifest does that 'system of interpretation' become, and the more do alternatives become invisible. Not only are dissenting views and opinions ruled out, as in the case of the Irish coverage of the North, but so too is much of the informative detail which is necessary to construct any alternative account. Another study of news about the north of Ireland (Elliott, 1977) found that reporting concentrated on the bare details of violent incidents – who, what, where and when, and that the concentration was more marked, the more controlled the medium. It was more marked in broadcast than press reports, and more marked in Irish than British broadcasting. The paradoxical problem for the broadcaster is that for all his devotion to the ideal of informing the democratic public, his ability to do so is likely to be least on those issues which matter most, those which call the democracy itself into question or threaten the stability of the state.

Why, then, would it not be possible to provide alternative accounts in a journalistic pluralism of competing reports? Reprieve subjectivity, in other words, and allow an explicit and open competition in broadcast news. As we have seen there is some variability in the way the objective criteria are applied to different subjects in different countries or as between subjects with differing significance for the state. Variation in the international genre of broadcast news takes place within specifically national contexts. As Anthony Smith (1973, pp. 108–9) has argued, 'Without its central *national* professional discipline, news becomes a different genre altogether ... The whole idea of news is that it is beyond a "plurality of viewpoints" ... Ten views of reality do not between them add up to a new "objectivity" to exchange for an old one.' Where broadcasting is not national and monolithic it is regional, and it is not the different views of different regions that are in contention, but of competing groups and classes. In other words, the restructuring of broadcast news to serve and give account of such competition requires the restructuring of broadcasting rather than of news. The very scale of broadcasting places it beyond the reach of those groups most likely to wish to challenge prevailing definitions of social values (Murdock and Golding, 1977). As broadcasting increasingly becomes the dominant news medium (by virtue both of audience size and of widespread credibility), the lingering pluralism of print media is less able to compete with the diffusion of these prevailing values.

If the restructuring of broadcasting to take account of competing views is one precondition for reformulating news, it remains to question whether such a task is possible or worthwhile. We have argued that broadcast news, as conventionally understood, is inherently incapable of adequately portraying social process. An alternative solution is to recognise these limitations and concentrate on alternative methods of satisfying the functions of news. By breaking down the unreal distinction between news and other 'current affairs' broadcasting more elbow room would be created for the extended presentation of abstraction and complexity. The massive application of resources to the speedy collection and packaging of television news could be reconsidered in the light of its dubious contribution to the enlightenment of audiences. Studies of comprehension and retention have repeatedly shown how little audiences get from broadcast news. Such studies are concerned with the short-term comprehension of facts, faces and events. Yet in the longer term broadcast news conveys a view of the world not easily amenable to this kind of study, but which we have suggested is partial, conservative and lacking in crucial dimensions. The solution to these problems lies outside the immediate confines of broadcast news itself. It necessitates a reconsideration of the role and structure of broadcasting as a knowledge-creating medium, and a radical questioning of the complex of relationships between broadcasting and society.

Notes

1. These first two solutions were widely canvassed in Britain recently by two television journalists (Birt and Jay, 1975, 1976). Though their views were far from radical, merely popularising a critique which had been familiar for many years, they were soundly castigated in many professional quarters. Their major arguments were that news required more background, that fact and comment were inseparable, and that

broadcasting required a 'new journalism' in an integrated system dissolving the old distinction between news and current affairs. These views were scorned as dangerous, unreadable and alarming by the Deputy Editor of *The Times*. He wrote that 'Apart from the danger of taking oneself too seriously, they surely cannot believe that a mass audience will watch a one-hour news and views programme every night and not switch to Match of the Day or the late movie. . . . There are facts and events which can be factually reported: indeed which must be factually reported without comment. Instant analysis and comment by pundits who cannot possibly know what really happened can diminish the impact of the event and can be dangerously misleading.' (Heren, 1976.)

2. It might be concluded that this line of thought suggests the inherent advantages of radio over television news. Radio is, of necessity, provided by talking heads, and its advantages as a news medium have often been advanced in recent years. We are left, however, with the problem that television news is by far the more popular source; radio news, though popular, is most popular in its brief, bulletin, or spot news format.

News staffing and output

Table App. 1.1 News Staffing

	Total station staff	News staff			News staff as % total
		Radio	TV	Combined	
S.R. (1971)	4,038		244		6.0
RTE (1973)	1,550			99	6.4
NBC (1973)	2,331	95*	17		4.8
WNBC (1972)	347	27	4		8.9
RTK (1973)	390			19	4.9

*Including states

Table App. 1.2 News department output

	Station hrs per week			News programmes per week§			News dept. output as % total		
	radio	TV	total	radio	TV	total	radio	TV	total
SR (1973)	360.3	84.5	444.8	34.5	14.4	48.9	9.6	17.0	11.0
RTE	115	54¶	169	6	4.5	10.5	5.2	8.3	6.2
NBC (1973)	130	45*	175	24 †	3.5	27.5	18.5	7.7	15.7
WNBC	129	42‡	171.5	13.75‖	3.5	17.5	10.7	8.2	10.1
RTK	131.5	37	168.5	26.25	3 †	29.25	20.0	8.1	17.4

*Including 10 schools
† Including translations in vernaculars and local bulletins
‡ Including 3 schools
§News including sports by news department and news background in news programmes
‖ Including 3.5 BBC relays
¶ Including 5.25 schools

News organisation charts

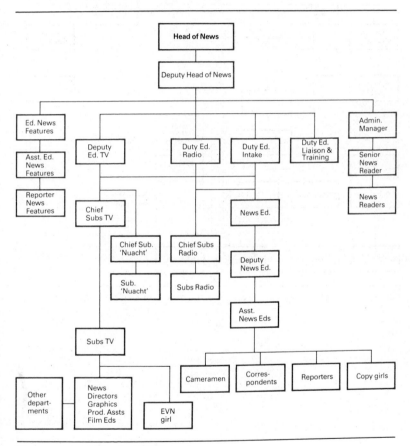

Fig. App. 2.1 RTE – April 1972

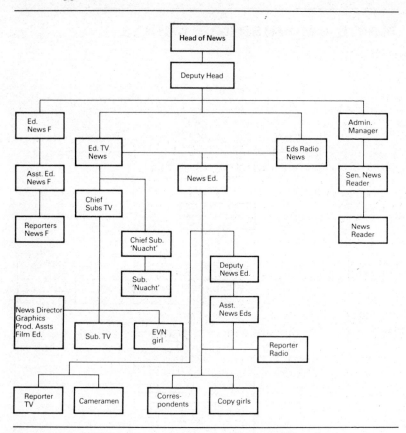

Fig. App. 2.2   RTE Newsroom organisation (as perceived October 1973)

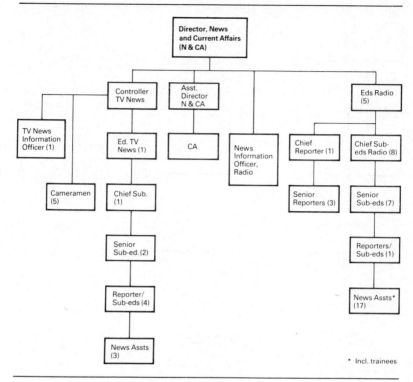

Fig. App. 2.3   NBC News Division (Lagos only) 1973

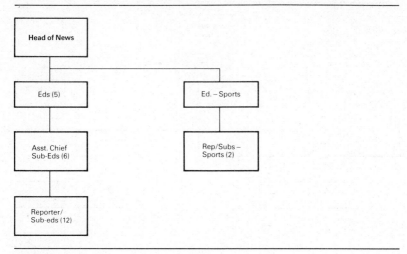

Fig. App. 2.4   WNBC News Division 1972

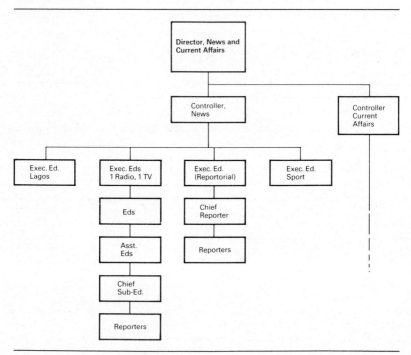

Fig. App. 2.5   WNBC News Division 1975

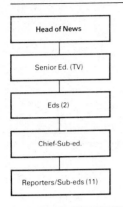

Fig. App. 2.6   RTK News Division 1973

Swedish News

Swedish News Production was formally organised in a similar way in all the various production units. Under the executives, journalists and reporters were divided into various groups – intake and output editors, domestic and foreign commentators and reporters, general reporters. These were theoretically of equal status but differed in the power they were able to exercise over the production of news partly because of their position in the news production process – output editors tended to be most powerful as they were in the end responsible for the output, and partly according to the style of the programme – this was most significant in deciding the relative position of the foreign and domestic groups. The production units varied from each other less in formal organisational differences than in the use they made of the formal structure.

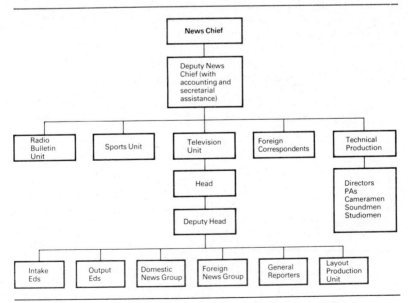

Fig. App. 2.7   Central News Department (prior to reorganisation in 1973)

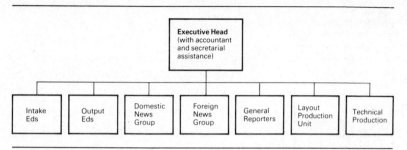

Fig. App. 2.8   Rapport

Bibliography

Adedeji, A. (ed.) (1968) *Nigerian Administration and Its Political Setting*, London, Hutchinson.

Ainslie, R. (1966) *The Press in Africa*, London, Gollancz.

Akenson, D. H. (1970) *The Irish Education Experiment: The National System of Education in the Nineteenth Century*, London, Routledge and Kegan Paul.

Aloba, A. (1959a) Journalism in Africa: I. Nigeria, *Gazette*, Vol. 5, No. 2, pp. 246–8.

Aloba, A. (1959b) Journalism in Africa: II. The tabloid revolution, *Gazette*, Vol. V, No. 4, pp. 409–12.

Aloba, A. (1959c) The African Press: III. Yesterday and today, *Gazette*, Vol. V, No. 3, pp. 317–21.

Alsop, J. & S. (1960) *The Reporter's Trade*, London, The Bodley Head.

Altheide, D. L. (1976) *Creating Reality – How TV News Distorts Events*, New York, Sage Publications.

Altheide, D. L. and **Rasmussen, P. K.** (1976) Becoming news: a study of two newsrooms, *Sociology of Work and Occupations*, May.

Andersson, I. (1956) *A History of Sweden*, London, Weidenfeld and Nicolsen.

Anderson, S. V. (1968) *The Nordic Council: A Study of Scandinavian Regionalism*, Seattle, University of Washington Press.

Anon. (1965) Producing the news, *New Left Review*, No. 32, July/August, pp. 32–9.

Anon. (1965) Africa listens in: the impact of broadcasting, *Round Table*, LX (June), pp. 234–41.

Anon. (1977) Nigerian Television Authority, *Combroad*, **36**, July–Sept., pp. 37–9.

Argyris, C. (1974) *Behind the Front Page*, London, Jossey-Bass.

Arikpo, O. (1967) *The Development of Modern Nigeria*, Penguin Books, Harmondsworth.

Arms, George L. (1961) Diary from Nigeria, *NAEB Journal*, Sept./Oct., pp. 11–21.

Arms, George L. (1963) Diary from Nigeria: the second year, *NAEB Journal*, Jan./Feb., pp. 9–14.

Arnold, B. P. (1974) The structure and content of news programmes, *EBU Review*, Vol. XXV, No. 5, pp. 28–31.

Aronson, J. (1971) *Packaging the News*, New York, International Publishers.

Austin, P. B. (1968) *On Being Swedish*, London, Secker and Warburg.

Awolowo, O. (1968) *The People's Republic*, London, Oxford University Press.

Awolowo, O. (1970) *The Strategy and Tactics of the People's Republic of Nigeria*, London, Macmillan.

Axinn, George H. and **Axinn, Nancy W.** (1968) Rural communications: preliminary findings of a Nigerian study, *Rural Africana*, Spring, Vol. V, pp. 19–27.

Axinn, George H. and **Axinn, Nancy W.** (1969) Communication among the Igbo: a folk-village society, *Journalism Quarterly*, Summer, pp. 320–4.

Azikiwe, N. (1970) *My Odyssey*, London, Hurst.

Bagdikian, B. H. (1971) *The Information Machines*, New York, Harper and Row.

Baggaley, J. and **Duck, S.** (1976) *Dynamics of Television*, Farnborough, Saxon House, Teakfield.

Barnes, A. M. (1957) Research in Radio and TV News, *Journalism Quarterly*, pp. 323–32.

Barton, F. (1966) *The Press in Africa*, IPI, Nairobi.

Barton, F. (1969) *African Assignment: The Story of IPI's Six-Year Training Programme in Tropical Africa*, Zurich, International Press Institute.

Barton, F. (n.d.) *The African Newsroom*, International Press Institute, Zurich.

Batscha, R. M. (1975) *Foreign Affairs and the Broadcast Journalist*, New York, Praeger.

Beckett, J. C. (1969) *The Making of Modern Ireland, 1603–1923*, Faber, London.

Benet, J. (1970) Interpretation and Objectivity in Journalism, in A. K. Daniels and R. Kahn-Hut (eds), *Academics on the Line*, San Francisco, Jossey-Bass, 1970.

Bensman, J. and **Lilienfeld, R.** (1973) *Craft and Consciousness*, London, Wiley Interscience.

Berg, M. *et al.* (eds) (1977) *Current Theories in Scandinavian Mass Communication Research*, Grenaa, Denmark, GMT.

Berelson, B. (1949) What missing the newspaper means, in P. Lazarsfeld and F. Stanton (eds), *Communications Research 1948–49*. New York, Harper and Bros.

Birt, J. and **Jay, P.** (1975, 1976) Series of articles, in *The Times*, 28 Feb. 1975; 30 Sept. 1975; 1 Oct. 1975; 2 Sept. 1976; 3 Sept. 1976.

Bleyer, W. G. (1927) *Main Currents in the History of American Journalism*, New York, Houghton Mifflin.

Bliss, E. Jr. and **Patterson, J. M.** (1971) *Writing News for Broadcast*, New York, Columbia University Press.

Blumler, J. G. (1969) Producer's attitudes towards television coverage of an election campaign: a case study, in P. Halmos (ed.), The Sociology of Mass Media Communicators. *The Sociological Review: Monograph No. 13*, pp. 85–115.

Board, J. R. (1970) *The Government and Politics of Sweden*, Houghton Mifflin, Boston.

Bogart, L. (1968–1969) Changing news interests and the news media, *Public Opinion Quarterly*, Vol. XXXII, No. 4, pp. 560–74.

Boorstin, D. J. (1963) *The Image*, Harmondsworth, Penguin Books.

Boretsky, R. A. and **Yurovsky, A.** (1970) *Television Journalism*, Prague, International Organisation of Journalists.

Bonnevier, H. (1978) Swedish radio and TV up for review, *EBU Review*, Vol. XXIX, March, pp. 17–19.

Boyce, G. (1978) The fourth estate: the reappraisal of a concept, in J. Curran, G. Boyce, P. Wingate (eds), *Newspaper History*, London, Constable, pp. 19–40.

Breed, W. (1956) Analysing news: some questions for research, *Journalism Quarterly*, pp. 467–77.

Breed, W. (1958) Mass communication and socio-cultural integration, *Social Forces*, pp. 109–16.

Brinkley, D. (1964) Interview, in *TV Guide*, 11 April.

Broadcast (1976) Protests as RTE axes '7 Days', 26 Sept. 1976, p. 5.

Broadcasting Review Committee (1974) *Report 1974*, Dublin, Stationery Office, Prl. 3827.

Brucker, H. (1973) *Communication is Power: Unchanging Values in a Changing Journalism*, New York, Oxford University Press.

Bryan, C. R. (1960) Enlightenment of the people without hindrance: the Swedish Press Law of 1766, *Journalism Quarterly*, Vol. 37, No. 3, pp. 431–4.

Burns, T. (1977) *The BBC: Public Institution and Private World*, London, Macmillan.

Bush, C. R. (1960) A system of categories for general news content, *Journalism Quarterly*, Vol. 37, pp. 206–10.

Carey, J. (1969) The communications revolution and the professional communicator, in P. Halmos (ed.), *The Sociology of Mass Media Communicators*. Sociological Review Monograph 13, Keele, pp. 23–38.

CBS News (1958) *Television News Reporting*, New York, McGraw-Hill.

Chibnall, C. (1977) *Law-and-Order News*, London, Tavistock Publications.

Chick, J. D. (1971) The Nigerian press and national integration, *Journal of Commonwealth Political Studies*, Vol. IX, pp. 115–33.

Chubb, B. (1970) *The Government and Politics of Ireland*, London, Oxford University Press.

Cipolla, C. M. (1969) *Literacy and Development in the West*, Harmondsworth, Penguin Books.

Cohen, B. C. (1963) *The Press and Foreign Policy*, Princeton, Princeton University Press.

Coker, I. (1952) *Seventy Years of the Nigerian Press*, Lagos, Daily Times.

Coker, I. (1960) The Nigerian press 1929–59, in report on international seminar, Dakar,

1960, on *Press and Progress in West Africa*, Distributed by Ibadan University, pp. 73–133.

Coker, I. (1968) *Landmarks of the Nigerian Press*, Cornell University Press, 1968.

Coker, O. S. (1968) Mass media in Nigeria, in R. D. Colle (ed.), *Mass Media Systems*, Ithaca, Cornell University Press.

Coleman, J. S. (1963) *Nigeria: Background to Nationalism*, Los Angeles, University of California Press.

Collins, R. (1976) *Television News*, London, BFI Television Monograph.

Colonial Office (1937) *Interim Report of a Committee on Broadcasting Services in the Colonies*, London, HMSO, Colonial No. 139.

Colonial Office (1954) *Colonial Reports: Nigeria 1952*, London, HMSO.

Coltart, J. M. (1963) The influence of newspapers and television in Africa, *African Affairs*, July, pp. 202–10.

Cox, G. (1965) Bringing more hard news to the screen, *EBU Review*, May, No. 91B, pp. 27–8.

Cranfield, G. A. (1962) *The Development of the Provincial Newspaper, 1700–1760* London, Clarendon Press.

Crawley, J. (1964) *The Work of a BBC Foreign Correspondent*, London, BBC Lunchtime Lectures.

Croll, P. and **Golding, P.** (1972) Letter: 'The sociology of television', *The Listener*, 26 Oct., Vol. 88, No. 2274, p. 541.

Curran, J. (1977) Capitalism and control of the press, 1800–1975, in J. Curran *et al.* (eds), *Mass Communications and Society*, London, Edward Arnold, pp. 195–230.

Darnton, R. (1975) Writing news and telling stories, *Daedelus*, 104. pp. 175–94.

Davis, M. (1977) *Interpreters for Nigeria: The Third World and International Public Relations*, Urbana, University of Illinois Press.

Day, R. (1970) Troubled reflections of a TV journalist, *Encounter*, May.

Day, R. (1975) *Day by Day*, London, William Kimber and Co. Ltd.

de Sola Pool, I. and **Shulman, I.** (1959) Newsmen's fantasies, audiences and newswriting, *Public Opinion Quarterly*, pp. 145–58.

Diamond, L. A. W. (1965) Bringing radio and television to Northern Nigeria, *EBU Review*, Sept., pp. 27–29.

Dizard, W. P. (1966) *Television: A World-View*, Syracuse University Press, New York.

Donohue, G. A., Tichenor, P. J. and **Olien, C. N.** (1972) Gatekeeping: mass media systems and information control, in F. G. Kline and P. J. Tichenor (eds), *Current Perspectives in Mass Communication Research*, London, Sage.

Dowling, J. and **Doolan, L.** (1969) *Sit Down and Be Counted*, Wellington, Dublin.

Edeani, D. O. (1970) Ownership and control of the press in Africa, *Gazette*.

Ehrenberg, A. *et al.* (1970) The news in May, *Public Opinion Quarterly*, Winter, pp. 546–55.

Elder, N. (1970) *Government in Sweden*, London, Pergamon.

Elias, T. O. (ed.) (1969) *Nigerian Press Law*, London, Evans.

Elliott, P. (1972a) *The Making of a Television Series: A Case Study in the Sociology of Culture*, London, Constable.

Elliott, P. (1972b) *The Sociology of the Professions*, London, Macmillan.

Elliott, P. (1977) Reporting Northern Ireland: a study of news in Britain, Ulster and the Irish Republic, in *Media and Ethnicity*, Paris, UNESCO.

Elliott, P. (1978) Professional ideology and organisational change: the journalist since 1800, in J. Curran, G. Boyce, P. Wingate (eds), *Newspaper History*, London, Constable, pp. 172–91.

Enahoro, P. (1973) Africa's beseiged press, *Africa*, No. 21, May, pp. 28–32.

Epstein, E. J. (1973) *News from Nowhere – Television and the News*, New York, Random House.

Epstein, E. J. (1975) *Between Fact and Fiction: The Problem of Journalism*, New York, Vintage Books.

Fairlie, H. (1968) The unreal world of television news, in D. M. White and R. Averson (eds), *Sight, Sound and Society*, Beacon Press, Boston, Ch. 9.

Fang, I. (1968) *Television News*, New York, Hasting House.

230   *Bibliography*

Fathi, A. (1973) Problems in developing indices of news values, *Journalism Quarterly*, Vol. 50, pp. 497–501.

Federal Ministry of Information (1970) *Second National Development Plan, 1970–1974*. Federal Ministry of Information Printing Division, Lagos, Nigeria.

Fisher, D. (1977) The New Broadcasting Legislation in Ireland, *EBU-Review*, Sept., pp. 47–50.

Fisher, D. (1978a) Broadcasting in Ireland: RTE changes fast, but with caution, *Intermedia*, Vol. 6, No. 1, Feb., pp. 8–9.

Fisher, D. (1978b) *Broadcasting in Ireland*, London, Routledge and Kegan Paul.

Forsyth, F. (1969) *The Biafra Story*, Harmondsworth, Penguin Books.

Frank, R. (1970) An anatomy of television news, *Television Quarterly*, Vol. 9, No. 1, Winter, pp. 11–23.

Frank, R. S. (1973) *Message Dimensions of Television News*, London, Lexington Books.

Friendly, F. W. (1967) *Due to Circumstances Beyond Our Control*, New York, Random House.

Fulcher, J. (1973) Class conflict in Sweden, *Sociology*, Vol. 7, No. 1, Jan., pp. 49–70.

Furhoff, L. (1968) The mass media in Scandinavian countries, *Scandinavian Political Studies*, Vol. 3.

Gabel, J. (1967) *La Falsa Conscienza*, Dedalo, Bari, quoted in Rositi (1975).

Galtung, J. and **Ruge, M.** (1965) The structure of foreign news, *Journal of Peace Research*, Vol. 1, pp. 64–90.

Gans, H. J. (1970) Broadcaster and audience values in the mass media: the image of man in American television news, *Transactions of the Sixth World Congress of Sociology*, Vol. IV, pp. 3–14. International Sociological Association, Milan.

Gelles, R. J. (1971) The television news interview: a case study in the construction and presentation of social reality, Mimeo.

Gerbner, G. (1961) Press perspectives in world communication, *Journalism Quarterly*, pp. 313–22.

Gerbner, G. (1964) Ideological perspectives and political tendencies in news reporting, *Journalism Quarterly*, pp. 495–509.

Gerbner, G., Holsti, O. and **Stone, P. J.** *et al.* (1969) *The Analysis of Communication Content: Developments in Scientific Theory and Computer Techniques*, New York, Wiley and Sons.

Glasgow University Media Group (1976) *Bad News*, London, Routledge and Kegan Paul.

Golding, P. (1974a) Media role in national development: critique of a theoretical orthodoxy, *Journal of Communication*, Vol. 24(3), Summer, pp. 39–53.

Golding, P. (1974b) *The Mass Media*, London, Longman.

Golding, P. (1977) Media professionalism in the Third World: the transfer of an ideology, in J. Curran, M. Gurevitch and J. Woollacott (eds), *Mass Communication and Society*, London, Arnold, pp. 291–308.

Golding, P. and **Murdock, G.** (1978) Confronting the market: public intervention and press diversity, in J. Curran (ed.), *The British Press: A Manifesto*, London, Macmillan.

Goldstein, W. (1967) Network television and political change: two issues in democratic theory, *Western Political Quarterly*, Vol. 20, pp. 875–87.

Gorham, Maurice (1967) *Forty Years of Irish Broadcasting*, Talbot, Dublin.

Grant, M. A. (1971) Nigerian newspaper types, *Journal of Commonwealth Political Studies*, IX, 2, pp. 95–114.

Grant, M. A. (1975) *The Nigerian Press and Politics Since Independence*, London University, unpublished PhD.

Gray, T. (1966) *The Irish Answer*, London, Heinemann.

Green, M. (1969) *Television News: Anatomy and Process*, Belmont, California, Wadsworth.

Guillou, J. (1974) A Swedish Watergate? *Index on Censorship*, Vol. 3, No. 2.

Gustafson, A. (1961) *A History of Swedish Literature*, Minneapolis, University of Minnesota Press.

Gustafsson, K. E. and **Hadenius, S.** (1976) *Swedish Press Policy*, Stockholm, Swedish Institute.

Hachten, W. A. (1971) *Muffled Drums: The News Media in Africa*, Iowa State University Press.

Hadenius, S. *et al.* (1968) The social democratic press and newspaper policy in Sweden 1899–1909, *Scandinavian Political Studies*, **3**.

Hahr, Henrik (1963) The code of broadcasting practice in Sweden, *EBU Review*, Vol. XIV.

Hall, S. (1970) A world at one with itself, *New Society*, 18 June, pp. 1056–8.

Hall, S. (1972) The limits of broadcasting, *The Listener*, 16 March, Vol. 87, No. 2242, pp. 328–9.

Hall, S. (1975) The 'structured communication' of events, in *Getting the Message Across*, Paris, UNESCO Press.

Halloran, J. D., Elliott, P. and **Murdock, G.** (1970) *Demonstrations and Communication: A Case Study*, Harmondsworth, Penguin Books.

Halloran, J. D. and **Gurevitch, M.** (eds) (1970) *Broadcaster/Researcher Co-operation in Mass Communication Research*, University of Leicester.

Hannan, Damian (1970) *Rural Exodus*, London, G. Chapman.

Harris, P. (1976) International news media authority and dependence, *Instant Research on Peace and Violence*, Vol. VI, No. 4, pp. 148–59.

Harris, P. (1977) *News Dependence: The Case for a New World Information Order: Final Report to UNESCO*. Mimeo. Centre for Mass Communication Research, Leicester.

Hartmann, P. (1976) *The Media and Industrial Relations*, unpublished, Leicester Centre for Mass Communication Research.

Head, S. W. (1963) Can the journalist be a professional in a developing country? *Journalism Quarterly*, Autumn, Vol. 40, No. 4, pp. 594–8.

Head, S. W. (1972) *Broadcasting in Africa*, Temple University Press, Philadelphia.

Hemanus, P. (1971) Development trends in the Scandinavian press, *Gazette*, Vol. XVII, No. 1/2, pp. 1–15.

Heren, L. (1976) The alarming flaws in the case for New Journalism, *The Times*, London, 9 Sept.

Hill, Lord (1972) Speech at Extel dinner, 10 April 1972, reported in *UK Press Gazette*, No. 328, 17 April, pp. 16–17.

Hill, Lord (1974) *Behind The Screen*, London, Sidgwick and Jackson.

Himmelstrand U. (1969) *Nigeria and Biafra: The Truth that Vanished*, Stanford, Valifornia, unpublished, Centre for Advanced Study in the Bahavioural Sciences.

Himmelstrand, U. and **Folster, K.** (1967) *Political persecution in the Lagos and Western Nigeria Press 1959–65*, Uppsala, unpublished.

Hirsch, F. and **Gordon, D.** (1975) *Newspaper Money*, London, Hutchinson.

Hohenberg, J. (1964) *Foreign Correspondence: The Great Reporters and Their Times*, New York, Columbia University Press.

Home Office (1977) *Report of the Committee on the Future of Broadcasting* (The Annan Committee), London, HMSO Cmnd 6753.

House of Commons (1851) *Select Committee on Newspaper Stamps: Minutes of Evidence*, London, HMSO.

Howe, R. W. (1966) Reporting from Africa, *Journalism Quarterly*, Summer.

Høyer, S., Hadenius, S. and **Weibull, L.** (1975) *The Politics and Economics of the Press: A Developmental Perspective*, Beverly Hills, Sage Publications.

Høyer, Svennik and **Lorentzen, Pål E.** (1977) The politics of professionalisation in Scandinavian journalism, in *Current Theories in Scandinavian Mass Communication Research*, Grenaa, Denmark, GMT.

Hughes, H. M. (1940) *News and the Human Interest Story*, Chicago, University of Chicago Press.

Hughes, H. M. (1942) The social interpretation of news, *Annals of the American Academy of Political and Social Science*, Vol. 219, pp. 11–17.

Inglis, B. (1954) *The Freedom of the Press in Ireland 1784–1841*, London, Faber and Faber.

Isaacs, J. (1968) Television journalism, *Encounter*, March.

Jacobs, R. (1970) The journalistic and sociological enterprises as ideal types, *The American Sociologist*, Vol. 5, pp. 348–50.

Janis, I. L. (1949) The problem of validating content analyses, in H. D. Lasswell *et al.*,

Language of Politics, Boston, MIT Press.
Janowitz, M. (1975) Professional models in journalism: the gatekeeper and the advocate, *Journalism Quarterly*, 52(4), Winter, 618–26.
Jenkins, D. (1969) *Sweden: The Progress Machine*, London, Hale.
Johnson, T. J. (1972) *Professions and Power*, London, Macmillan.
Johnstone, J. W. *et al.* (1972–1973) The professional values of American newsmen, *Public Opinion Quarterly*, Winter, pp. 522–40.
Johnstone, J. W. C., Slawski, E. J. and **Bowman, W. W.** (1976) *The News People*, Urbana, University of Illinois Press.
Jolliffe, H. R. (1956) A semantic slant on objectivity vs interpretation, *Journalism Quarterly*, Vol. 33, pp. 189–93.
Jones- Quartey, K. A. B. (1959) Anglo-African journals and journalists in the nineteenth and early twentieth centuries, *Transactions of the Historical Society of Ghana*, 4(1), 47–56.
July, R. (1968) *The Origins of Modern African Thought*, London, Faber and Faber.
Kandil, H. (1975) Towards Arabvision, *EBU Review*, Vol. XXVI, No. 3, May, pp. 58–61.
Kaplan, A. (1943) Content analysis and the theory of signs, *Philosophy of Science*, Vol. 10, pp. 230–47.
Karnekull, T. (1964) *The Intellectual Face of Sweden*, Uppsala, Ergo International.
Katz, E. and **Wedell, G.** (1978) *Broadcasting in the Third World: Promise and Performance*, London, Macmillan.
Kim, C. L. and **Oh, J. H.** (1964) Perceptions of professional efficacy among journalists in a developing country, *Journalism Quarterly*, Spring.
Kinkel, J. T. (1968) Broadcast journalism: tribulations of a one man gang, *Journal of Broadcasting*, Vol. 12, pp. 131–6.
Kolade, C. (1968) Mass Communications in Africa, *Asian Broadcasting Union Newsletter*, **40**, 20, July.
Kolade, C. (1974) Nigeria, Section 5.1, pp. 78–88, in S. Head (ed.), *Broadcasting in Africa*, Temple University Press.
Lang, K. and **Lang, G. E.** (1953) The unique perspective of television and its effect: a pilot study, *American Sociological Review*, 18(1), Feb., pp. 3–12.
Lang, K. and **Lang, G. E.** (1955) The inferential structure of political communicators, *Public Opinion Quarterly*, pp. 168–83.
Lang, K. and **Lang, G. E.** (1970) *Politics and Television*, Chicago, Quadrangle.
Lansipuro, Y. (1975) Joint Eurovision/Intervision news study, *EBU Review*, Vol. XXVI, No. 3, May, pp. 37–40.
Leroy, D. J. and **Sterling, C. H.** (eds) (1973) *Mass News: Practices, Controversies and Alternatives*, Englewood Cliffs NJ, Prentice-Hall.
Lippmann, W. (1920) *Liberty and the News*, New York, Harcourt, Brace and Howe.
Lippmann, W. (1922) *Public Opinion*, Free Press, New York.
Lippmann, W. and **Merz, C.** (1920) A test of the news, *New Republic*, 4 August.
Lloyd, P. C. (ed.) (1966) *The New Elites of Tropical Africa*, London, Oxford University Press.
Lubell, S. (1962) Personalities and issues, in S. Krause (ed.), *The Great Debates*, Indiana University Press.
Lyle, J. (1967) *The News in Megalopolis*, San Francisco, Chandler.
MacDonald, D. (1971) Is objectivity possible? *The Center Magazine*, Sept.–Oct., Vol. 4, Pt. 5, pp. 29–43.
MacDougald, D. (1944) *The Language and Press of Africa*, Philadelphia, University of Pennsylvania Press.
Mackay, I. K. (1964) *Broadcasting in Nigeria*, Ibadan, Ibadan University Press.
MacNeil, R. (1968) *The People Machine*, London, Eyre and Spottiswoode.
McQuail, D. (1969) Uncertainty about the audience and the organisation of mass communications, in P. Halmos (ed.), *The Sociology of Mass Media Communicators*, Sociological Review: Monograph No. 13, Keele, pp. 75–84.
McRedmond, L. (1976) *Written on the Wind: Personal Memories of Irish Radio 1926–1976*, Dublin, Gall and Macmillan.
MacRorie, K. (1956) The process of news reporting, *ETC*, Vol. 13, pp. 254–64.

Madden, R. R. (1867) *The History of Irish Periodical Literature*, 2 vols., London, T. C. Newby, reprinted Johnson Reprints, 1968.

Mahoney, J. (1975) The news exchange: the agency dimension, *EBU Review*, Vol. XXVI, No. 3, pp. 32–4.

Mazrui, A. (1972a) *Cultural Engineering and Nation Building in East Africa*, Evanston, Northwestern University Press.

Mazrui, A. (1972b) The press, intellectuals and the printed word, in E. Moye and S. Rayner (eds), *Mass Thoughts*, Kampala, Makerere University.

Meehan, J. (1970) *The Irish Economy Since 1922*, Liverpool University Press.

Mencken, H. L. (1955) *Prejudices*, New York, Vintage Books.

Merrill, J. C. (1968) Global patterns of elite daily journalism, *Journalism Quarterly*, pp. 99–105.

Merrill, J. C. (1974) *The Imperative of Freedom – A Philosophy of Journalistic Autonomy*, New York, Hastings House.

Meyer, T. P. and **Miller, W. C.** (1970) Emphasis and non-emphasis radio newscast delivery, *Journalism Quarterly*, pp. 144–7.

Mills, C. W. (1956) *White Collar*, New York, Oxford University Press.

Molotch, H. and **Lester, M.** (1974) News as purposive behaviour, *American Sociological Review*, Vol. 39 (Feb.), pp. 101–12.

Mott, F. L. (1962) *American Journalism: A History, 1690–1960*, New York, Macmillan.

Munter, R. (1967) *The History of the Irish Newspaper, 1685–1760*, Cambridge, Cambridge University Press.

Murdock, G. (1973) Political deviance: the press presentation of a militant mass demonstration, in S. Cohen and J. Young (eds), *The Manufacture of News*, pp. 156–75, Constable, London.

Murdock, G. and **Golding, P.** (1977) Beyond monopoly – mass communications in an age of conglomerates, in P. Beharrell and G. Philo (eds), *Trade Unions and the Media*, London, Macmillan,pp. 93–117.

Nayman, O. B. (1973) Professional orientations of journalists: an introduction to communicator analysis studies, *Gazette XIX*, 4.

Newfield, J. (1974) Journalism: old, new and corporate, in R. Webster (ed.), *The Reporter as Artist: A Look at the New Journalism Controversy*, New York, Hastings House, pp. 54–65.

Nigerian Broadcasting Corporation *Annual Reports*, NBC, Lagos.

Nigerian Broadcasting Corporation (1969) Ten years of service: a story of expansion, *ABU Newsletter*, Asian Broadcasting Union, Vol. 46, 15.

Nigerian Broadcasting Corporation (1977) *The First Twenty Years, 1957–1977*, NBC, Lagos.

Nilsson, N. G. (1971) The Origin of the Interview, *Journalism Quarterly*, **48**, pp. 707–13.

Nkrumah, K. (1963) Address to Second Conference of African Journalists, Accra.

Nord, B. A. (1966) Press freedom and political structure, *Journalism Quarterly*, pp. 531–34.

Nordenstreng, K. (1970) Policy for news transmission, reprinted in D. McQuail (ed.), *Sociology of Mass Communication*, Harmondsworth, Penguin Books, 1972, pp. 386–405.

Nott, K. (1961) *A Clean, Well-Lighted Place*, London, Heinemann.

Oakley, S. (1966) *The Story of Sweden*, London, Faber.

O'Boyle, L. (1968) The image of the journalist in England, France and Germany 1815–1848, *Comparative Studies in Society and History*, Vol. X, pp. 290–317.

Ohlstrom, B. (1966) Information and propaganda: a content analysis of editorials in four Swedish daily newspapers, *Journal of Peace Research*, Vol. 3, pp. 75–88.

Olson, K. E. (1966) *The History Makers*, Baton Rouge, Louisiana State University Press.

Olsson, C. O. and **Weibull, L.** (1973) The reporting of news in Scandinavian countries, *Scandinavian Political Studies*, Vol. 8, pp. 141–67.

Omu, F. I. A. (1965) *The Nigerian Newspaper Press, 1859–1937: A Study of origins, growth and influence*, PhD, University of Ibadan.

Omu, F. I. A. (1968) The dilemma of press freedom in colonial Africa: the West African example, *Journal of African History*, pp. 279–98.

Omu, F. I. A. (1978) *Press and Politics in Nigeria 1880–1937*, London, Longman.

Opubor, A. (1973) Mass communications in Nigeria, Ch. 14, in U. Damachi and H. Seibel (eds), *Social Change and Economic Development in Nigeria*, New York, Praeger.

Orlik, P. B. (1976) Systematic limitations to Irish broadcast journalism, *Journal of Broadcasting*, Vol. 20:4, Fall, pp. 467–80.

Ortega Y Gassett, J. (1944) *Mission of the University*, London, Routledge and Kegan Paul.

Oton, E. V. (1966) The training of journalists in Nigeria, *Journalism Quarterly*, Spring, pp. 107–9.

Patel, D. B. (1973) Mass communications and development in Africa, in A. Mazrui and H. H. Patel (eds), *Africa in World Affairs*, New York, The Third Press.

Peltola, P. (1973) News transmission, past and present, in K. Nordenstreng (ed.), *Informational Mass Communications*, Helsinki, Tammi.

Pers, A. V. (1966) *Newspapers in Sweden*, Stockholm Swedish Institute, Swedish Newspaper Publishers Association.

Pietila, A. (1971) Swedish editors views on government support of the press, *Journalism Quarterly*, Winter, pp. 724–9.

Piotrowski, B. (1973) The press in Sweden today, *The Democratic Journalist* (Prague), 9, 1973, pp. 11–14.

Ploman, E. (1976) *Broadcasting in Sweden*, London, Routledge and Kegan Paul.

Plotnicov, L. (1970) Rural–urban communications in contemporary Nigeria: the persistence of traditional social institutions, in P. C. W. Gutkind (ed.), *The Passing of Tribal Man in Africa*, Leiden.

Powers, R. (1978) *The Newscasters: The News Business as Show Business*, New York, St Martin's Press.

Rosengren, K –E. (1970) International news: intra and extra media data, *Acta Sociologica*, Vol. 13, No. 2.

Rosengren, K-E. (1974) International news: methods, data and theory, *Journal of Peace Research*, pp. 145–56.

Roscho, B. (1975) *Newsmaking*, Chicago, University of Chicago Press.

Rositi, F. (1975) The television news programme: fragmentation and recomposition of our image of society. Report presented to Prix Italia, Florence.

Rowand, E. (1972) *Press and Opinion in British West Africa 1855–1900*, Birmingham University, unpublished PhD.

Rydbeck, O. (1965) Co-ordinating news services, *EBU Review*, May.

Samuelsson, K. (1968) *From Great Power to Welfare State*, London, Allen and Unwin.

Samuelson, M. (1962) Measuring job satisfaction in the newsroom, *Journalism Quarterly*, pp. 285–91.

Sarkar, C. (1972) Development and the new journalism, *Vidura*, Oct., pp. 335–8, New Delhi.

Saxer, U. (1969) News and publicity, *Diogenes*, No. 68, Winter, pp. 53–79.

Schlesinger, P. (1978) *Putting 'Reality' Together: BBC News*, Constable, London.

Schramm, W. (1949) The nature of news, *Journalism Quarterly*, Sept., pp. 259–69.

Schutz, W. C. (1958) On categorising qualitative data in content analysis, *Public Opinion Quarterly*, 1958, pp. 503–15.

Scott, G. (1968) *Reporter Anonymous*, London, Hutchinson.

Shaw, D. L. (1967) News bias and the telegraph: a study of historical change, *Journalism Quarterly*, 44(1), Spring, pp. 3–12, 31.

Sherman, C. E. and **Ruby, J.** (1974) The Eurovision news exchange, *Journalism Quarterly*, Autumn.

Siebert, F. S., Peterson T. and **Schramm, W.** (1956) *Four Theories of the Press*, Urbana, University of Illinois Press.

Sigelman, L. (1973) Reporting the news: an organisational analysis, *American Journal of Sociology*, Vol. 79 (1), July, pp. 132–51.

Simmel, G. (1964) Superordination and subordination, in K. Wolff, *The Sociology of G. Simmel*, New York, Free Press.

Simon, N. (1966) *The Odd Couple*, New York, Random House.

Skornia, H. J. (1968) *Television and the News*, Pacific Books, California.

Small, W. (1970) *Television News and the Real World*, Hastings House Publishers, New York.

Smith, A. (1973) *The Shadow in the Cave*, London, George Allen and Unwin.

Soja, E. W. (1970) Communications and change, in E. Soja and J. Paden (eds), *The African Experience*, Evanston, Northwestern University Press.

Soyinka, W. (1972) *The Man Died*, Rex Collings, London.

Steinberg, S. H. (1974) *Five Hundred Years of Printing*, Penguin Books. Harmondsworth.

Sternquist, N. (1967) *Sweden in the '60s*, Stockholm, Almquist and Wiksell.

Stephenson, W. (1963) A critique of content analysis, *The Psychological Record*, pp. 155–62.

Stewart, J. H. (1962) The Irish press during the French Revolution, *Journalism Quarterly*, 39, pp. 507–18.

Stokke, Olav (ed.) (1971) *Reporting Africa*, The Scandinavian Institute of African Studies, Uppsala.

Stothard, Blaine (1975–77) Sweden: the limits of press freedom, *Index on Censorship*, Vol. 4, No. 3, 1975, *Index on Censorship*, Vol. 6, No. 3, 1977.

Sveriges Radio *Structures and Programming for the 1970s*, Stockholm.

Swallow, N. (1966) *Factual Television*, Focal Press, London.

Swedish Broadcasting Commission (1977) *Radio and TV, 1978–1985*, Ministry of Education, Stockholm.

Talese, G. (1971) *The Kingdom and the Power*, London, Calder and Boyars and New York, Bantam.

Taylor, H. A. (1965) The British concept of the freedom of the press, *Gazette*, pp. 23–38.

Thoren, S. (1968) The flow of foreign news into the Swedish press, *Journalism Quarterly*, pp. 521–5.

Tracey, M. (1977) *The Production of Political Television*, London, Routledge and Kegan Paul.

Tuchman, G. (1972) Objectivity as strategic ritual: an examination of newsmen's notions of objectivity, *American Journal of Sociology*, pp. 660–79.

Tuchman, G. (1973a) The technology of objectivity, *Urban Life and Culture*, April, pp. 3–26.

Tuchman, G. (1973b) Making news by doing work: routinising the unexpected, *American Journal of Sociology*, Vol. 79, No. 1, pp. 110–31.

Tunstall, J. (1970) *The Westminster Lobby Correspondents*, London, Routledge and Kegan Paul.

Tunstall, J. (1971) *Journalists at Work*, London, Constable.

Tunstall, J. (1977) *The Media Are American*, London, Constable.

Turnbull, G. S. (1936) Some notes on the history of the interview, *Journalism Quarterly*, 13, pp. 272–9.

Turner, L. W. and Byron, F. A. W. (1949) *Broadcasting Survey of the British West African Colonies – in Connection with the Development of Broadcasting Services for the African Population*, unpublished, Colonial Office, London, August.

Tyrrell, R. (1972) *The Work of the Television Journalist*, London, Focal Press.

Ugboajah, F. O. (1972) Traditional-urban media model: stocktaking for African development *Gazette, XVIII*, No. 2, pp. 76–95.

Ugboajah, F. O. (1977) Nigeria's key journalists: a profile, *Unilag Communication Review*, Vol. 1, No. 1, pp. 4–6.

Ullrich, W. (1974) Mass media and their role in revolutionary Africa, *The Democratic Journalist*, 1974, No. 11, pp. 13–17.

Vängby, S. (1971) *Opartiskhet Och Saklighet*, Stockholm, Sveriges Radio.

Varis, T. (1974) *Television News in Eurovision and Intervision*, Report to EBU Working Party on Television News, Lisbon.

Varis, T. and Jokelin, R. (1976) *Television News in Europe: A Survey of the News-Film Flow in Europe*, research report No. 32, Institute of Journalism and Mass Communications, University of Tampere, Finland.

Warner, M. (1971) Organisational context and control of policy in the television newsroom: a participant observation study, *British Journal of Sociology*, 22(3), Sept., pp. 283–94.

Westerståhl, J. (1972) *Objective News Reporting*, Mimeo.

Westerståhl, J. and Carl-Grunner, J. (1958) *The Political Press*, Gothenberg University.

Westley, B. H. and **Barrow, L. C.** (1959) An investigation of news-seeking behaviour, *Journalism Quarterly*, Vol. 36, pp. 431–8.

Whale, J. (1967) *The Half-Shut Eye*, London, Macmillan.

Whale, J. (1970) News, *The Listener*, 15 Oct., pp. 510–12.

Whale, J. (1972) *Journalism and Government*, London, Macmillan.

White, D. M. (1950) The gatekeeper: a case study in the selection of news, *Journalism Quarterly*, **27**, Fall, pp. 383–90.

White, T. de Vere (1968) *Ireland*, London, Thames and Hudson.

Whyte, J. H. (1971) *Church and State in Modern Ireland*, Dublin, Gill and Macmillan.

Wilcox, D. L. (1974) The press in Black Africa: philosophy and control, unpublished PhD, University of Missouri, Columbia.

Wilkerson, M. (1970) *News and Newspapers*, London, Batsford.

Williams, F. (1957) *Dangerous Estate: The Anatomy of Newspapers*, London, Longman.

Williams, F. (1969) *The Right to Know: The Rise of the World's Press*, London, Longman.

Williams, R. (1974) *Television: Technology and Cultural Form*, London, Fontana/Collins.

Wilson, D. (1974–5) News from nowhere, *Sight and Sound*, Winter, pp. 45–8.

Windahl, S. and **Rosengren, K-E.** (1976) The professionalisation of Swedish journalists, *Gazette*, Vol. XXII, No. 3, pp. 140–9.

Wintour, C. (1972) *Pressures on the Press*, London, Andre Deutsch.

Wyndham Goldie, G. (1972) The sociology of television, *The Listener*, 19 Oct., Vol. 88, No. 2273, pp. 517–19.

Wyndham Goldie, G. (1977) *Facing the Nation: Television and Politics, 1936–1976*, London, Bodley Head.

Index